# PRAISE FOR
# GIRLS WRITE NOW 2012 ANTHOLOGY

"Writing doesn't have to be a solo act. Here, in their own words, we have girls and their mentors giving us the lowdown on love, friendship, family and identity—a writing friendship that produces powerful works with flair, fun and courage."

– LIZZIE SKURNICK,
*SHELF DISCOVERY: THE TEEN CLASSICS WE NEVER STOPPED READING*

"The young women of Girls Write Now are creative from deep in their minds and hearts out to the tips of their fingers—original and engaged in how they observe the world, how they reflect on it, and how they express their thoughts and feelings about it on the page. Their fiction, memoir and poetry brim with eloquence, honesty and insight."

– SARAH SAFFIAN,
*ITHAKA: A DAUGHTER'S MEMOIR OF BEING FOUND*

"The vital work done by the women of Girls Write Now helps ensure that their girls will be all right for many years into the future."

– JANICE ERLBAUM, *GIRLBOMB*

"To discover new voices is always a thrill. To meet them in the heady mixture of the Girls Write Now community is not only thrilling, but also an introduction to the power of mentorship."

– NANCY K. MILLER,
*WHAT THEY SAVED: PIECES OF A JEWISH PAST*

"Girls Write Now consistently produces some of the most uplifting, original work I've seen. They have a way of reaching into the invisible city and making visible what is so quintessential to the human experience, particularly of growing up female in New York."

– COURTNEY E. MARTIN,
*DO IT ANYWAY: THE NEW GENERATION OF ACTIVISTS*

Girls Write Now, Inc.

247 West 37th Street, Suite 1800

New York, NY 10018

info@girlswritenow.org

girlswritenow.org


Printed in the United States

ISBN 978-0-615-64344-1

List price: $20.00 (USD)

GIRLS WRITE NOW
2012 ANTHOLOGY

## ANTHOLOGY EDITORIAL COMMITTEE

MELISSA GIRA GRANT,
*EDITOR*

MEGHAN McNAMARA,
*DIRECTOR OF PROGRAMS*

MAYA NUSSBAUM,
*FOUNDER + EXECUTIVE DIRECTOR*

KIRTHANA RAMISETTI,
*PROGRAM ADVISORY
COMMITTEE COMMUNICATIONS
CHAIR*

JENNIFER BACON

SIOBHAN BURKE

AMY DiLUNA

JILLIAN GALLAGHER

HEATHER M. GRAHAM

NORA GROSS

WHITNEY JACOBY

JENNIFER TENCH

## DESIGN
JENIFER CARTER

## COPYEDITING
BETH HICKS

ANGELICA SGOUROS

## PHOTOGRAPHY
JEN CHU

Founded in 1998, Girls Write Now (GWN) is the first organization in the United States with a writing and mentoring model exclusively for girls. From young women exploring writing to seasoned professionals practicing their craft every day, GWN is a community of women writers dedicated to providing the guidance, support and opportunities for high school girls to develop their creative, independent voices, and write their way to a better future. 100% of GWN's seniors graduate and move on to college—bringing with them portfolios, awards, scholarships, new skills, and a sense of confidence. Mentees from the Class of 2012 won an astounding 27 regional and national awards in the Scholastic Arts & Writing competition, along with full scholarships through Posse and Questbridge, among others.

For fifteen years, Girls Write Now has built a record of achievement and innovation that has been recognized twice by the White House, by *The New York Times, NBC Nightly News*, the MacArthur Foundation, and the global branding firm Siegel+Gale. In the past year, GWN has been admitted as a grantee partner into the New York Community Trust-funded Hive Learning Network, the Catalog for Giving of New York City, the New York Women's Foundation, and the Edmund de Rothschild Foundations. In 2012, Youth, I.N.C. honored GWN as one of the three most enterprising and innovative nonprofits improving the lives of New York City youth.

*We wish to thank the following individuals for their support of Girls Write Now and for making the work in this anthology possible:*

BOARD OF DIRECTORS
Kamy Wicoff, *Board Chair*; Lisa Chai, *Treasurer*; Marjorie Coismain, *Secretary*; Lee Clifford; Sang Lee; Nancy K. Miller; Maya Nussbaum; Chelsea Rao; Linda Winston

PROGRAM ADVISORY COMMITTEE
Erin Baer, *Pair Support Chair*; Jessica Benjamin, *Digital Media Chair*; Maya Frank-Levine, *Curriculum Co-Chair*; Andrea Gabbidon-Levene, *Mentee Enrollment Chair*;

## GIRLS WRITE NOW 2012 HIGHLIGHTS

### HIGHER ED

100% of seniors headed to college including: Amherst College, Barnard College, Bennington College, Howard University, and UCLA in Fall 2012

### HONORS

Distinguished by President's Committee twice in 2 years; Won Youth, I.N.C.'s Innovator award in January 2012

### AWARDS

Mentees received 27 Scholastic Art & Writing Awards, including two national medals, plus full scholarships through Posse and Questbridge, among others

### DIGITAL MEDIA

Partnered with Figment, Open Road Integrated Media, Parsons the New School for Design, and the Hive Digital Learning Fund in the New York Community Trust

Anuja Madar, *Pair Support Co-Chair*; Julie Polk, *Curriculum Co-Chair*; Kirthana Ramisetti, *Communications Chair*; Heather Smith, *Mentor Enrollment Chair*; Elaine Stuart-Shah, *Fundraising Chair*; Moira Taylor, *College Prep Advisor*

### YOUTH BOARD

Diamond Arriola, Brittany Barker, Ximena Castillo, Rocio Cuervas, Emma Fiske-Dobell, Cherish Smith, Joy Smith, Yolandri Vargas, Samantha White

### STAFF

Maya Nussbaum, *Executive Director*; Meghan McNamara, *Director of Programs*; Jessica Wells-Hasan, *Director of Development & External Affairs*; Anusha Mehar, *Program Coordinator*; Ashley Young, *Program Coordinator*

### INTERNS

Nicole Bayard, Ximena Castillo, Kamelia Kilawan, Nadia Misir, Lauren Seaman

### DORKSHOP LEADERS

Mónica Arias, Lauren Slowik, Julia Vallera, Lara Warman

### WORKSHOP TEAMS

FICTION: Allison Adair Alberts, Therese Cox, Kate Jacobs, Wendy Lee, Kathleen Scheiner

POETRY: Colleen Barry, Mayuri Chandra, Jackie Clark, Sara Femenella, Emily Hazel, Lynn Melnick

MEMOIR: Amanda Berlin, Kristen Demaline, Amanda Orenstein, Michele Thomas, My-Thuan Tran, Kate Trebuss

JOURNALISM: Grace Bastidas, Susan Burton, Amy Feldman, Gillian Reagan, Ingrid Skjong, Allison Yarrow

SCREENWRITING: Christina Brosman, Kristi Goldade, Heather Kristin, Nancy Mercado, Katherine Nero, Jessica Pishko

TRANSMEDIA STORYTELLING: Alex Berg, Jana Branson, Jalylah Burrell, Tobi Elkin, Jessi Hempel, Mary Pat Kane

### READINGS COMMITTEE

Meg Cassidy, Samantha Carlin, Rachel Friedman, Ashley Howard, Hilary Leichter, Jess Pastore, Alissa Riccardelli, Rory Satran

### MENTOR ENROLLMENT COMMITTEE

Nancy Hooper, Demetria Irwin, LaToya Jordan, Patricia Lespinasse

### MENTEE ENROLLMENT COMMITTEE

Rachel Cohen, Karen Kawaguchi, Nakisha Williams

# REMIX
## GIRLS WRITE NOW
### 2012 ANTHOLOGY

**FOREWORD**

**CHIMAMANDA NGOZI ADICHIE**

While growing up in Nigeria, I was surrounded by confident, enterprising women—my mother the university administrator, my aunt the restaurant owner, my mother's friends who were traders, professors, hairdressers. They made me see the many possibilities, the many things I could dare to be and do.

Now, as an adult, I realize how fortunate I was to have them; many girls are not so fortunate.

I have been writing since I was old enough to spell. I think of writing as a mix of magic and craft. The magic is the transformation that happens when the writing is going well, when hours pass without my noticing and characters sometimes speak to me. The craft is the choice I make to sit down for hours and write and re-write, until my neck aches and the prose is acceptably polished. I was almost 20 before I attended my first writers' workshop, and it was important in teaching me about craft. I received positive and negative feedback from other writers, learned to see my work through the eyes of others, and, even more important, felt a sense of validation. Other people like me also cared about writing and reading stories.

Two years ago, I was invited to read at CHAPTERS, the monthly reading series produced by Girls Write Now, featuring young women writers and their adult professional mentors. I said yes. I admired the idea of women mentoring girls, particularly a mentorship focused on writing. And I expected to be mildly entertained.

I remember sitting in the front of the room at the Center for Fiction and watching as girl after girl came up to read from their work. I remember the girl who read a piece about her family, the honesty of her emotion, her searching, questioning spirit. I remember another girl who read words so polished and stylized, I thought she had to be older than she was. I watched the mentors and how proud they looked of their mentees. I imagined the patience that must come with their mentoring, the moments of frustration and missed connection, but also the sense of fulfillment in witnessing the growth of a girl's confidence. I saw in some of them the women that those girls would become.

There was, in all the readings that evening, a sense of urgency and necessity. They seemed to me to be poems and stories written not because the girls had some extra time on their hands, but because they had to be written. They mattered. They mattered to the girls who wrote them and they mattered to me, as a listener and reader.

Afterwards, the only word I could think of that best captured how I felt, a word I don't often use, was "inspired." Watching those girls, I felt as though there was reason to believe in the power of writing again, as though things long tarnished had suddenly become shiny, and I returned to my own writing with a sense of renewed purpose.

The writing in this anthology is a glimpse of that evening. Some of the pieces are astonishing in their talent and promise, others even more so in how fully formed they seem. Reading them is a treat. I wish for every reader who opens this book the same feeling I had that evening when I first met Girls Write Now: Inspiration.

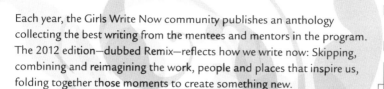

Each year, the Girls Write Now community publishes an anthology collecting the best writing from the mentees and mentors in the program. The 2012 edition—dubbed Remix—reflects how we write now: Skipping, combining and reimagining the work, people and places that inspire us, folding together those moments to create something new.

Remix acknowledges that writing is a communal act. It's also the exchange of ideas and the transformation that occurs within the mentor/mentee relationship that is at the core of Girls Write Now programs. Mentees are stunningly diverse teen girls from all five boroughs of New York City, many originally from countries around the globe; mentors are professional women writers who stand as shining, real-life examples of exactly who their girls can be as women and as writers. The six chapters that make up the body of Remix are the culmination of their year's work together, a peek into their portfolios, sequenced, mixed and matched.

We've labeled each chapter with a hashtag to guide you around. Some of the pieces gathered under one hashtag link to pieces under another—you can skip back and forth between them like tracks, shuffling each chapter as a playlist. Think of it like a DJ's set, taking you up and down and back around.

Along the way, you'll get together with the people (#TIESTHATBIND) who shape us (#WHOWEARE) as we grow and we change (#TRANSFORMINGINTO), and we test our limits (#ATACROSSROADS). From our visions (#OTHERWORLDS), we build something all our own (#ANDWEREHOME), and for each other. Not only are the chapters remixed, but some of the pieces themselves are, too: Mentors remixing their mentees work; mentees remixing the work of other writers.

Mentoring the next generation of women writers also means mentoring them to write in a digital world. In #PROFILES, we'll introduce you directly to our mentors and mentees as they embrace (and resist) digital modes of expression. Scan the section for their tweet-sized pull quotes then go with them #BEHINDTHESCENES to see how they workshop their writing in our remix culture.

When we pause for a moment in the rush of our work in the city, and with each other, we feel the future taking shape. It's made up of many voices, many tools, many platforms, many possibilities. It's often overwhelming, but it's also our opportunity to seize. Last spring when 10 mentees representing Girls Write Now were invited to the White House for a celebration of literature, former Poet Laureate Billy Collins urged them to read widely in search of writing that makes them "furiously jealous," then imitate it, adapt it and "have fun with language." They and their fellow mentees have heeded the call in Remix. We hope you will be intrigued and in awe, absorb new techniques and abandon others, and above all, JOIN THE NEXT GENERATION OF WOMEN WRITERS IN CONTINUING THE REMIX CYCLE.

—THE 2012 GIRLS WRITE NOW ANTHOLOGY EDITORIAL COMMITTEE

# TATYANA ALEXANDER

YEARS AS MENTEE: 2011, 2012

GRADE: 11

HIGH SCHOOL: Academy for Conservation and the Environment, Brooklyn, NY

BORN: New York, NY

LIVES: Brooklyn, NY

AWARDS: Scholastic Art & Writing Awards Silver Key for Personal Essay/ Memoir

# JILLIAN GALLAGHER

YEARS AS MENTOR: 2011, 2012

OCCUPATION: Writer at FutureBrand, New York, NY

*Tatyana says:* In the short months I've spent with my mentor Jillian, I learned not only about writing, but about life as well. Jillian taught me that in order to write a story that makes sense, you have to freewrite something that doesn't. She also taught me not to overwork myself, that ideas will flow into your head when you least expect it. I consider Jillian my friend because we have so much in common, but are two very different people. I WILL ALWAYS REMEMBER WHEN SHE SAID "NOT ALL WRITERS HAVE THE BEST HANDWRITING."

tatyana appears in: #atacrossroads

*Jillian says:* I was relieved during our first meetings when it turned out that Tatyana and I had more in common than I'd imagined we would. But beyond our similarities, I've been able to draw such inspiration from her example. TATYANA EMBRACES THE TOUGH STUFF THAT LOTS OF WRITERS WOULD PREFER TO SWEEP AWAY, and tells stories of these things with incredible poise, maturity, and beauty. I remember that now when I'm writing and tempted to tone down an idea to make it less scary. I've learned from her that the hardest things can be the most beautiful.

jillian appears in: #atacrossroads

# ERIKA ALFARO

YEARS AS MENTEE: 2012

GRADE: 12

HIGH SCHOOL: Flushing International High School, Queens, NY

BORN: Long Island, NY

LIVES: Queens, NY

SCHOLARSHIPS: Scholarship for Academic Excellence

# GRACE BASTIDAS

YEARS AS MENTOR: 2007, 2008, 2009, 2010, 2012

OCCUPATION: Freelance Journalist based in New York City

PUBLICATIONS: *New York* magazine, *The New York Times, New York Post*

*Erika says:* At every meeting she's there at Communitea, a cafe in Long Island City, waiting for me, ready to hear about the crazy week I just had. We start by doing a writing exercise that we share with each other. Anecdotes always come up, and I discover new things about her. IN THE BLINK OF AN EYE AN HOUR HAS PASSED, AND IT'S NEVER ENOUGH. During workshops, she's there to inspire me to share my work, which I always hesitate to do. Then I find out, it's not that hard after all.

erika appears in: #otherworlds, #andwerehome

*Grace says:* Erika told me that when she first moved to the United States from El Salvador, she would read the dictionary every day to brush up on her English. Now that's dedication! I think about that when I write. I MAY NOT ALWAYS FEEL LIKE I HAVE THE TIME TO TACKLE THE BLANK PAGE, BUT HER WORDS KEEP MY PEN MOVING.

grace appears in: #andwerehome

# LASHANDA ANAKWAH

YEARS AS MENTEE: 2011, 2012

GRADE: 12

HIGH SCHOOL: Marble Hill School for International Studies, Bronx, NY

BORN: New York, NY

LIVES: Bronx, NY

AWARDS: Scholastic Art & Writing Awards National Gold Medal for Writing Portfolio; Scholastic Art & Writing Awards Gold Key for Personal Essay/Memoir; Scholastic Art & Writing Awards Silver Key for Flash Fiction

# RACHEL COHEN

YEARS AS MENTOR: 2011, 2012

OCCUPATION: General Assignment Sports Reporter, *The Associated Press*

*Lashanda says:* Rachel Cohen. Or as I like to call her, Rache. My sisters ask me why I call her that. It's not much of a nickname; it's just her actual name without the L. They wouldn't understand. It's been two years since we first met. I WENT FROM VIEWING HER AS MY GIRLS WRITE NOW MENTOR TO VIEWING HER AS THE PERSON WHO ALWAYS HAS MY BACK and one of the few people I can count on. So please let me call her Rache, because removing the L from her name shows how much we've been through and how close we now are.

lashanda appears in: #whoweare

*Rachel says:*

    1:16 a.m. Me: how's it going?
    1:17 a.m. Lashanda: good. but i feel bad. i hope ur not waiting for me
    1:19 a.m. Me: it's ok. i want to see this through to the end.
    1:20 a.m. Lashanda: aw!

That's from the actual Google chat when she was frantically scrambling to finish her memoir piece for the Scholastic Art & Writing Awards. Four hours later, it was done. Yes, after 5 a.m. I'm way too old for this. But WHEN YOU SEE SOMEONE COMMIT SO DEEPLY TO TELLING A HARD, FRANK STORY, SUDDENLY SOMETHING THAT CRAZY FEELS JUST RIGHT.

rachel appears in: #transforminginto

# BEGINA ARMSTRONG

YEARS AS MENTEE: 2012

GRADE: 12

HIGH SCHOOL: A. Phillip Randolph Campus High School, New York, NY

BORN: New York, NY

LIVES: Brooklyn, NY

WILL ATTEND: Columbia College of Chicago, Chicago, IL

# JACKIE CLARK

YEARS AS MENTOR: 2012

OCCUPATION: Editor and Curator, *Coldfront Magazine*

PUBLICATIONS: *Red Fortress (H_NGM_N), Office Work* (Greying Ghost Press), and *I Live Here Now* (Lame House Press, Winter 2012)

*Begina says:* My mentor and I combine practicals with dynamics in our writing. I have learned many things from working with my mentor. She has challenged me to take editing and time management more seriously. We also worked together to create and edit big writing projects that I wanted to send out to contests. The biggest writing project we worked on was editing a nine-page story I wrote. The piece required a lot of attention and I DEFINITELY APPRECIATED HAVING SOMEONE ELSE AROUND TO READ MY WORK. TWO HEADS ARE BETTER THAN ONE.

begina appears in: #otherworlds

*Jackie says:* As a first year GWN mentor, MY ENTIRE MENTORING EXPERIENCE HAS BEEN A BIT OF A REMIX/SHAKE UP. I have been reminded of all the amazing opportunities that await young, talented writers like my mentee! I have learned from and admired my mentee's ambition and involvement with other organizations aside from GWN, such as viBe Theater. It has been so refreshing and personally motivating to spend time with someone who has the world ahead of her and not only knows it but is constantly taking pragmatic steps towards finding her place in it.

jackie appears in: #otherworlds

# SARAI ARROYO

YEARS AS MENTEE: 2012

GRADE: 12

HIGH SCHOOL: New Design High School, New York, NY

BORN: New York, NY

LIVES: Brooklyn, NY

WILL ATTEND: Long Island University (LIU), Brooklyn, NY

# ALLISON YARROW

YEARS AS MENTOR: 2012

OCCUPATION: Staff Writer at *Newsweek Daily Beast*

PUBLICATIONS: The Huffington Post, *Newsweek*, Slate, CNN.com, *Poets & Writers magazine*, *The Forward*

*Sarai says:* For me, having a mentor in my life is an experience I hope to repeat one day. I remember wondering after our first meeting, "What if she thinks my writing is childish? What if my stories are not impressive?" When I finally mustered up the courage to present a rough draft of a story I was working on, one comment took me by surprise, "It's very dreamlike, very wise beyond its years." IT WASN'T THE FIRST TIME SOMEONE COMPLIMENTED MY WRITING, BUT IT WAS THE FIRST TIME THAT I TOOK IT TO HEART AND CONTINUED WITH AMBITION.

sarai appears in: #atacrossroads

*Allison says:* Sarai writes beautifully and honestly, and with a voice that seems at once wise and curious. But she's a very perceptive reader, too. This year, before we worked on writing (and then during and after), we read. We read stories out loud to each other on the floor of a bookstore, and in the loud buzz of a coffee shop. Franz Kafka, Flannery O'Connor, and Grace Paley were some of the writers we explored. IT WAS ALWAYS SUCH A TREAT TO SEE A STORY THROUGH HER EYES, to witness her consuming something anew that I had long loved, and to learn more about it through her new lens.

# ANDREINA AVALOS

YEARS AS MENTEE: 2012

GRADE: 11

HIGH SCHOOL:
Urban Assembly School
for Law and Justice,
Brooklyn, NY

BORN:
Brooklyn, NY

LIVES:
Brooklyn, NY

# HEATHER M. GRAHAM

YEARS AS MENTOR: 2011, 2012

OCCUPATION: Deputy Editor at iVillage

PUBLICATIONS: Mediabistro.com, *New York Moves* magazine, DailyGlow.com, Lifescript.com, EverydayHealth.com

*Andreina says:* I love my mentor. She has helped me become more persistent when it comes to my writing. I have written more pieces in different genres. My grammar has improved because I have my mentor teach me how to edit my work. WE HAVE A STRONG CONNECTION AND I COULDN'T HAVE ASKED FOR A BETTER ROLE MODEL. She has taught me not to give up and because of that I have won various trophies in Speech and Debate tournaments. I'm happy to say I'm going to Albany, NY to compete! Thank you, Heather!

andreina appears in: #atacrossroads

*Heather says:* Andreina is an inspiration to me. She is a smart, creative, brave young woman who has reminded me how important it is for girls and women to feel empowered. OUR WRITING RELATIONSHIP HAS BLOSSOMED INTO A QUITE A PARTNERSHIP—we talk about the goal for each piece we work on and then take that into the editing process. She has shown me the importance of allowing her to develop her own voice while still guiding her and passing on the writing skills taught to me. Her excerpt will make you want to read more of her work! I do.

heather appears in: #atacrossroads

# MARIAH
# TERESA AVILES

Years as mentee: 2011, 2012

Grade: 11

High school: Young Women's
Leadership School of East
Harlem, New York, NY

Bron: New York, NY

Lives: Bronx, NY

# ALLISON
# ADAIR ALBERTS

Years as mentor:
2011, 2012

Occupation: Doctoral Candidate at Fordham University, New York, NY

Publications: *Rhetorikós: Excellence in Student Writing*

*Mariah says:* Constantly running late, Allie receives the same text message from Riah:
"Allie, I'm running a little late. I'll be there soon." It's become more of a routine and an
expectation—a habit, rather than a "once in a blue moon" kind of thing. Nonetheless, our
smiles shine through the Starbucks on the corner of Metropolitan and Wood Avenues,
greeting each other with our famous, "Hey how are you?" Transformation. Growth.
Our conversations and sessions may remain the same as always, but our ideas have more
structure, our writing has progressed. *More. More. More.* Thank you Allie.

mariah appears in: #andwerehome

*Allison says:* She with her pencil, and I with my pen, discuss poetics and narrative art. We are
in a bubble, in a cacophonous Bronx Starbucks. In a time away from real life, our time is a
time to create, to recreate, to cross out when necessary. Our words interweave and overlap,
remixing, re-visioning, reimagining. Year two flows more easily: we are serious writers now.

allison appears in: #andwerehome

## TUHFA BEGUM

Years as mentee: 2012

Grade: 10

High school: Vanguard High School, New York, NY

Born: Sylhet, Bangladesh

Lives: Bronx, NY

## JOSLEEN WILSON

Years as mentor: 2009, 2010, 2011, 2012

Occupation: Writer based in New York City

Publications: Many magazine articles, essays, more than 30 definitive nonfiction books, and several award-winning short documentaries

*Tuhfa says:* Start writing. Erase. Restart. I crumple up the paper, and then shoot for the wastebasket. I miss. I empty out the wastebasket and relive the writer's block. And then it all comes clear. Homer's *Iliad* becomes a poem about war. I rush out to meet Josleen. It is Friday. We sit down over coffee and talk about Isaac Asimov and photography. Inspiration hits me; something to write. Maybe I'll write a poem from the warrior's point of view. My mind is unscrambled. Thanks, Josleen. I start to rewrite. Remix: writing reignited.

tuhfa appears in: #otherworlds

*Josleen says:* We write our GWN Anthology pieces separately. I don't know what "remix" means and I resist the GWN Guidelines. Tuhfa explains it to me, and I start seeing it everywhere, like *The LEGO Ideas Book*, a bestseller for six-year-olds. This isn't the first time Tuhfa's taught me something I don't know. (I'll skip the day she explained a parabola: $y = a(x-h)^2 + k$. Who knew?) I read her short poem, several times. It is deep and complex. Side by side, I read my essay, but don't show it to her. I am stunned. Mentally, I circle a single word in her poem, pluck it out, and insert it in my own.

josleen appears in: #otherworlds

## SHYANNE MARIA FIGUEROA BENNETT

YEARS AS MENTEE: 2012

GRADE: 12

HIGH SCHOOL: Brooklyn College
Academy High School,
Brooklyn, NY

BORN: Brooklyn, NY

LIVES: Brooklyn, NY

AWARDS: Scholastic Art
& Writing Awards Gold
Key for Flash Fiction;
Scholastic Art &
Writing Awards Gold
Key for Poetry

SCHOLARSHIPS: New York State Academic Excellence Award

WILL ATTEND: Wheaton College, Norton, MA

## NORA GROSS

YEARS AS MENTOR: 2011, 2012

OCCUPATION: Masters Candidate in Sociology of Education at New York University
Steinhardt School of Culture, Education, and Human Development, New York, NY

*Shyanne says:* As I walked into the coffee shop I saw Nora, who greeted me with a smile
and hug. My mind was reeling from a discussion in my Puerto Rican and Latino Studies
class on how racism can be covert. I recounted the discussion; NORA IS ONE OF THE FEW
PEOPLE I FEEL COMFORTABLE AROUND TO RAMBLE ON ABOUT MY INTELLECTUAL CURIOSITIES. After
listening intently, she challenged me to focus my thoughts into a freewrite. The resulting
poem, "Pelo Malo/Bad Hair," revealed unconscious feelings about my identity that were
startling—things I may not have known without Nora's push.

shyanne appears in: #tiesthatbind, #transforminginto

*Nora says:* In one of our earliest sessions, I encouraged Shyanne to do a freewrite—the kind
where she wasn't allowed to pick up her pen from the paper. We were both surprised
and delighted to reread what she'd written after only five minutes and discover not
only a bold and provocative idea, but beautifully constructed sentences full of imagery
and imagination. EVERY TIME I READ SHYANNE'S WRITING WORK, I AM INSPIRED BY ITS BEAUTY, ITS
CREATIVITY, AND ITS BRAVERY. I have tried to bring some of that to my own writing practice.

nora appears in: #tiesthatbind, #andwerehome

# JESSICA BORDON

YEARS AS MENTEE: 2012

GRADE: 10

HIGH SCHOOL: Fiorello H. LaGuardia High School of Music & Art and Performing Arts, New York, NY

BORN: Bronx, NY

LIVES: Bronx, NY

# INGRID SKJONG

YEARS AS MENTOR: 2010, 2011, 2012

OCCUPATION: Digital Editor

PUBLICATIONS: *Departures* magazine

*Jessica says:* My mentor Ingrid has "remixed" me by helping and encouraging me to do well in my future. Ingrid has helped me feel more confident in my work and inspired me, through her own experiences, to look forward to college. She's helped me feel more confident and relate to other people, especially older people! WHO KNEW A FIFTEEN-YEAR-OLD COULD RELATE TO AN OLDER WOMAN (NOT TOO OLD, THOUGH) SO MUCH! This is my first year at Girls Write Now and so far it's been a tremendous new experience that I have enjoyed immensely, thanks to my mentor Ingrid!

jessica appears in: #otherworlds

*Ingrid says:* Jessica has an imagination that knows no bounds. From her magic realism writing (talking flowers!) to her touching and often hilarious tales of her mother and grandmother who live in Puerto Rico, she has an insatiable desire for detail. I do, too, and she brings it out in me. SHE WEARS CAT-EYE MAKEUP—LINED EYES WITH AN ARTFUL FLICK AT EACH CORNER—THAT FASCINATES ME. She rolled up to our weekly meeting one day with a huge plastic bag of books that she'd picked up on the street because she just couldn't resist them. How could she? Think of all the details in them to find...

ingrid appears in: #otherworlds

## CHRISTINA BUTAN

YEARS AS MENTEE: 2012

GRADE: 11

HIGH SCHOOL: The Young Women's Leadership School of Astoria, Queens, NY

BORN: Queens, NY

LIVES: Queens, NY

AWARDS: Scholastic Art & Writing Awards Silver Key for Journalism

## AMY DILUNA

YEARS AS MENTOR: 2012

OCCUPATION: Senior Editor at TODAY.com

PUBLICATIONS: *New York Daily News*

*Christina says:* GIRLS WRITE NOW DIDN'T PAIR ME UP WITH A MENTOR; THEY PAIRED ME UP WITH A SUPERHERO. I firmly believe that Amy DiLuna is Wonder Woman in disguise. That's the only logical explanation I have because she has saved my life one too many times. Amy lets my mind and soul breathe for the first time every week—she saves me from the burning building that is my hectic life and puts the fire out as well. She remixes my life weekly by teaching me everything from how to keep my tone consistent in my writing to why the Vitamin C in grapefruit calms your nerves before a math test. I think it's a little selfish that she's keeping this superhero business a secret—I'm convinced she can fly, and I'm waiting for my lesson.

christina appears in: #andwerehome, #behindthescenes

*Amy says:* I was never like Christina. I don't know anyone who was—self-possessed, sure of what she believes in, confident, wildly talented, uncompromising. And WHAT A WICKED MAGIC FLOWS THROUGH HER FINGERS WHEN SHE WRITES. She's remixed my notion of just how wide-open and bright with possibility the horizon can be. I imagine the other girls at school look at her the way I do: with awe and wonder and hope that she'll remember us when she's running the world.

amy appears in: #whoweare, #andwerehome

# CINDY CABAN

YEARS AS MENTEE: 2011, 2012

GRADE: 11

HIGH SCHOOL: Millennium High School, New York, NY

BORN: New York, NY

LIVES: Brooklyn, NY

# WENDY LEE

YEARS AS MENTOR: 2011, 2012

OCCUPATION: Publishing Director at Lantern Books, Brooklyn, NY

PUBLICATIONS: *Happy Family,* a novel (Grove Press, 2008)

*Cindy says:* During our pair icebreaker, I told Wendy that I wanted to experiment with songwriting. HER EYES LIT UP, AS THEY ALWAYS DO WHEN SHE COMES UP WITH AN AMAZING IDEA. She said she would bring her guitar and teach me basic chords so we could write a song about where we lived. We wrote in prose first and then combined lines while also singing together. Her creativity and harmony not only inspired my writing, but allowed me to create my own song. Now every time I look at a bridge, my mind will burst into her song "Hell's Gate Bridge."

cindy appears in: #transforminginto

*Wendy says:* When I first met Cindy I was surprised to find she liked Nirvana and Doc Martens—just like I did, when I was a teenager in the 1990s. However, when I was her age, I definitely didn't have Cindy's poetic voice. I'VE BEEN INSPIRED BY CINDY'S POWERFUL, LYRICAL IMAGERY TO EXPLORE MY OWN VOICE, in poetry and in song. She has shown me that out of moments of quiet and reflection can come words of incredible beauty and strength.

wendy appears in: #transforminginto

# FANTA CAMARA

YEARS AS MENTEE: 2012

GRADE: 12

HIGH SCHOOL: Bronx International High School, Bronx, NY

BORN: Guinea

LIVES: Bronx, NY

AWARDS: The Henry Clay Award for Social Unity & Compromise at Bronx International High School

# MEG CASSIDY

YEARS AS MENTOR: 2012

OCCUPATION: Senior Publicist, Free Press Books, New York, NY

*Fanta says:* I remember the first time meeting Meg, I wondered, will she be patient? Because I felt like my English could be frustrating to someone who doesn't want to listen. But I found that she was different from what I feared. Meg is someone any young woman would like to be with, and they will learn the most important things from her, like how to take care of themselves in their own world. WITH HER, I FOUND COURAGE TO WRITE IN MY JOURNAL, which I never did outside of school before. Because of her, I now feel free to share my writing with confidence.

fanta appears in: #whoweare, #atacrossroads

*Meg says:* Our favorite place to meet, now that the weather's warm, is 16 Handles—a FroYo spot that lets you self-serve as many combinations of flavors and toppings imaginable. My inclination—with writing as with FroYo—is to choose way too many. Fanta knows how to keep both of hers simple. She can convey intense emotion with a single phrase, and as we're eating I'll often look longingly at her dish, thinking that the simplicity of it looks much more appealing than the mess I've created. LESS SPRINKLES, MORE SUBSTANCE IS WHAT FANTA REMINDS ME, ON THE PAGE AND OFF, EVERY TIME WE MEET.

meg appears in: #whoweare

# KAYTLIN CARLO
(far right)

YEARS AS MENTEE: 2012

GRADE: 11

HIGH SCHOOL: Pace High School, New York, NY

BORN: New York, NY

LIVES: Brooklyn, NY

# COLLEEN BARRY

YEARS AS MENTOR: 2012

OCCUPATION: Publishing Assistant, Random House, New York, NY

PUBLICATIONS: *Whatcom County First Prize Essay Anthology*, Robot Melo, BestPoem

*Kaytlin says:* COLLEEN INSPIRES ME TO "GO THERE." She's always telling me to not be afraid of my mind and the connections it makes. She has helped me to reveal myself in my work and to make my writing richer with detail. Every week she brings something new to our sessions, whether my edited resume, a new poet to read, or a website of flash nonfiction, I always know I will be inspired.

kaytlin appears in: #transforminginto

*Colleen says:* I love watching Kaytlin discover the way life can open and expand through words—one moment she's telling me about her 16th birthday and the first time she gets to wear heels, and the next moment she's telling me about her love for the ecstatic nature of Emily Dickinson's poems. It's an honor to be a part of each little piece of writing she creates; SHE INSPIRES ME ANEW EACH WEEK.

colleen appears in: #transforminginto

# SOPHIA CHAN

YEARS AS MENTEE: 2012

GRADE: 11

HIGH SCHOOL: NYC Lab High School for Collaborative Studies, New York, NY

BORN: Brooklyn, NY

LIVES: Brooklyn, NY

# SIOBHAN BURKE

YEARS AS MENTOR: 2012

OCCUPATION: Associate Editor, *Dance Magazine*; freelance dance critic based in New York City

PUBLICATIONS: *The New York Times, The Brooklyn Rail*, Hyperallergic, *The Columbia Journal of American Studies*

*Sophia says:* Is it bad to always want change? Is it bad to live recklessly? What do I mean by "bad"? Where will I be if I keep up this mindset? I am indecisive, spontaneous, jumbled, an EFPN (or so the personality test tells me). Questions are constantly nagging me. Is this the plan I really want? Will I be happy? Though I am still "a child with a huge future ahead of me," I envy those who have found their unintended place of happiness. Will I get there? I AM SCARED OF THE RISKS, EXHILARATED BY THE THRILL OF THE UNKNOWN. "How did you become a journalist, Siobhan?"

sophia appears in: #whoweare, #behindthescenes

*Siobhan says:* We're sitting across from each other at the 7th Avenue coffee shop that has become our Thursday-afternoon haunt. My pen hovers above the paper, my mind straining to find just the right words, while Sophia scribbles away, thoughts streaming onto the page. As a recovering perfectionist, I've been carefully observing her: SHE DOESN'T OVER-THINK; SHE'S NOT AFRAID TO CHANGE DIRECTIONS; and as she told me once, with typical candor and composure in the course of a conversation about SAT scores, "I just don't care to compare myself to others."

siobhan appears in: #transforminginto, #whowear

# MONICA CHIN

YEARS AS MENTEE: 2011, 2012

GRADE: 11

HIGH SCHOOL: Baruch College Campus High School, New York, NY

BORN: New York, NY

LIVES: New York, NY

AWARDS: Scholastic Art & Writing Awards Gold Key for Poetry; Scholastic Art & Writing Awards Silver Key for Poetry

# ELAINE STUART-SHAH

YEARS AS MENTOR: 2011, 2012

OCCUPATION: Freelance Writer based in New York City

PUBLICATIONS: *The New York Times, The Wall Street Journal*, and *Dance Magazine*

*Monica says:* "What have I gotten myself into?" That was the only thought running through my head during one of my first workshops in GWN. My interests were reading fiction, writing fiction, and breathing fiction. I never knew I would be remotely interested in journalism or, dare I say, autobiography! ELAINE REALLY ENCOURAGES ME TO PUSH PAST MY FEARS OF NONFICTION WRITING. At the beginning of most sessions she comes up with a creative twist to incorporate memoir into fictional writing. I remember at one of our meetings she suggested we write a short story using ourselves as the main character. As a journalist and nonfiction writer, she's made me a lot more comfortable with the genre.

monica appears in: #atacrossroads, #behindthescenes

*Elaine says:* At an early pair session this year, Monica told me she wanted to work on the "so what?" factor in her writing. "The what?" I asked. "No. 'So what?'" she replied, explaining that this is the reader reaction she wants to avoid. IF SOMEONE STOPS TO ASK THEMSELVES, "SO WHAT? WHY DO I CARE?" YOU'VE ALREADY LOST THEM. With this in mind, we've explored ways to capture and hold the reader's attention, from a fast-paced plotline to lyrical language. Now whenever I write something for grad school or work, I ask myself, "Is that a so-what lead, a so-what section?" It has made us both better storytellers.

elaine appears in: #atacrossroads

## TAYSHA MILAGROS CLARK

YEARS AS MENTEE: 2012

GRADE: 12

HIGH SCHOOL: Aquinas High School, New York, NY

BORN: Bronx, NY

LIVES: Bronx, NY

SCHOLARSHIPS: Scholastic Art & Writing Awards Gold Key for Poetry

WILL ATTEND: Barnard College, New York, NY

## MAYURI CHANDRA

YEARS AS MENTOR: 2011, 2012

OCCUPATION: Curriculum Writer for New York City arts programs

*Taysha says:* What I love most about Mayuri is how supportive she is. Because of the time I spend with her, I'm able to write about so many things. SHE CONVINCES ME TO STEP OUT OF MY SHELL AND WRITE ABOUT TOPICS THAT I WOULD OTHERWISE COWER FROM. Mayuri has helped me to be a more courageous writer and the honesty seen in her work inspires me to write about topics that are honest to my emotions.

taysha appears in: #whoweare

*Mayuri says:* The amazing thing about Taysha is how personal she is in her writing—SHE IS COMPLETELY UNAFRAID TO BARE HERSELF IN HER WORDS. At our meetings, she could just "enter" a piece immediately as herself, whereas I always need time to charge up my thoughts and pen. She has definitely taught me to be open-minded in my writing and ease some of the pressure off my writing—that it can and should be more free-flowing.

mayuri appears in: #whoweare

# SULEYMA CUELLAR

YEARS AS MENTEE: 2012

GRADE: 11

HIGH SCHOOL: School of St. Jean Baptiste, New York, NY

BORN: Puebla, Mexico

LIVES: New York, NY

AWARDS: Second Place Hobby Awards, School of St. Jean Baptiste

SCHOLARSHIPS: The Friends of Nic Base, in writing

# JENNIFER BACON

YEARS AS MENTOR: 2012

OCCUPATION: Assistant Professor of Special Education, Iona College, New Rochelle, NY

PUBLICATIONS: *Journal of Poetry Therapy, phati'tude Literary Magazine,* Teachers College Record

*Suleyma says:* "Suleyma, this is Jennifer, your mentor." Jennifer looked at me and smiled with a smile that made my nervousness go away. I sat down and smiled back and in five minutes from that first "hi," I had opened up to her, sharing all my personal feelings. I COULD NOT BELIEVE THAT I OPENED UP SO FAST TO SOMEONE I HAD MET ONLY A FEW MINUTES AGO. But since then, Jennifer has showed me that you have to be able to trust people. She has become more than a mentor to me—she's someone I can turn to for advice or just to listen to me. That is something that is hard to find, yet I found it in her.

suleyma appears in: #whoweare

*Jennifer says:* I remember Suleyma from our first mentee/mentor workshop. There were several things that stood out to me the very first time I heard her speak, but one of the most memorable was her "quiet boldness." Suleyma was a natural—she would just stand up in this large room of strangers with a beaming smile and speak. One of the funniest stories that she shared during the first workshop, with a mischievous grin, was her knack for writing love poems for others who would eagerly ask her to help them write a romantic poem to win someone over. But it was not until our first individual meeting that I had the privilege of learning the depth of her boldness. NOT ONLY WAS SULEYMA TALENTED, SWEET, AND FUNNY, SHE WAS POWERFUL! Her story, wisdom, and presence were such an inspiration and tribute to all of the gifts and talents that she has and will continue to offer this world.

jennifer appears in: #whoweare

# KRISTASIAH DANIELS

YEARS AS MENTEE: 2011, 2012

GRADE: 11

HIGH SCHOOL: Brooklyn School for Music and Theatre, Brooklyn, NY

BORN: New York, NY

LIVES: Brooklyn, NY

# JODI NARDE

YEARS AS MENTOR: 2012

OCCUPATION: Blog Editor and Online Marketing Manager, NYU Press

PUBLICATIONS: *New Orleans Review, New York Moves* magazine

*Kristasiah says:* My mentor and I have just met and are still getting to know each other. I like all her ideas for stories, and we recently tried a writing game that turned out to be somewhat hard but somewhat easy at the same time. So far in our meetings she's influenced me to revisit the nonstop vortex of my own creation: "Blood and Fangs." Because of her, I'm starting to get out of my writer's block and back into the life of Crystal and Jay. I hope in the future we have more fun and do more stories. LOOKS LIKE I MIGHT HAVE A NEW FRIEND.

kristasiah appears in: #otherworlds

*Jodi says:* Remixing Krissy's piece from Jay's perspective was a bit of a challenge. After all, he was the mysterious, complex, wolf-boyfriend of her beloved protagonist. Krissy rarely gave him a voice on purpose, focusing instead on Crystal's inner voice as she came of age as a (half) vampire. I didn't think I'd be able to characterize him without some disappointment. But Krissy was excited by my first draft, kindly correcting me on physical details and ENCOURAGING ME TO "FOCUS ON FEELING"—A PIECE OF ADVICE I HOPE TO APPLY TO ALL OF MY WRITING.

jodi appears in: #otherworlds

# SHANNON DANIELS

YEARS AS MENTEE: 2012

GRADE: 10

HIGH SCHOOL: Stuyvesant
High School, New York, NY

BORN: New York, NY

LIVES: New York, NY

AWARDS: Scholastic Art
& Writing Awards
Gold Key for Personal
Essay/Memoir

# WHITNEY JACOBY

YEARS AS MENTOR: 2012

OCCUPATION: Account Manager-Independent Bookstores, Simon & Schuster,
New York, NY

*Shannon says:* As we walked into Chinatown, I pointed out a tenement. "That's where my grandmother lived."

We both felt a strong sense of cultural identity with our grandmothers. This, along with our mutual love for coming-of-age novels and plaid brought us together. We gushed over how many childhood memories took place in the same streets.

WHITNEY HAS DARED ME TO WRITE MORE FICTION, AND I CHALLENGED HER TO DIP HER TOES INTO THE OCEAN OF POETRY.

shannon appears in: #transforminginto, #behindthescenes

*Whitney says:* The first time I saw Shannon perform was at the portfolio check-in. I hear her read every week during our one-to-one sessions, but it's not quite the same when you're in a cafe surrounded by people doing their own work.

When Shannon practiced her CHAPTERS' piece at the check-in, I saw her in a whole new light. SHE RADIATED BEAUTY WITH HER CONFIDENCE AND POISE, AND WAS TRANSFORMED INTO A WOMAN BEFORE MY EYES.

The spirit Shannon exemplifies in her writing and performing inspires me to have the same outlook on my own work.

whitney appears in: #tiesthatbind, # otherworlds

# GINA DiFRISCO

YEARS AS MENTEE: 2011, 2012

GRADE: 11

HIGH SCHOOL: Urban Assembly School for Green Careers, New York, NY

BORN: New York, NY

LIVES: Bronx, NY

# KATE TREBUSS

YEARS AS MENTOR: 2012

OCCUPATION: Doctoral candidate in English and Comparative Literature at Columbia University, New York, NY

*Gina says:* I sit at my desk thinking, how has my mentor remixed me? I say to myself, "I'm too tired for this." I light a candle and some incense. Sitting at my desk, with the light of a candle and my empty computer screen, the smoke of the incense catches my sight. I blow at it, creating patterns in the air. I AM THE SMOKE AND KATE IS THE WIND THAT REMIXES ME. It's been everything. The things we talk about to the things we see and write. She teaches me new things and gives me new ideas. I am turned into a new pattern at every meeting.

gina appears in: #transforminginto, #andwerehome, #behindthescenes

*Kate says:* Two weeks ago I suggested to Gina—for what felt like the millionth time—that it might be helpful to use an agenda so she wouldn't be caught off guard by deadlines. Gina gave me a withering look and told me I was being ridiculous—clearly she'd just lose an agenda. I was a little dismayed by Gina's fatalistic logic but dropped the subject. I felt more than a little sheepish when Gina and I exchanged the following texts the day before the GWN Anthology deadline. Gina, who already finished her submission, was checking in to see how my piece was coming along:

Gina: Hey, hows the anthology piece going?
Me: good! still working on it! :(
Gina: Awe. Work hard and good luck then
Me: thanks! i am a terrible influence. sorry i haven't been more on top of this!! i promise it WILL be done on time!! xo
Gina: Its okay, just get it done. :)

IN SPITE OF MY CHAGRIN, I'VE NEVER BEEN PROUDER.

kate appears in: #atacrossroads, #andwerehome

# KARMA DOLKAR

YEARS AS MENTEE: 2012

GRADE: 11

HIGH SCHOOL: Flushing International High School, Queens, NY

BORN: Toelung, Tibet

LIVES: Queens, NY

# AMANDA ORENSTEIN

YEARS AS MENTOR: 2012

OCCUPATION: Editorial Assistant, John Wiley & Sons, Hoboken, NJ

PUBLICATIONS: *New York Family* magazine

*Karma says:* Amanda is a great mentor who has been giving me so much support in all the work that I've done. SHE TAUGHT ME THAT WRITING COMES FROM DEEP DOWN IN YOUR HEART. Writing keeps people attached to their inner selves and it doesn't have to be boring. She has opened up my interest in trying out different kinds of fun writing activities, which has helped me to be as creative as I can be.

karma appears in: #atacrossroads

*Amanda says:* Karma continually inspires me with her creativity and imagination. She prefers I surprise her with our pair session activity, and without any preparation, always manages to create something unique and original. HER STYLE OF WRITING HAS MADE ME THINK ABOUT THE BOUNDARIES I IMPOSE ON MY OWN WORK and ways in which I could loosen those restrictions and just have more fun with my writing. Working with Karma has given me the motivation to approach my writing from many different angles and try to mix it up!

amanda appears in: #tiesthatbind

# SHARLINE DOMINGUEZ

YEARS AS MENTEE: 2011, 2012

GRADE: 12

HIGH SCHOOL: Brooklyn College Academy, Brooklyn, NY

BORN: Dominican Republic

LIVES: Brooklyn, NY

AWARDS: Scholastic Art & Writing Awards Gold Key for Writing Portfolio

SCHOLARSHIPS: Questbridge Scholarship to Amherst College

WILL ATTEND: Amherst College, Amherst, MA

# NANCY MERCADO

YEARS AS MENTOR: 2010, 2011, 2012

OCCUPATION: Executive Editor, Roaring Brook Press/Macmillan Children's Group, New York, NY

*Sharline says:* Nancy's humorous personality and her openness to new ideas amazed me from the first time we sat down to have coffee. Although we have never really taken advantage of the fact that we write in different genres, I THANK NANCY FOR ALWAYS ACCEPTING THE WAY IN WHICH I WRITE ABOUT MY LIFE and the complaints I make about society. Every time I sit down to write with Nancy, she makes sure that I get as much as I can down on paper. Even when we were pressured to meet the deadline for our CHAPTERS reading piece, I still remember laughing and poking fun at our last-minute submission, promising that we would never do it again. Of course, this is a lie in Nancy and Sharline's world. What can I say? We know how to have fun beyond our love of writing.

sharline appears in: #andwerehome

*Nancy says:* "I don't know even know where the heck this piece came from." That's pretty much what Sharline and I say every time we finish a freewrite. Sharline's openness to whatever flows out of her pen in any given moment has totally infected me and I now come to our freewrites with a similar open mind.

We laugh at the strangeness of our subconscious and where it takes us, most of the time without much instruction from our conscious mind. IT'S CERTAINLY AN ODD LITTLE WORLD INSIDE OUR HEADS, BUT THE MIXING AND THE JUDGMENT-FREE SHARING OF THESE WORLDS IS THE EXCITING PART.

nancy appears in: #andwerehome

# RUBY FELIZ

YEARS AS MENTEE: 2012

GRADE: 12

HIGH SCHOOL: The Urban Assembly Bronx School for Law, Government, and Justice, Bronx, NY

BORN: Santo Domingo, Dominican Republic

LIVES: Bronx, NY

AWARDS: Principal's Honor Roll, The Urban Assembly Bronx School for Law, Government, and Justice, Bronx, NY

SCHOLARSHIPS: Los Padres Foundation Scholarship

WILL ATTEND: SUNY Plattsburgh, Plattsburgh, NY

# JALYLAH BURRELL

YEARS AS MENTOR: 2012

OCCUPATION: Doctoral Candidate at Yale University, New Haven, CT

PUBLICATIONS: *Vibe*, The FADER, *Village Voice, Portland Mercury,* and *Encore,* among others

*Ruby says:* THE RULE-BREAKER. THAT'S WHAT I CALL HER. Once our comfort level was sparked, that spark grew into flames. And the moment she felt comfortable she started breaking the rules of our freewrites. "You have to know the rules to break them." I lingered on these words after one meeting. While it was just another statement to Jalylah, it was a challenge I took on. Jalylah has inspired me to play on the horizon of different styles I thought were against the rules—rules I had set for myself. Slowly but dangerously our relationship has grown into a rule-breaking frenzy.

ruby appears in: #tiesthatbind, #whoweare

*Jalylah says:* Spring is just two days old, it's already almost hot and 125th street is bustling. We meet at the corner of Lexington, and Ruby's red hair glows as we walk to Marcus Garvey Park. No shaded benches remain but Ruby spots an unoccupied chess table. We put down our bags, dig out our poems, and start rehearsing for our upcoming reading. BY HER POEM'S MIDPOINT, A MOTLEY FEW CROWD RUBY AND SHE MEETS THESE STRANGER'S GAZES WITH SMILING EYES, steady voice, and unhampered verse. Applause. And then a query, "Can we use this chess table?" We laugh. "Of course."

jalylah appears in: #tiesthatbind

# TEAMARÉ GASTÓN

YEARS AS MENTEE: 2012

GRADE: 10

HIGH SCHOOL: Central Park East High School, New York, NY

BORN: New York, NY

LIVES: New York, NY

AWARDS: Scholastic Art & Writing Awards Gold Key for Dramatic Script

SCHOLARSHIPS: Alliance Summer Arts Program (ASAP) Award

# KATHERINE NERO

YEARS AS MENTOR: 2011, 2012

OCCUPATION: Writer and Director based in New York City

*Teamaré says:* My mentor and I came up with our pieces after a long discussion about mirrors and their history. She told me of the stories she heard growing up about the monsters that lived beyond what we see, and that was what gave me the idea for "Mirror Horror." A scary movie buff myself, I automatically jumped on this project as a great way to get in touch with my twisted side; and for that I HAD TO LOOK AT THE ME BEYOND ME.

teamaré appears in: #otherworlds

*Katherine says:* During a recent meeting, Teamaré shared one of her dreams with me. We discussed the dream's significance and later explored possible interpretations through a writing exercise. That process helped me realize how negligent I had become. THANKS TO TEAMARÉ, I AM NOW MORE DILIGENT ABOUT RECORDING AND ANALYZING MY DREAMS. She reminded me how important it is to explore your subconscious thoughts in order to write truthfully.

katherine appears in: #otherworlds

## NATHALIE GOMEZ

YEARS AS MENTEE: 2011, 2012

GRADE: 11

HIGH SCHOOL: North Queens Community High School, Queens, NY

BORN: Providence, RI

LIVES: Queens, NY

## AMANDA BERLIN

YEARS AS MENTOR: 2011, 2012

OCCUPATION: Writer and Life Coach

PUBLICATIONS: Forbes.com, *Teen Identity magazine, Renew,* Volunteerism.org, *Your Bella Life*

*Nathalie says:* Amanda is like the sister I wish I had. Is that mean to say when I have three sisters already? She's always so supportive of everything I do. I'm constantly putting pressure on myself, but she can always get me to relax. She understands my weird logic whenever I'm writing. I can write something that doesn't make sense to me, but she'll know where I could go with it. SHE INSPIRES ME TO GO WITH THE FLOW, AND TO REMEMBER TO JUST BREATHE. I'm on the boat with only one sail and she's the breeze that nudges me to strive for greatness.

nathalie appears in: #tiesthatbind

*Amanda says:* If you were to meet my mentee Nathalie, you'd think she's like the smooth groove of an R&B song. On the surface, she's calm, collected, amiable, and strong. I've come to know Nathalie as much more. I'VE REALIZED NATHALIE IS A FIGHT SONG, AN 80S HAIR BAND POWER BALLAD. She's all, "Here I go again on my own / goin' down the only road I've ever known / I've made up my mind. / I ain't wastin' no more time!" fist pumping in the air, long hair streaming down her back. This is the part of Nathalie that I can only hope to remix into myself. Nathalie is courage. And I know she has so much of it, she can share a little of it with me.

amanda appears in: #tiesthatbind

# MENNEN GORDON

YEARS AS MENTEE: 2012

GRADE: 9

HIGH SCHOOL: Institute for Collaborative Education, New York, NY

BORN: Brooklyn, NY

LIVES: Bronx, NY

# RORY SATRAN

YEARS AS MENTOR: 2012

OCCUPATION: Content Director at Opening Ceremony, New York, NY; Freelance Writer & Editor

PUBLICATIONS: *Self Service* magazine, *The Washington Post, Marie Claire, Lula* magazine, *About Face: Women Write What They See When They Look in the Mirror* (Seal Press, 2008), *Opening Ceremony* (Rizzoli, fall 2012)

*Mennen says:* While in a park near Lafayette Street, we sat while Rory read over my piece for the CHAPTERS Reading Series. In need of something relevant to do, I WAS ASSIGNED THE TASK OF WRITING ABOUT THE MORNING ROUTINE OF SOMEONE IN THE PARK. Uninspired, I just wrote about this boy wearing a striped shirt, Adidas shoes, and khakis. He played intently and was adorable, so I wrote about him. There was another girl near him, who seemed rambunctious, and she turned into the character of his felon-enamored sister.

mennen appears in: #tiesthatbind

*Rory says:* Mennen will be the first to tell you that I don't always come to our pair sessions with a plan. I'M A BIG PROPONENT OF SPONTANEOUS EXERCISES (for admittedly lazy reasons). So while reading over her work one day, I had her write about the morning routine of someone at the park where we were working. The resulting piece is 'Stripes,' which I later remixed, focusing on another character.

rory appears in: #tiesthatbind

Recognition for
*The 2011 Girls Write Now Anthology*

**Independent Publisher Book Awards**
Outstanding Book of the Year *and*
Independent Voice Award

**National Indie Excellence Book Awards**
Finalist, Anthology

**New York Book Festival**
Honorable Mention, Wild Card

# DANNI GREEN

YEARS AS MENTEE: 2012

GRADE: 12

HIGH SCHOOL: Academy for Young Writers, Brooklyn, NY

BORN: New York, NY

LIVES: Brooklyn, NY

WILL ATTEND: Lewis and Clark, Portland, Oregon

# KATHLEEN SCHEINER

YEARS AS MENTOR: 2012

OCCUPATION: Freelance writer, editor, and proofreader based in New York City

PUBLICATIONS: *Dance International, L'Ecran Fantastique, Toxic, Publishers Weekly,* and the anthology *Memoirs of Meanness* (Pergola Publishing, 2009)

*Danni says:* There are many glaring differences between Kathleen and I. She prefers prose—fantasy and horror fiction, specifically. I gravitate toward poetry to express the vulnerable parts of myself. Kathleen is enamored with horror movies. I don't watch horror movies and don't plan on starting. ONE THING THAT IS NOT DIFFERENT ABOUT US IS THAT OUR MOMS HAVE BEQUEATHED US THINGS THAT WE WOULD RATHER HAVE NOT RECEIVED. We took our topic and remixed our writing to be in the other's genre—achieving my goal of writing in prose thanks to Kathleen as my mentor.

danni appears in: #tiesthatbind

*Kathleen says:* This year I am proud to have met and worked with Danni Faith Green. I LOVE HER MIDDLE NAME FAITH BECAUSE TO ME THAT IS THE ESSENCE OF WHO DANNI IS. Danni is direct and forthright; she believes in saying and writing about what is on her mind, while I prefer to work with nuance, metaphor, and those unsayable things that usually come out as creepy-crawlies. We've worked together a lot on editing and refining, my forte, but I must say I have learned quite a lot from Danni about saying just what needs to be said.

kathleen appears in: #tiesthatbind

# MARCELA GRILLO

YEARS AS MENTEE: 2012

GRADE: 12

HIGH SCHOOL: Institute for Collaborative Education, New York, NY

BORN: Brooklyn, NY

LIVES: Brooklyn, NY

AWARDS: Scholastic Art & Writing Awards National Silver Medal for Writing Portfolio; Scholastic Art & Writing Awards Gold Key for Flash Fiction; and Scholastic Art & Writing Awards National Silver Key for Flash Fiction

WILL ATTEND: Connecticut College, New London, CT

# HILARY LEICHTER

YEARS AS MENTOR: 2012

OCCUPATION: Freelance writer and workshop teacher, Columbia University, New York, NY

PUBLICATIONS: *Indiana Review* and *The L Magazine* online

*Marcela says:* I found out early on that Hilary and I would work really well together—whether it's at a bagel shop or a French restaurant. Most of the time she understands my own writing better than I do! IT'S ALWAYS GREAT TO BE ABLE TO SHARE YOUR WORK WITH SOMEONE YOU TRUST. This year, Hilary taught me to see my words beyond the first glance, and that there is always something underneath the surface worth pursuing.

marcela appears in: #transforminginto, #behindthescenes

*Hilary says:* After a side of fries, two cups of coffee, and a long afternoon of hard work, the owner of the cafe could tell that Marcela and I were on a deadline! When she turned in her portfolio for the Scholastic Art & Writing Awards a little later, I was amazed. Not only at her focus, drive, and determination, but at the talent brimming over in every piece she submitted. SHE IS A FORCE TO BE RECKONED WITH, AN INSPIRATION, AND MOST OF ALL, AN AMAZING WRITER. I have been so lucky to work with her this year.

hilary appears in: #whoweare

# PRISCILLA GUO

YEARS AS MENTEE: 2011, 2012

GRADE: 10

HIGH SCHOOL: Hunter College High School, New York, NY

BORN: New York, NY

LIVES: Queens, NY

# MY-THUAN TRAN

YEARS AS MENTOR: 2012

OCCUPATION: Global health consultant

*Priscilla says:* Throughout our weekly pair sessions, My-Thuan has always been kind and patient to me. She has held my hand as we made the tough decisions in my writing and has inspired and encouraged me to take bold risks. WE HAVE BONDED OVER FAVORITE FOODS, INTERESTS IN MUSIC, AND OUR TRIALS AND TRIBULATIONS WITH OUR HAIR. My-Thuan has not only mentored me in my writing, but mentored me in my life. I look up to her as a role model, a fellow writer, and best of all, a best friend.

priscilla appears in: #whoweare, #atacrossroads

*My-Thuan says:* When I first met Priscilla at the Crime Fiction Workshop, she made the entire room laugh. Instead of a dramatic piece, she wrote a funny confession scene where Odysseus' son admits to being his father's killer. The motive: Because in all other Greek myths, the son kills the father. WOW, I THOUGHT, THIS GIRL HAS GOT SO MUCH CREATIVITY AND HUMOR. I couldn't wait to see where we could go with our pair writing sessions. As we have worked together over the last year, I've seen a lot of this creativity and humor get remixed in my own writing.

my-thuan appears in: #whoweare, atacrossroads

# LARISSA HERON

YEARS AS MENTEE: 2011, 2012

GRADE: 10

HIGH SCHOOL: School of the Future, New York, NY

BORN: New York, NY

LIVES: New York, NY

PUBLICATIONS: The Clinton Chronicle, Future Times: The Newspaper at School of the Future, High 5, The Huffington Post, Indypendent.org, and Theater Development Fund

# TOBI ELKIN

YEARS AS MENTOR: 2012

OCCUPATION: Writer at eMarketer, Inc., New York, NY

PUBLICATIONS: AOL sites, Advertizing Age, Brandweek, MediaPost Communications Publications, The Huffington Post, The Lo-Down, Verbicide

*Larissa says:* Before Tobi became my mentor, poetry was my preferred form of writing. I had never written a reported piece and felt uncertain when I started. My first reported pieces, for which I conducted a series of interviews (and later transcribed them), were on the Occupy Wall Street movement. Tobi assisted me in deciding which quotes to use and which to drop, how to create transitions and find the heart and theme of the piece. UNDER HER GUIDANCE, MY JOURNALISM HAS BEEN PUBLISHED IN THE *CLINTON CHRONICLE* AND ON THE INDYPENDENT.ORG.

larissa appears in: #transforminginto, #behindthescenes

*Tobi says:* I had become accustomed to providing feedback, suggestions and editing assistance to Larissa on her writing, but hadn't produced much new writing of my own. I found her eager and receptive to offering input on my prose poem "My Everest," which explores how a person can often be more real in your thoughts and recollections than in reality. I remixed snippets of conversation, emails, and text messages to write "My Everest," after composing it in my head in various permutations. I AM CONTINUALLY IMPRESSED WITH, AND INSPIRED BY, THE EASE WITH WHICH LARISSA WRITES POETRY and applies herself to all creative endeavors.

tobi appears in: #transforminginto

# CHANDRA HUGHES

YEARS AS MENTEE: 2011, 2012

GRADE: 11

HIGH SCHOOL: Millennium High School, New York, NY

BORN: China

LIVES: New York, NY

# CLAUDIA PARSONS

YEARS AS MENTOR: 2011, 2012

OCCUPATION: Editor, Reuters

*Chandra says:* This being my second year with Claudia, we were able to follow a different path with our writing. We still collaborated on a story, but this time we worked on a radio play instead of a novel. BEING IN THE GWN REMIX DORKSHOPS AT PARSONS WITH CLAUDIA IS WONDERFUL. Being able to remix one piece in different ways (audio, animation, and video) is fun. I'm able to see what my mentor does and apply it to my own ideas. Using the tools learned in the Workshops, Claudia and I are able to apply them back to our radio project, creating a wonderful new piece.

chandra appears in: #otherworlds, #behindthescenes

*Claudia says:* ONE DAY I'LL BE WATCHING THE OSCARS AND THEY'LL ANNOUNCE THAT CHANDRA HUGHES HAS WON THE ACADEMY AWARD for animated movie, and I'll tell everybody "I know her." Chandra spends many a night recording and editing scripts to remix anime films. We were part of the Digital Remix Portfolio Pilot with GWN this year, and I found myself asking her to show me how the software worked. While I was struggling with the basics, Chandra was making words fly, literally fly, in her animation of a poem called "If These Wings Could Fly." Now, if only these words could fly...

claudia appears in: #otherworlds

# KATHRYN JAGAI

YEARS AS MENTEE: 2009, 2010, 2011, 2012

GRADE: 12

HIGH SCHOOL: Hunter College High School, New York, NY

BORN: New York, NY

LIVES: Brooklyn, NY

AWARDS: TED talk, *Teen Ink* Editor's Choice Award, Scholastic Art & Writing Awards National Gold Medals, 4 times, and Gold Keys, 5 times (2010, 2011, 2012)

WILL ATTEND: Bennington College, Bennington, VT

# THERESE COX

YEARS AS MENTOR: 2011, 2012

OCCUPATION: Writer, Performer, Artist, and Adjunct English Instructor at CUNY

PUBLICATIONS: *The Brooklyn Rail*; 2012 Irish Writers' Centre First Novel Award

*Kathryn says:* Therese is a constant stream of amusement and information, her brain a plethora of obscure Irish factoids and liberal doses of caffeine. OUR LOVE FOR WRITING IS AUGMENTED BY OUR SHARED APPRECIATION OF VISUAL ART AND MUSIC, the varying styles complimenting each other as we move through writing exercises and editing forays. Our research and field trips have lent an adventurous whimsy to our time together, perusing old sketchbooks and museums, and I look forward to whatever our meetings divulge every week.

kathryn appears in: #otherworlds

*Therese says:* KAT'S IMAGINATION IS AS VISIONARY AS A TESLA INVENTION, as ornamental as a Gaudi cathedral, and as much fun to spend time with as a steampunk comic book. One aspect of Kat that's inspired me most is her willingness to take brave imaginative leaps in her writing. Her latest novel features a huge cast of characters dealing with past lives, supernatural creatures and crises of biblical proportions. As a result, I'm starting my new novel with a jam-packed cast and an eye on big issues—a daunting undertaking, but I'm sure she'll help me out when I get stuck.

therese appears in: #otherworlds, #behindthescenes

# FLORA LI

YEARS AS MENTEE: 2012

GRADE: 10

HIGH SCHOOL: Hunter College High School, New York, NY

BORN: Guangzhou, China

LIVES: Queens, NY

# MARY PAT KANE

YEARS AS MENTOR: 2012

OCCUPATION: Writer and Storyteller

PUBLICATIONS: *Philadelphia Daily News, The Christian Science Monitor, AIDS and the Arts in Philadelphia* (a PEW Foundation project); storyteller with *The Moth* and *Speakeasy Storycast*; blogs *Ms. CRANKY* and *WISPS*

*Flora says:* Mary is a very optimistic person. THE FIRST TIME I SAW HER, I WAS ATTRACTED BY HER HEARTY LAUGHTER AND SMILES. Her poetry always gets in touch with life and the way people feel. Mary has helped me improve my English a lot. Similarly, she is a very industrious person—she shares her work and life experiences with me. She has taken me places I've never been, even watching the show that developed before my eyes. I have learned a lot from her, and see the beauty of life.

flora appears in: #whoweare

*Mary Pat says:* I've learned so much working with my mentee, Flora, about determination and work ethic, tinged sometimes with loneliness (she is away from her parents who are in China) and worries about fitting in because English is still new to her. But she just forges on, signing up for every program she can to better herself.

I think, maybe in comparison, I had made peace with my lack of more success. I was resigned to it; didn't send out my work as much. MAYBE, BECAUSE OF FLORA, I WILL DUST MYSELF OFF AND START OUT AGAIN. Why not?

mary appears in: #andwerehome

# JOANNE LIN

YEARS AS MENTEE: 2011, 2012

GRADE: 12

HIGH SCHOOL: Millennium
Highschool, New York, NY

BORN: New York, NY

LIVES: New York, NY

# LATOYA JORDAN

YEARS AS MENTOR:
2011, 2012

OCCUPATION:
Assistant Director of
Communications/PR Manager for New York Law School, New York, NY

PUBLICATIONS: *Mobius: The Journal for Social Change, The November 3rd Club, The Splinter Generation,* and *qarrtsiluni.*

*Joanne says:* SUNDAYS AT BARNES & NOBLE CAN BE SUMMED UP IN THREE WORDS: BACON, BABIES, AND BOOKS. While I sit across from LaToya, my mentor, I am surrounded by the laughter we share and the books piled on every shelf. This year, as LaToya is preparing for her new baby's first steps in this world, she also helps me find my first steps in a genre of fiction that I have never explored: dark fiction. However, our writing sessions are never dark. We always end up on a light tone, either about babies or bacon...the perfect ending to a long week.

joanne appears in: #atacrossroads, #behindthescenes

*LaToya says:* Joanne and I are in our second year together. We meet on the same day, at the same time, at the same location as last year. But this year has definitely been different, in part because of the various changes in our lives—lots of baby talk because of my pregnancy, and college talk as she tackles her junior year. JOANNE HAS BEEN TAKING RISKS WITH HER WRITING; I love that she has delved into fiction, flash fiction, and darker subject matter for her stories and poetry. I often write about darker subject matter and have instead been writing lighter pieces, inspired by Joanne to switch things up a little.

latoya appears in: #whoweare

# SUSSY LIZ

YEARS AS MENTEE: 2012

GRADE: 12

HIGH SCHOOL: Manhattan Bridges High School, New York, NY

BORN: Santiago, Dominican Republic

LIVES: Bronx, NY

# AMY FELDMAN

YEARS AS MENTOR: 2011, 2012

OCCUPATION: writer, editor and journalist based in New York City

PUBLICATIONS: *Bloomberg Businessweek, Fast Company, Forbes, Inc., Institutional Investor, Money, The New York Times, the New York Daily News, Reuters, Time,* and other publications

*Sussy says:* As I look back, I remember my first session with Amy. I remember setting our goals and, of course, getting to know her at a McDonald's near Columbus Circle. Within a month we already had a plan for my college applications and had started working on them. College essays, scholarships, applications—you name it, we did it all. IT'S BEEN A DELIGHTFUL JOURNEY WITH AMY, GETTING TO KNOW MY WRITING, AND UNDERSTANDING THE POWER OF WORDS.

sussy appears in: #tiesthatbind

*Amy says:* Sussy and I first bonded over the fact that we both like Junot Diaz. But much of our time together has been more practical than literary: Sussy was a senior when we met, and college application deadlines loomed. Together, we hit them. College applications, check. FAFSA, check. Gates scholarship, check. HEOP (Higher Education Opportunity Program), check, check, check. ALL TOLD, SUSSY WROTE 17 ESSAYS, WHICH WE REVISED, EDITED AND WHIPPED INTO SHAPE. Watching Sussy get the job done was inspiring. We celebrated getting through it by going to the theater. I hope we'll soon celebrate the prize—that she gets into the college she wants.

amy appears in: #atacrossroads

# ALICIA MALDONADO

YEARS AS MENTEE: 2011, 2012

GRADE: 12

HIGH SCHOOL: NYC iSchool, New York, NY

BORN: New York, NY

LIVES: New York, NY

WILL ATTEND: St. Bonaventure University, St. Bonaventure, NY

# KRISTI GOLDADE

YEARS AS MENTOR: 2012

OCCUPATION: Masters Candidate in Literary Reportage Concentration at NYU's Arthur L. Carter Journalism Institute, New York, NY

PUBLICATIONS: *Epiphany* magazine, *Capital New York, Brooklyn Based*

*Alicia says:* The most memorable meeting I have had with Kristi was when we went to this 1970's-themed cafe. I was standing outside texting Kristi to see where she was. She told me, "Alicia, I will be there in 2 shakes." I was confused because I have never heard of that restaurant. When she arrived I asked, "KRISTI, WHAT RESTAURANT IS TWO SHAKES? I HAVE NEVER HEARD OF IT." Kristi looked at me confused and said, "That is not a restaurant; it means 'I will be there soon.'" We both started laughing, but it made me remember that Kristi and I are from two different places. She moved here to try to succeed in her writing and seeing her try so hard inspires me to work hard for the goals I want to reach in life.

alicia appears in: #whoweare

*Kristi says:* I remember the first time I met Alicia. It was an early Saturday morning at our first genre workshop. We were both groggy. Already I regretted my decision to join the AM workshop group and wondered if others felt the same. Alicia wore a plaid button-down and Ugg boots. I noticed her beside a girl in braces across the sunny room. They were giggling. When the staff announced, "Alicia, your mentor is Kristi," our eyes met again. She got up from her chair, walked across the room and introduced herself. She was still smiling from earlier. I smiled too, AND FROM THAT MOMENT, I KNEW WE'D CLICK. Right then, we decided to meet at the Delancey Street Starbucks for our pair sessions. And we still do. Alicia is always 10 minutes earlier than me, waiting at the window, never annoyed by my persistent tardiness. I appear, out of breath, having yet again miscalculated. We smile, say hello, and tell each other what has happened since the last time we met.

# ALEXANDRA MANGUAL

YEARS AS MENTEE: 2012

GRADE: 11

HIGH SCHOOL: Herbert H. Lehman High School, Bronx, NY

BORN: New York, NY

LIVES: Bronx, NY

# JESSICA PISHKO

YEARS AS MENTOR: 2012

OCCUPATION: Teacher, Columbia University, New York, NY

PUBLICATIONS: anderbo, elimae, and Mr. Beller's Neighborhood

*Alexandra says:* I was afraid of working with someone and opening up my most valuable possession to her: I'm writing a novel and it means more to me than anything. When I told her it was based on a daydream about the Jonas Brothers, she didn't react the way everyone else does. She was a bit intrigued. I felt so much more comfortable after that. I opened up and let her judge my novel. I CAN TAKE HER CRITICISM EASILY, BECAUSE IT'S MOLDING ME INTO A BETTER WRITER DAY BY DAY. She's more than a mentor, she's my friend.

alexandra appears in: #tiesthatbind

*Jessica says:* Alex brings so much enthusiasm, from her interests to her writing. HER FAVORITE WORD IS "FEARLESS" AND I CAN SEE WHY. She dives into her fiction with so much of herself, with a real lack of all the neuroses and anxieties that I often bring to my own writing.

jessica appears in: #tiesthatbind

## BRIANNA MARIE MARINI

YEARS AS MENTEE: 2012

GRADE: 10

HIGH SCHOOL: Young Women's Leadership School of Queens, NY

BORN: New York, NY

LIVES: Queens, NY

AWARDS: Scholastic Art & Writing Awards Silver Key for Short Fiction

## KRISTEN DEMALINE

YEARS AS MENTOR: 2011, 2012

OCCUPATION: Social Media and Communications Coordinator at GRACE Communications Foundation, New York, NY

PUBLICATIONS: *Eco Centric* blog, *Cleveland Plain Dealer*, *Akron Beacon Journal*, Smithsonian National Air and Space Museum Flyer, *Penny Ante*, Idealist Milano Graduate School blog

*Brianna says:* I think both my mentor and I have come a long way when it comes to "remixing" and learning from each other. KRISTEN HAS STARTED TO TEACH ME HOW TO BE MORE CONFIDENT AND SURE IN MY WORK. She's also shown me that not everything I do needs to be edited and fixed and changed to be worth something. I've learned a lot from her, not only in terms of my writing, but also in terms of being more confident about anything I do and enjoying whatever it is.

brianna appears in: #tiesthatbind

*Kristen says:* Writing is our refuge; I think we're both most ourselves on the page. Brianna inspires me to take more literary risks, a quality I needed to get back in touch with as a writer. I'M ENCOURAGED BY HER JOYFUL LEAPS INTO LANGUAGE, even when writing emotionally difficult material. We finish each others' sentences, scribble all over our pieces, and we text about *Glee.*

kristen appears in: #whoweare

# AMANDA DAY McCULLOUGH

YEARS AS MENTEE: 2012

GRADE: 10

HIGH SCHOOL: Hunter College High School, New York, NY

BORN: New York, NY

LIVES: Queens, NY

AWARDS: Scholastic Art & Writing Awards Gold Key for Poetry, Scholastic Art & Writing Awards Gold Key for Personal Essay/Memoir

# SAMANTHA CARLIN

YEARS AS MENTOR: 2012

OCCUPATION: Executive Assistant, GOJO Industries

PUBLICATIONS: The Norman Mailer Writer's Colony, the Taglit-Birthright Alumni Essay Contest, Barnard College, The New South Young Playwright's Festival, Susquehanna University's *The Apprentice Writer,* The Scholastic Art & Writing Awards

*Amanda says:* I'm always excited to get feedback from Samantha. She takes my writing seriously and we share our work with one another freely. I don't know how many times she's told me "think about word choice." The message is finally sinking in. Every word Samantha writes is deliberate, and she's taught me to manipulate language to strengthen my ideas. The greatest lesson I've learned from her is that there is no boundary to what I can do with my writing. SAMANTHA IS THE REASON THAT I BELIEVE IN MYSELF AS A WRITER.

amanda appears in: #tiesthatbind

*Samantha says:* At our first pair meeting, Amanda and I set a goal to confront fears in our writing—from our personal fears, to taking risks with content and subject matter in our work. Over the year, I've admired Amanda's courage to go there more and more in her writing. When I was writing this anthology story, the ending that I was imagining scared me. As I held my breath, quivering at the idea, I ASKED MYSELF, "WOULD AMANDA DO IT?" THE ANSWER CAME BACK TO ME IN A CLEAR "YES." Following Amanda's lead, I took the leap.

samantha appears in: #tiesthatbind

# SHYANNE MELENDEZ

YEARS AS MENTEE: 2011, 2012

GRADE: 12

HIGH SCHOOL: Millennium High School, New York, NY

BORN: New York, NY

LIVES: New York, NY

SCHOLARSHIPS: St. John's Scholarship, PACE

WILL ATTEND: John Jay College, New York, NY

# SARA FEMENELLA

YEARS AS MENTOR: 2012

OCCUPATION: Advertizing Manager at *Poets & Writers Magazine,* New York, NY; Contributing Editor at *Dossier Journal,* Brooklyn, NY

PUBLICATIONS: *Denver Quarterly, Jerry Magazine, Pleiades, Verse, Normal School, St. Ann's Review, Dossier Journal*

*Shyanne says:* When my mentor Sara introduced me to Poets House in Battery Park I didn't know what to expect. However, when I walked in and saw that it was a huge library full of poetry books, I was really excited. After taking out about seven books and acquiring different tones from different poets, I ended up writing three poems over the course of our hour and a half session. EXPLORING MY SKILLS AS A POET HAS DEFINITELY BECOME MORE COMFORTABLE since Sara is a skilled writer. Having her as my mentor allows me to learn to add different tweaks to my poems. I hope that she and I remain close after this GWN year comes to an end.

shyanne appears in: #transforminginto

*Sara says:* On a bitter February Saturday I met Shyanne at Poets House, located all the way downtown on the water, hoping she wouldn't hate me for dragging her to what is basically the coldest, windiest corner of Manhattan, on what was basically the coldest day of the whole winter. Once inside, WE FOUND A SUNSPOT ON A COUCH BY THE WINDOW, WHERE WE CURLED UP WITH STACKS OF POETRY BOOKS AND READ AND WROTE ALL AFTERNOON, while the wind howled outside (and it even snowed a little). It was a memorable day, and one that I hope will stick with her and much as it will stick with me.

sara appears in: #transforminginto

# SAMANTHA PERSEPHONE MOZES

YEARS AS MENTEE: 2012

GRADE: 10

HIGH SCHOOL: Bard High School Early College, New York, NY

BORN: New York, NY

LIVES: New York, NY

AWARDS: Scholastic Art & Writing Awards Silver Key for Poetry

# SUSAN BURTON

YEARS AS MENTOR: 2012

OCCUPATION: Former editor of *Harper's* and former producer of *This American Life*, currently at work on a memoir to be published by Random House

PUBLICATIONS: *Slate, Mother Jones, New York, The New Yorker,* and *The New York Times Magazine.* Co-author, with Hyder Akbar, of *Come Back to Afghanistan: A California Teenager's Story* (Bloomsbury USA, 2005).

*Say Samantha and Susan:*

| STREETS ON WHICH WE HAVE MET | for | AND |
|---|---|---|
| Houston | tea | BREAKFAST AT TIFFANY'S |
| Sullivan | coffee | *The Merchant of Venice* |
| Crosby | $8 hot chocolates | Joni Mitchell |
| Amsterdam | ricotta and toast | *The Little Mermaid* |
| W. 83rd | molten chocolate brownie | *My Own Private Idaho* |
| Prince | chocolate fudge cake | *3/8 of a Kiss* |
| | blue bottles of Saratoga | |
| | sparkling water | |

samantha appears in: #otherworlds

susan appears in: #tiesthatbind

## AVA NADEL

YEARS AS MENTEE: 2012

GRADE: 11

HIGH SCHOOL: Millennium High School, New York, NY

BORN: Brooklyn, NY

LIVES: Brooklyn, NY

## JESSI HEMPEL

YEARS AS MENTOR: 2012

OCCUPATION: Senior Writer, *Fortune* magazine, New York, NY

*Ava says:* "Ready to pick one?" Jessi says as I sip on my iced chai. I nod and reach into the pouch of paper slips in the back of Jessi's notebook. I read the prompt and make a face. "I'm not really sure if I like this one," I say hesitantly. It's hard to write about something you're not used to. "C'mon," Jessi replies, "Let's try it out." Ten minutes later, I read out my response as Jessi listens. ONCE I FINISH, JESSI SAYS, "WOW, THAT WAS REALLY BEAUTIFUL," I smile, feeling the satisfaction of stepping out of my comfort zone. Don't underestimate yourself.

ava appears in: #transforminginto

*Jessi says:* The timer dings and Ava and I both put down our pens. As we nibble chocolates at the Cocoa Bar where we meet every Monday evening, we compare notes on our ten minute writing warm up. Last September when we began, our ideas felt forced. We'd labor over a few sentences and read them to each other tentatively. Tonight we've written two pages each. I listen to Ava's rich descriptions of a meal she enjoyed. "Maybe I should write an essay about that," she says, BECAUSE WE HAVE BOTH LEARNED, EVERY EVENT IS AN OPPORTUNITY FOR A STORY.

jessi appears in: #transforminginto

# AMANDA NERVAIS

<small>YEARS AS MENTEE:</small> 2012

<small>GRADE:</small> 10

<small>HIGH SCHOOL:</small> Academy
for Young Writers,
New York, NY

<small>BORN:</small> Brooklyn, NY

<small>LIVES:</small> Brooklyn, NY

<small>AWARDS:</small>
Scholastic
Art & Writing
Awards Silver
Key for Poetry

# KATE JACOBS

<small>YEARS AS MENTOR:</small> 2011, 2012

<small>OCCUPATION:</small> Editor, Roaring Brook Press, New York, NY

*Amanda says:* Coming into Girls Write Now, I have to admit, I was a little skeptical about the whole thing. All the other girls seemed different from me, and I didn't really click with anyone from the interview process. But when they told me I had to switch to the PM workshop and I MET KATE, EVERYTHING CHANGED. I WROTE MORE, READ MORE, EVEN WENT OUTSIDE MORE. Not to mention, we live across the street from each other! I can't wait to continue on this great friendship and journey to become a better writer in general.

amanda appears in: #whoweare

*Kate says:* Mandy is full of ideas. SHE COMES TO OUR WRITING SESSIONS WITH ALL THE ENTHUSIASM OF HER INSPIRATION. "Do you have a writing prompt today?" she asks. "Because I have an idea!" I find myself buoyed by her raw talent. Instead of thinking endlessly, I write. The two of us sit on my couch, scribbling away. "And then what happens?" she asks me when we share our work. "I don't know," I admit, "that's why I stopped there." She laughs and we're off again, onto her next idea, our pens flying across the page.

kate appears in: #whoweare

# BRE'ANN NEWSOME

YEARS AS MENTEE: 2012

GRADE: 9

HIGH SCHOOL: The Urban
Assembly Bronx Studio for
Writers and Artists,
Bronx, NY

BORN: New York, NY

LIVES: Bronx, NY

# CHRISTINA BROSMAN

YEARS AS MENTOR:
2011, 2012

OCCUPATION: Talent Department at ID, New York, NY

PUBLICATIONS: *And Then She DIES at the End* (FringeNYC 2012), *Obelisk Road, Standard Deviants*

*Bre'ann says:* I remember one of my first experiences openly sharing a piece with my mentor Christina. It was a poem that was very heavy on symbolism and had not yet been seen by another pair of eyes. Once she read over it and gave me her opinion about it, I felt silly for ever being afraid to share it. MY MENTOR HAS REMIXED MY WRITING AND TAUGHT ME THAT IT'S OKAY, SOMETIMES, TO BE BLUNT. It can make a piece come alive. That note has changed my attitude towards writing. Thanks to Christina, I've learned to never second guess whether what I feel is acceptable.

bre'ann appears in: #tiesthatbind, #atacrossroads, #behindthescenes

*Christina says:* Poetry is the furthest thing from whatever would be considered my wheelhouse. So when we received the anthology prompt this year and Bre said she wanted to write a poem, however great I thought that'd be for her, my feelings were mildly overshadowed by how much I didn't want to attempt the same thing myself. Then my dread multiplied when she came to me with a stellar piece that I was meant to remix. I gave it a shot, and very timidly presented my poem to her. OUR ROLES HAD REVERSED, AND SHE HELPED ME TRY SOMETHING NEW AND HELPED IT TAKE SHAPE. It was an amazing experience, and I'm so excited to see how our relationship continues to unfold.

christina appears in: #tiesthatbind

# CHANTAREYA PAREDES

YEARS AS MENTEE: 2011, 2012

GRADE: 12

HIGH SCHOOL: Millennium High School, New York, NY

BORN: Okinawa, Japan

LIVES: Brooklyn, NY

WILL ATTEND: Savannah College of Art and Design, Savannah, GA

# ALISSA RICCARDELLI

YEARS AS MENTOR: 2011, 2012

OCCUPATION: Communications Manager for the New York City Teaching Fellows program, New York, NY

*ChanTareya says:* We had to go to Italy this year. Really, we did. It was necessary. I found someone to write about but she wasn't from America. SO WE, MEANING ALISSA AND I, HAD TO LEAVE THE STATES. ONLY THROUGH OUR WRITING, THOUGH. I don't know Italian so Alissa was always there with some input. And me, I just wanted to learn about Italian culture. Unfortunately, it was only for a while. The person I wrote about came back to the U.S. So we had to, too. Best mental vacation ever.

chantareya appears in: #whoweare

*Alissa says:* This year I learned to be brave from my mentee TT. I'd been hiding behind something with my writing, and being candid and fearless herself, she could tell. This year we worked primarily on her novel in progress, a project into which TT dove fearlessly. AS I ENCOURAGED HER TO KEEP GOING, MORE OFTEN THAT NOT, SHE WAS ALSO ENCOURAGING ME. Not just to write, but to write something honest, something true. For that, I am incredibly grateful. Her motivation and skill is so endlessly inspiring to me that I've been pushing myself forward, just as TT so consistently does, to write something that she'll be proud of.

alissa appears in: #tiesthatbind, #behindthescenes

# EMELY PAULINO

YEARS AS MENTEE: 2010, 2011, 2012

GRADE: 11

HIGH SCHOOL: Young Women's Leadership School of Astoria, Queens, NY

BORN: Queens, NY

LIVES: Queens, NY

AWARDS: Scholastic Art & Writing Awards Gold Key for Poetry; and Scholastic Art & Writing Awards Silver Key for Poetry

# JESS PASTORE

YEARS AS MENTOR: 2010, 2011, 2012

OCCUPATION: Fundraising Coordinator for the American Civil Liberties Union Foundation, New York, NY

*Emely says:* Our first trip to the Nuyorican Poets Cafe was on a cold, rainy Saturday. After hearing about a performance with Australia's slam poetry champion, Jess eagerly told me about the event. As a fan of performance poetry, it was inspiring to visit such a famous cafe and listen to Luka Lesson. We both agreed that his poem 'Athena' was our favorite. IT INSPIRED BOTH OF US TO WRITE POEMS ABOUT OUR ANCESTORS, JUST LIKE HE DID. Through our pair meetings, Jess has helped me set and accomplish writing goals as well as motivated me to continue writing and performing poetry.

emely appears in: #andwerehome

*Jess says:* It's after 9 p.m. and we're sitting side by side on the R train. Purses propped on laps and notebooks propped on purses, we're both eagerly writing. Our common pose tonight-- subway scribbling, both wearing those slouchy knit hats again-- isn't the only thing we've shared. We're fresh from a performance at the Nuyorican Cafe, where the powerful words, beats, and images of Australia's poetry slam champion washed over us. Those beats and similes are still echoing in my head, and I can tell that Emely's reeling, too. Stepping out of my comfort zone and into the realm of spoken expression of the written word has pushed my pen to hit paper more often this year, and that wouldn't have happened if Emely hadn't shared this passion with me and encouraged events like this. As the weeks go by I REALIZE HER UNBRIDLED OPTIMISM AND SENSE THAT ANYTHING IS POSSIBLE IN HER WORK IS WHAT I'M TRYING TO REMIX INTO MY OWN WRITING THIS YEAR. She hasn't built walls that preclude an option, a genre, a venue where her writing could take her. I'm so excited that she sees tonight's performance as somewhere she could go, and I'm pinning some of her optimism to my own pages, hoping that together we can write her way there.

jess appears in: #andwerehome

# YODALIN PERALTA

YEARS AS MENTEE: 2012

GRADE: 11

HIGH SCHOOL: Bronx International High School, Bronx, NY

BORN: Dominican Republic

LIVES: Bronx, NY

# NAKISHA WILLIAMS

YEARS AS MENTOR: 2011, 2012

OCCUPATION: Freelance Writer and Reporter based in New York City

PUBLICATIONS: *US Weekly* magazine, InStyle.com, BET.com

*Yodalin says:* Once I entered the GWN office I knew how challenging this experience was going to be, but I never thought that such an amazing person as Nakisha was going to make this experience memorable. I won't deny it, I was pretty scared to share my writing, something so personal and that few people have read, but I'm so grateful to be paired with such an inspiring person who helps me experience new genres and conquer my fears. SHE'S MORE THAN A MENTOR; SHE'S LIKE A BEST FRIEND. I will always remember all of her advice that's helped me to succeed.

yodalin appears in: #atacrossrods, #behindthescenes

*Nakisha says:* I was surprised to discover that the soft spoken Yodalin I met on day one was actually bursting with passionate, thought-provoking opinions about the world around her! BUT THAT'S YOLY—A QUIET STORM—AND I'VE BEEN BLOWN AWAY LISTENING TO HER EXPRESS HER IDEAS AND WATCHING HER TRANSLATE THEM TO PAPER (sometimes literally). Besides teaching me about political topics like the DREAM Act, Yodalin has expanded my Spanish vocabulary. She takes risks with writing and has inspired me to write about the things that stir me up the most, even when the words take me out of my comfort zone.

nakisha appears in: #transforminginto

# IDAMARIS PEREZ

YEARS AS MENTEE: 2011, 2012

GRADE: 12

HIGH SCHOOL: St. Jean Baptiste High School, New York, NY

BORN: New York, NY

LIVES: New York, NY

# DEMETRIA IRWIN

YEARS AS MENTOR: 2011, 2012

OCCUPATION: Freelance Writer based in New York City

PUBLICATIONS: *New York Amsterdam News, City Limits, BlackEnterprise.com, The Boston Globe*

*Idamaris says:* It seemed like I could never let my words flow naturally like the wind. "I always stutter in my writing and I hate it," I complained when I couldn't finish one of Demetria's timed writing prompts. "It takes time and practice to become a confident writer," she said smiling. "DON'T BE HARD ON YOURSELF, IDA. TONI MORRISON DID NOT WRITE *BELOVED* IN ONE DAY." She was right. I have to remix my writing style, stop trying to be a perfectionist and just write. When I looked at her, I thought how glad I am to have her as my mentor.

idamaris appears in: #tiesthatbind

*Demetria says:* In Ida's screenplay "Teen Thirst for Justice," one character calls some other characters a bunch of "no-lives." THE INSTINCT WAS TO CHANGE THAT TO "LOW-LIVES," BUT THEN "NO-LIVES" BEGAN TO MAKE SENSE TO ME and it was an interesting turn of phrase that caught my ear. That dash of creativity coupled with recent headlines about Trayvon Martin being murdered, inspired me to write a poem called "The No-Lives" about all of these black children that have died tragically at the hands of authority figures and even their own peers.

demetria appears in: #atacrossroads, #behindthescenes

# MARY PORTES

YEARS AS MENTEE: 2012

GRADE: 12

HIGH SCHOOL: The Urban
Assembly Bronx
School for Law,
Government and
Justice, Bronx, NY

BORN: New York, NY

LIVES: Brooklyn, NY

SCHOLARSHIPS:
Los Padres
Foundation
Scholarship, College Assistance Program, Artistic Award from the Youth Leadership Council at HEAF

WILL ATTEND: Manhattan College, New York, NY (on full scholarship)

# GILLIAN REAGAN

YEARS AS MENTOR: 2012

OCCUPATION: Public Editor and Director of Marketing and Special Projects at *Capital New York*, New York, NY

PUBLICATIONS: *Capital New York, New York Observer, The New York Times, Businessweek, The Business Insider,* among others

*Mary says:* "Friendship is born at that moment when one person says to another: 'What! You too? I thought I was the only one.'"—C.S. Lewis.

Gillian began talking to me about everything and anything. Things I thought only I did. WHO KNEW MAKING FRIENDS WAS SO EASY? It was this sense of ease that sparked our relationship. Not only do we love to write, but we inspire each other to try new things. Because of our many meetings, I discovered that I actually like poetry! Without Gillian, I wouldn't have fallen in love with freewriting. She has made me see writing in a whole new light.

mary appears in: #otherworlds

*Gillian says:* Mary, in the back of the Girls Write Now workshop room, was a shining light —shy and polite but with glittering eyes. Her quiet confidence broke through and glowed under the gnawing fluorescence of a Crown Heights library, week after week. THIS YOUNG WOMAN, FANTASTIC FANTASY FICTION NOVELIST, ANDROID APP DEVELOPER, ROCKSTAR CUPCAKE BAKER, VOLUNTEER AND SCHOOL LEADER, loving daughter, and sister (and mom to a one-eyed cat called Cookie), future healing doctor and ace lawyer, CONTINUES TO INSPIRE ME. I am a better person and a better writer under Mary's shimmering brilliance.

gillian appears in: #otherworlds

# TEMA REGIST

YEARS AS MENTEE: 2012

GRADE: 10

HIGH SCHOOL: Midwood High School, Brooklyn, NY

BORN: New York, NY

LIVES: Brooklyn, NY

# LYNN MELNICK

YEARS AS MENTOR: 2012

OCCUPATION: Poet based in New York City

PUBLICATIONS: *If I Should Say I Have Hope, The Paris Review, A Public Space, LIT* magazine, *jubilat, Gulf Coast, The Brooklyn Rail, Boston Review, The Awl, Poetry Daily, Narrative* magazine, *Guernica*

*Tema says:* Lynn is an amazing person. Lynn has remixed me, enabling me to grow as a writer by expanding my writing skills. The practice of combining poems that at first don't seem to have any common ground was an extraordinary method that she taught me and has helped me open up and lengthen my poems. During one of our pair sessions, I mentioned to Lynn that one of my writing goals was to improve upon my titles because they never had enough meaning, but now my titles are wonderful. BECAUSE OF LYNN, MY PASSION FOR WRITING HAS INCREASED VERY MUCH.

tema appears in: #transforminginto

*Lynn says:* What I try to remix from Tema into my own writing practice is her remarkable ability to just start writing. She doesn't waste time second-guessing herself or her ideas; she just opens her notebook and begins to write inspired and beautiful poems. WHEN I SIT DOWN TO WRITE AND FEEL UNSURE OF WHERE TO GO, I OFTEN THINK OF TEMA AND I JUST START WRITING. Because of her, I have learned to relax a bit more and let the words lead me where they will.

lynn appears in: #transforminginto

# NAJAYA ROYAL

YEARS AS MENTEE: 2012

GRADE: 9

HIGH SCHOOL: Benjamin Banneker Academy for Community Development, Brooklyn, NY

BORN: Brooklyn, NY

LIVES: Brooklyn, NY

# ANUJA MADAR

YEARS AS MENTOR: 2008, 2009, 2012

OCCUPATION: Content Strategist at Marriott International, New York, NY

PUBLICATIONS: Marriott International

*Najaya says:* One thing that I have learned from my mentor and remixed into myself is to not be afraid to change things up, whether dealing with writing or life itself. SHE SHOWED ME THAT A BLOCK IN THE ROAD IS NOTHING BUT OURSELVES HOLDING US BACK MENTALLY, and there is always a way around it, even if it's something as small as changing a few lines. The outcome can be incredible.

najaya appears in: #whoweare

*Anuja says:* Whether she's speaking her mind in school or transforming an ordinary pair of jeans into something fashion-forward, there is one element that runs consistently through Najaya's life–SHE KNOWS WHO SHE IS AND WHAT SHE WANTS, AND IF WHAT SHE WANTS DOESN'T EXIST, SHE'LL SET FORTH TO CREATE IT. At twice her age, I am in the midst of this journey, and I am amazed, inspired, and encouraged by her sense of self.

anuja appears in: #whoweare

# EMILY SARITA

YEARS AS MENTEE: 2010, 2011, 2012

GRADE: 12

HIGH SCHOOL: NYC iSchool, New York, NY

BORN: Brooklyn, NY

LIVES: Brooklyn, NY

WILL ATTEND: Russell Sage College, Troy, NY

# JANA BRANSON

YEARS AS MENTOR: 2010, 2011, 2012

OCCUPATION: Publicist at The Door Marketing Group, New York, NY

*Emily says:* I walk into Starbucks and see Jana waiting for me, and I smile at her, giving her a long hug. Ever since I came back from the Dominican Republic, I wanted to tell Jana about my vacation and how much fun I had. Plus, I wanted to tell her about my idea of writing a memoir based on my adventures. I REALLY LIKE TELLING JANA ABOUT MY IDEAS BECAUSE SHE GIVES GREAT ADVICE and gives me a sense of what I need to focus on.

emily appears in: #transforminginto

*Jana says:* Emily and I have been working together for three years and every year has been different. We have both grown so much in who we are, and in our writing. One of the first times we met, Emily talked about how she wanted to explore different genres and not stick to just one. Since then, she's written poetry, memoir, fiction, nonfiction, a scene from a play—you name it, she hasn't been afraid to try it. HER WILLINGNESS TO EXPLORE AND TAKE THE PLUNGE HAS CERTAINLY INSPIRED ME TO DO THE SAME—in my writing and beyond.

jana appears in: #transforminginto

# NYIESHA SHOWERS

YEARS AS MENTEE: 2012

GRADE: 12

HIGH SCHOOL: High School of Graphic Communication Arts, New York, NY

BORN: Queens, NY

LIVES: Brooklyn, NY

AWARDS: Summer Media Challenge via HarlemLIVE

SCHOLARSHIPS: R.A.C.E. Program Scholarship

WILL ATTEND: Howard University, Washington, D.C.

# PATRICIA LESPINASSE

YEARS AS MENTOR: 2012

OCCUPATION: Post-doctoral Fellow in the English Department at Rutgers University, New Brunswick, NJ

*Nyiesha says:* Seated inside of the very cozy Krik Krak, a Haitian restaurant in Upper Manhattan, was when it hit me. Patricia brought me to a Haitian restaurant to introduce me to some of Haiti's best dishes that I could use as inspiration for my food memoir. Being from a Caribbean island myself, I was not at all intimidated by tasting Haitian food. (By the way, the food was superb.) After leaving the restaurant, I REALIZED THAT OUR RELATIONSHIP IS NOT ONLY ABOUT OR RELATED TO WRITING, IT IS RELATED TO LIFE. I have taken her experiences as a student at Ivy League schools as a testament to do my best in whatever I can. I have also taken her love for poetry and dabbled in poetry a lot this year.

nyiesha appears in: #whoweare

*Patricia says:* Before meeting face to face, Nyiesha and I had an introductory phone conversation. I still remember one of her first questions: "What is your ethnic background?" Nyiesha was very curious about my ethnicity because she wanted a mentor that she could relate to. When I revealed to her that I was Haitian-American she was elated that we shared a West Indian background. Throughout the year, we discovered that we shared many other things, including an interest in identity politics. IDENTITY BECAME A RECURRING THEME IN OUR PAIR WRITING SESSIONS. I enjoyed the challenge of writing about identity beyond the confines of class, race, and gender.

patricia appears in: #whoweare

# GEORGIA SOARES

YEARS AS MENTEE: 2012

GRADE: 12

HIGH SCHOOL: Manhattan Village Academy, New York, NY

BORN: Brazil

LIVES: New York, NY

AWARDS: 1st place in a regional writing contest in Brazil, Conhecendo o Judiciario

SCHOLARSHIPS: Posse Scholarship to University of Southern California, Los Angeles, CA

WILL ATTEND: University of Southern California, Los Angeles, CA

# KAREN KAWAGUCHI

YEARS AS MENTOR: 2012

OCCUPATION: partner/owner of K Works Global

PUBLICATIONS: *Every Teacher's Toolkit* (Pearson Longman, 2010) and co-author of *Texas ELPS Toolkit* (Pearson Longman, 2009)

*Georgia says:* The first time I met Karen, I couldn't foresee the strong friendship and trust we would develop. SINCE OUR FIRST WRITING SESSION, I FOUND IN KAREN THE SUPPORT AND ATTENTION I NEEDED TO GROW AS A WRITER. Someone to read my stories and point out strengths and weaknesses; someone to encourage me to express my feelings through words even when they seem indescribable; someone to care for me as if we'd known each other forever. Karen teaches me not only writing lessons, but life lessons: I learned to face obstacles in life—something that has given me more to write about.

georgia appears in: #whoweare, #behindthescenes

*Karen says:* In the earliest days of our partnership, we worked feverishly on Georgia's college admission essay. From those efforts, I learned that she wrote beautifully. I learned of her passion for mastering English, even as a young girl in Brazil. I SAW HER BRILLIANT MIND, HER DRIVE TO ACHIEVE, AND HER COURAGE. She quoted from her favorite song: "Suddenly I see / this is what I want to be." Suddenly I saw Georgia and all that she could be. She won a Posse scholarship and will attend USC. She has given me renewed courage to take chances and embrace life.

karen appears in: #whoweare

# SADE SWIFT

YEARS AS MENTEE: 2012

GRADE: 11

HIGH SCHOOL: Beacon High School, New York, NY

BORN: New York, NY

LIVES: New York, NY

# LINDA CORMAN

YEARS AS MENTOR: 2011, 2012

OCCUPATION: Senior editor, Jennison Associates, New York, NY

*Sade says:* Linda is an amazing mentor. I never in a million years thought that I, of all people, would be able to teach someone older than me something she never knew or expose her to something she'd never experienced. The best thing about everything was the fact that we both shared things about our lives that really inspired some memorable pieces, some that I WILL LOOK BACK AT AND THINK "WOW, THAT REALLY CHANGED MY LIFE." She always stuck by me, not only through my work, but through every aspect of my life and I'm forever thankful for that!

sade appears in: #tiesthatbind, #behindthescenes

*Linda says:* I can remember the moment when I felt like this writing partnership could click, though not the most crucial detail. I'd been feeling that I had little to offer BECAUSE SADE IS SO CONFIDENT, SO MOTIVATED, AND SO SURE OF WHAT SHE WANTED TO DO. But, at one pair meeting in the fall, I said something about her writing (what, exactly, is what I can't remember) that Sade said was very helpful, and it caused her to want to dig into her writing more, to elaborate and to revise. Pair sessions got much easier, and more fun, after that.

# LUCY TAN

YEARS AS MENTEE: 2011, 2012

GRADE: 12

HIGH SCHOOL: Stuyvesant High School, New York, NY

BORN: New York, NY

LIVES: Brooklyn, NY

AWARDS: Scholastic Art & Writing Awards Gold Key for Writing Portfolio, and Scholastic Art & Writing Awards Silver Key for in Poetry; Intel Science Talent Search 2012 Semi-finalist

WILL ATTEND: Case Western Reserve University, Cleveland, OH

# EMILY HAZEL

YEARS AS MENTOR: 2010, 2012

OCCUPATION: Associate Editor, Lee & Low Books, New York, NY; freelance poet, writer, and editor

PUBLICATIONS: collection of poetry, *Body & Soul*; prose in *Brown Alumni Magazine* and *Brio*; poetry in *Creating Space, RedeemerWrites*, and *The Francestown News*, and forthcoming in *The Mochila Review*

*Lucy says:* Always arriving early to our weekly meetings, Emily is fully prepared with writing prompts, GWN handouts, and poems to discuss. IN THE MIDST OF OUR READINESS, WE ALSO CATCH A LOT OF SURPRISES AS WE EXPERIENCE NEW YORK CITY TOGETHER—a scenery of whirling snowflakes while we stand on the steps of the Metropolitan Museum; 1990s pop music blasting in the background while we write poems in Central Park; or tourists standing two inches away and towering over us as we carry conversation in public atriums. Our thought-provoking and cognitive conversations often leave me pondering on my own writing career.

lucy appears in: #whoweare, #andwerehome

*Emily says:* At orientation I was intrigued by the metaphor Lucy chose to introduce herself: a microscope that writes poems. She is an observer—I love how she sees connections between scientific discovery and creative writing. LUCY'S POEMS ARE UNCLUTTERED EFFICIENCY APARTMENTS, CLEVERLY ARRANGED, UNUSUALLY DECORATED. Mine tend to be longer, railroad style apartments, leading listeners from one room to the next. Between the two of us, I am the relentless reviser, seldom finished when Lucy is—yet I have learned to share with her my messy rough drafts, even as I struggle to read these fragments of myself, the ink still wet.

emily appears in: #whoweare, #andwerehome

# IRIS TORRES

YEARS AS MENTEE: 2012

GRADE: 10

HIGH SCHOOL: The Young Women's Leadership School of Manhattan, New York, NY

BORN: New York, NY

LIVES: New York, NY

# HEATHER KRISTEN

YEARS AS MENTOR: 2008, 2009, 2010, 2011, 2012

OCCUPATION: Freelance Writer based in New York City

PUBLICATIONS: *Glamour, The Huffington Post, Slate, Smith, St. Petersburg Times, Narrative, New York Press, Oprah's Lifeclass, Live and Let Love* (Gallery, 2011)

*Iris says:* Small red fan shining underneath the hot, bright lights of Forever 21. The small red fan in a yellow bag. The coldness of winter trapping itself into the yellow bag. The small red fan in Heather's hand, the olive green walls of Starbucks with its coffee aroma watching it all unfold. The small red fan around her neck. A SMALL SILVER ELEPHANT SHINING ON MY FINGER. Gifts that are foreign in our Starbucks cafe on that winter day with snowflakes falling quietly to the sidewalk.

iris appears in: #atacrossroads

*Heather says:* A gloomy gray green Starbucks greets us. A mix of jazz and black coffee propels our pens to write of cultures Iris and I want to explore. Asia and India are on a remixed tape that goes on and on. At Christmas we trade gifts of a red China fan necklace and elephant ring. WE HAVE MANY DIFFERENCES, BUT WE ARE LINKED BY WANDERLUST OF THE UNEXPECTED.

heather appears in: #tiesthatbind

# YESENIA TORRES

YEARS AS MENTEE: 2012

GRADE: 12

HIGH SCHOOL: Christ the King Regional High School, Queens, NY

BORN: New York, NY

LIVES: Brooklyn, NY

WILL ATTEND: SUNY Oswego, Oswego, NY

# JENNIFER TENCH

YEARS AS MENTOR: 2012

OCCUPATION: Executive Editor in the K-12 division of Houghton Mifflin Harcourt, New York, NY

*Yesenia says:* We sit side by side staring at one of the GWN program leaders. Her flaming red hair peeks out of her hat. She asks, "So how is your relationship with your mentor?" It didn't take long for me to explain what I felt. From the writing and good criticism she gives me to the long conversations about boys and family, MY MENTOR HAS BECOME AN OLDER SISTER. We trade stories from our own experiences so that no matter what coffee shop or deli we meet at, our long talks always allow me to leave confident in my writing and with new advice to follow in my life.

yesenia appears in: #atacrossroads

*Jennifer says:* Yesenia is courageous and writes from the heart. WHEREVER WE MEET, WE TALK ABOUT BOOKS AND WRITING AND BOYS AND FRIENDS. We share books and poems we've read. I admire her candor and her approach to life. Sometimes after we meet, she sends me poems from the subway about what she sees. She makes me laugh, and more importantly, she makes me think in new ways about writing and life.

jennifer appears in: #tiesthatbind, #atacrossroads

# YANIBEL VERAS

Years as mentee: 2012

Grade: 11

High school: Frederick Douglas Academy, New York, NY

Born: Dominican Republic

Lives: New York, NY

# ASHLEY ROSE HOWARD

Years as mentor: 2012

Occupation: Freelance Writer; Event Coordinator for Tribeca Events, New York, NY; Professional Blogger

Publications: NJ.com, *Health & Fitness*, Life2PointOh.com

*Yanibel Says:* "So, Yanibel. What are your writing goals?" Ashley asked me at our first meeting, over tea. I told her I was looking to improve my grammar and also to do more creative writing. I WAS HAPPY TO HEAR THAT HER GOALS WERE VERY SIMILAR. When first meeting Ashley, I have to admit I didn't think we'd have anything in common. But I'm happy to say I was wrong and I look forward to our weekly meetings.

yanibel appears in: #transforminginto

*Ashley Says:* Like a first date, we met at a tea place and we were both a bit nervous. I took a long swig of my earl grey and asked Yanibel about her writing goals. She then asked me mine. By the end of our first hour together we were talking about life and giggling between sips of compatibility and trust. I'VE FOUND MENTORING NOT ONLY HELPED MAKE A DIFFERENCE IN SOMEONE ELSE'S LIFE, IT HELPED ME GROW AND DISCOVER ALL THE POSITIVE QUALITIES I HAVE TO OFFER. While I continue to be an anchor of support in Yanibel's life, she gives me the courage to fearlessly sail forward through my own insecurities.

ashley appears in: #transforminginto

## SAMANTHA YOUNG CHAN

Years as mentee: 2011, 2012

Grade: 11

High school: Baruch College Campus High School, New York, NY

Born: New York, NY

Lives: New York, NY

## ALEX BERG

Years as mentor: 2012

Occupation: Associate Producer of video at *Newsweek* and *The Daily Beast*

Publications: *The New York Times,* The Huffington Post, *The Washington Post,* and iVillage

*Samantha says:* The minute I met Alex, I knew I wanted her to be my mentor. We had lots of qualities in common: we are adventurous, willing to try out new mediums to show our work through, and we both deal with some form of visual medium. Throughout our entire partnership, she's been supportive of all my ideas and provided me with lots of help and feedback that has allowed me to really tap into my creative juices. She was able to help me find multiple ways to remix my radio play, and now it has taken on other written forms and perspectives.

samantha appears in: #otherworlds, #behindthescenes

*Alex says:* The notion of remix has taken on two forms in working with Samantha. The first is that we have literally remixed her piece that appears in this anthology, from a play to prose to video. This process has been creatively stimulating, however a second figurative form of remix—the idea of remixing one's approach to writing—has been the most inspiring. Samantha's fearlessness and drive to tackle any style or genre brings a play-like quality to writing together. I've been able to tap into her sense of adventure to reinvigorate the approach to my own work, be it writing or working in a visual medium.

alex appears in: #atacrossroads

# #TIESTHAT BIND

What are the ties that bind us together? In this chapter, you will read how our mentors and mentees feel about relationships between lovers, friends, and family. Sometimes these ties bring us together, but they may also pull us apart.

Writer Cheryl Lu Lien Tan, who offered a craft talk on Food Memoir to our writers, says:

> *"The phrase* Ties That Bind *makes me think of family, naturally, but also people I love who may not be related to me by blood but will stand by me through thick and thin. My first book* A Tiger in The Kitchen *really grew out of a yearning to reconnect with my family—specifically the women in my family, with whom I'd felt a little distanced in my 13 or so years in the United States. I had moved to America to pursue my dream of being a journalist, and years after achieving many things I'd set out to achieve, I realized that there was a hole in my life. For me, that hole manifested itself very symbolically in food and the memories of the dishes that my grandmothers, my mother and my aunties had always lovingly made for me. The fact that I had no idea how to make any of these dishes drew me back home to Singapore to finally learn— but also to rediscover my family and spend time with them. There is so much depth and richness to even the most ordinary of families. If you can adequately paint that richness in your pages, it's very compelling."*

— *Jennifer Tench*
2012 Mentor and Anthology Committee Member

# PDA
## BRE'ANN NEWSOME

Christina says: *Bre brought this new piece, her poem "PDA," to one of our recent pair meetings. Because it was about the exciting initial spark in a relationship, we thought it would be fun if the remix element took this new relationship from her poem into the future. So, in that spirit, my poem, "kiss #2000," describes what happens a few years into a relationship, when that spark has mellowed and become a part of the foundation of something deeper.*

I feel them watching
All of the spectators in the crowd
Watching me as I love you out loud
Their faces in awe
Eyes round, soundless

I don't even feel like me
I'm anything and everything you ever said I could be
I'm diving into their pupils
And even deeper in their memory

I just hope they forever remember me...
With this beautiful person in front of me

I don't mind letting go of my pride
As long as I can hold on to you
I don't mind if they judge me right here and now
I'm just gonna keep falling into you
Crashing into you

If anyone above can see this
They might think it sinful
But really, I've never felt so heavenly
Like angels closing and pushing me even closer to you

No need to look back at them
Just let those people see
It's not like we can really tell them to stop
Besides, I kinda like it when they watch

# KISS #2000
## CHRISTINA BROSMAN

sweatpants and couch cushions
bookcases for walls
splitting utility bills
setting the coffee pot timer
arguments over who's washing more dishes
and overcrowding the dvr
hogging the shower

or memorized curves
shorthand speech
and movie dates
and "i love you, have a good day"
and "sleep well" / "don't stay up too late"
bookends of warm rituals

no one remembers kiss#2000
but it's comfort in close quarters
the grace to be able to stop counting
and know that you're mine

# MEMORIES IN MUSIC
## MARCELA GRILLO

He passes my shop every day around 6. Honest to God every time the man passes by the window, I notice he is wearing a black overcoat, black slacks, and boots. He knocks and knocks, but I won't answer the door.

The shop has been closed for a few weeks, and I couldn't care less. I don't really care about anything anymore. It took me forever to even step down here: The floorboards still creak under my feet, as the smell of dust seeps into my nose. I can name every single instrument that's hidden in every corner of this shop. Most of them I repaired and built from nothing with my bare hands. I've got guitars, banjoes, harmonicas, congas, pianos, and... clarinets. Well, I've got one clarinet. It's still sitting in the same spot, but I can't look at it because it's one of the last things that Jake ever touched. He never liked practicing, but when he did, it was magical. On quiet nights I can almost still hear the whistling music traveling up the stairs.

I can still almost hear Jake's frantic footsteps, the way he would wave a piece of sheet music at me and ask for help in reading the notes. I would always say the same thing: "Look at the music. It'll tell you."

There's only one working light above my head. I wanted to fix the others, but then my life turned upside down and I just never got around to it. So I spend the days sitting in my shop. Usually I'm all alone. Except when that guy stops by.

Even when it's pouring rain out, this guy stands there. It was on his third coincidental visit that I noticed he was carrying an instrument. I was sitting one day trying to fix the strings on an old ukulele when I heard footsteps above my head.

"What's wrong with this one, Dad?" Jake's hopeful voice floated through the thin air of the workshop. He sipped on soda from a can and watched me work.

I stood over a beautiful Steinway and my fingers ran over it delicately. "Several keys are missing."

"Whose is it?"

"Mine." I turned to Jake and rolled up my sleeves. "Are you gonna help me or not? I could use you."

"Okay!"

I gently lifted the piano top. "Hold this side." As Jake reached to help me, I watched in horror as his elbow knocked over the soda. Everything spilled over the smooth keys. "Jake!" I yelled. "Damn it!"

Jake's eyes widened. I saw his legs begin to shake. "Sorry!"

I reached for an old rag and wiped the keys down, but I knew that my luck was gone. "What the hell did you do that for? It's all ruined!"

"I didn't mean to!"

"Step away!" I shouted. "You know what, just go away. To your room, wherever. I don't care!"

I turn down my stereo and John Coltrane softens to a murmur. My cigarette's end has burned into a fading light. I walk up the steps and round the corner; a shadow is standing in front of me. I can finally see the man with the long overcoat up close: He's got glasses and his boots are soaked from all the rain.

"We're closed." I'm thinking this will get the guy to leave, but he doesn't. I can't help but think that he's seeking some sort of retribution from me. I'm already punishing myself enough. People can judge me all they want.

"It says you're open."

"Well, we're not open right now." I'm lying. Straight out lying.

The man stares at me. All of a sudden I am transparent, and he can see right through me. "I need you to repair my clarinet."

I take a deep breath. "I don't fix those. I used to, but I don't anymore. You should go somewhere else."

"This is the only place in the neighborhood!" The man insists. "Please. It's for my son."

Right away, it seems like without anything the man has me entirely exposed. Everything around me has faded, and all I see now is that speeding blue van in the pouring rain, and Jake caught right in front of it. All that remained was his green baseball cap. I feel just as hopeless as I did then. My words are caught in my throat, and I feel my eyes burning with tears. "Let me see it," I find myself asking.

The man looks concerned but hands over the instrument anyway. I hold the clarinet in my hands. It's smooth under my fingers.

"He never likes practicing," the man says.

My fingers try not to shake as I remember the very last day I had with my son. We were in the workshop for hours. Jake had finally learned that damn song while I played accompaniment on the Steinway even though the keys were still sticky. The music was pure and beautiful and helped us forget all the evils of the outside world. Just for a little while.

# A BURNED HEART
## RUBY FELIZ

Jalylah says: *Ruby brought a draft of "A Burned Heart" to a pair session, and I was so taken with the opening line and theme, that I wrote a response. We revised the pieces in dialogue.*

Love is fire.
Whether it warms your heart
or burns your house down,
you never know.
It is a mystery.
But whether it is worth discovering
the secrets it holds
or letting its wonders wander
your mind,
Love is art.
A decision.
But whether it is a step towards a warming sensation
or disaster,
only those who take it
will experience its beauty.
Love with everything you have got
or do not love at all.

Wise words from a healing heart.

# EQUINOX
## JALYLAH BURRELL

Summer Saturdays, Rumsey Playfield exposes Freak-folkers, Fela-pretenders and their mannered fans to afternoon sears. Cold water is currency. Veterans freeze their bottles Friday evenings and they drip condensation at the edge of raffia mats, Brooklyn Flea blankets and repurposed flat sheets — a flash mob quilt the harried trample in their rush to winding vendor lines. Mulling options, some sing, some shuffle scuffed Keds to the abundant beat, we tweet Foursquare check-ins. Greenpoint-based breweries hawk craft beers, a Long Island City charcuterie, fennel sausage. There are also undersalted, oversized organic pretzels, your regretful selection, and limeade, mine, but no Volvic, not even Poland Springs.

These are our ways. And the humidity hovers like your embrace. This is a song to be reprised on fall dawns. It whistles tea kettles. It peels silver streaks of paint from pre-war radiators. By spring, it sparks from frayed space heater cords into a faint chill. There is no better recipe for disaster. Comfort too. Love is fire.

# EVERYTHING MUST GO
## HEATHER KRISTIN

Heather says: *At first, My nonfiction piece was inspired by Idra Novey's lecture on erasures at the GWN Found Poetry Workshop*

Maybe they were keys to something, maybe mom was about to reveal a box filled with secrets about our father whom I had never met. Since birth, mom told us a few tall-tales about him. First he was an airline pilot, then a spy for an unnamed foreign government. I wanted to believe her.

Ripped the envelope and out fell three diamond rings tied together with string. They were from our great-great-grandma. Incredible. Huge, with white sparkles locked inside that turned to rainbows. I slipped on one of the diamonds.

"Mom... Can we sell these and maybe the land someday?"

"Don't you dare!" The glow had left her eyes. outside she suddenly looked hollow and sad. She continued, "I am kept here by God to protect and preserve."

Days later, I lived a world away from Mom. After years of drifting, she was trying desperately to put the pieces back together. And I was falling apart. I wanted to protect her, take away her feelings of loss and paranoia, and make her better.

When I returned to my apartment, I called mom and told her to move back to New York.

"I'm the provider. You don't need to make everything okay." She believed she was making up for what we lost when we were homeless.

Didn't need those things. I wanted a mother who was involved in my life.

I watched from my window neighbors illuminate their dwellings with candles, neon signs, and remembered mother's heart racing through her thin jacket, touching mine. No matter how many years or miles separated us, her warm embrace a shelter for my fears.
Tears down my cheeks. The anger, hurt, and trauma wash over me. The city glowed back, lives down below, escaping wars at home or in foreign countries, their best. I had to forgive my mother and accept she did the best she knew how.

And then I did what my mother was unable to do: I let go of everything.

# THOSE SHAPES LOSE THEIR MEANING
## AMANDA DAY McCULLOUGH

*Samantha says: When going through our Girls Write Now notebooks, Amanda and I discovered we'd used the same line in our "found poems" at the poetry workshop. With this in mind, we decided to explore the meaning of the shared line "You are a constant barricade" in short stories. As a writing exercise, we began with writing letters to the "you" in that line. Then for our stories, we flipped the perspective again, writing from the point of view of the character who was receiving the letter and being called "a constant barricade." These are the final stories.*

You are a constant barricade.
Impeding her progress,
Even now that
You have gone.

But she does not
Want to break
You down,
And that is
The only reason
You are still
Standing.

# A SHOOTING RANGE
## SAMANTHA CARLIN

So are all the constant, bitter things:
The wind striking
between skyscrapers.
Icicle swords are weapons
of the city's winter crusade
against stillness.

The Lipton tea
steeped ten minutes
too long.
Because you were fighting with me
about the socks in the dryer and
which subway to take to Brooklyn.

The bathroom door
left ajar as you shower,
An invitation?
But you barely blink.

You are a constant barricade.

# OVER COFFEE
## BRIANNA MARIE MARINI

Brianna says: *"Waiting, holding my breath," "Choking down words,"* and *"From heart to fingertips to tongue"* were lines that I took from my mentor Kristen's piece she drafted during the poetry workshop. I used them to make lines in my short story.

Coffee, cold, dark, sip. Bitter, no milk, too lazy to go grab the milk *thing* sitting on the counter against the wall with the sugar and everything else anyone would need.

Thoughts — jumbled. *(Check.)* The call had been weird and ominous, and she didn't really know what to think.

Heels, pointed, pinching her feet. The drive had been long and rather agonizing with way too much traffic on the roads and why had she worn heels again?

*Starbucks, of all places.*

She needed coffee, a muffin, for fuel. She could only last on fumes for so long.

She hadn't gotten a feeling like the one she had now since her boyfriend had cheated on her the year before. Yeah, they were in a good place now, but she still remembered that weird clenching in her chest and her lungs feeling frozen and choked with cold, dirty air.

~~Brother~~ Harry del Sarto — through the door, jingle. *(Check.)* Twenty seven, college grad, suit and tie, wife and newborn baby girl at home, trust fund kid – what did he know of hardship?

*~~Half-brother~~* Harry. Light bulb — they didn't have the same lives, but that didn't matter. Not when they had a mother in common. It was a link, thin and practically nonexistent, a thread sticking out of a well-worn homemade scarf, but it was enough.

Liquidy — light brown, liquidy, and full of ice. Sweet, probably. She judged by what he drank — petty. *(Check.)*

*Was that whipped cream?*

"It's mom."

No "hi," "how are you?," "how's life?" Straight to the point.

She didn't grow up with the woman, but it was a blood thing, right?

"From what?" The words were clunky, the sounds from an old car in desperate need of repair.

"You're too quick to kill her off, love."

No six-feet-unders in the ~~family~~ people she was forced to claim. Okay. Good. She didn't need to pull out her funeral dress anytime soon —

"Lung cancer. Stage four. She didn't want to tell you until now."

Coffee. Dark, bitter. Sip. Cold. Grounding, in a way. Kept her from insanity for a bright second.

"How long does she have?"

"Pardon?"

Was he stupid? What else could that mean? Light bulb. *(Check.)* He thought for a second, sizing her up.

"Five months."

Heart — beating. *(Check.)* Fingers — tingling. *(Check.)* Tongue — heavy. *(Check.)*

They say that there's a time and a place for everything. What on earth made ~~her half brother~~ Harry think that this news was something to hear over coffee?

The taste of graveyard soil was in her mouth. She could feel the texture of it on her fingers, the day she had taken a handful of it to throw it on ~~her father's~~ Dr. Richards' coffin. The imaginary grains of it were sticking to her sweaty palms right now.

"Why?"

"Why what, angel? Why is she dying? Heck if I know."

"Why didn't she want me to know until now?"

"She didn't want you to stress."

Sugar coated lines of nothing, ropes of melted candy canes on Christmas cookies falling from his lips. She didn't know the woman well enough for that to be the reason.

Seventeen. She was seventeen. Driver's license, high school diploma, freshman in college, seventeen. Five months, and she'd still be seventeen. Nine, she needed nine months.

Ice — rushing in her veins. *(Check.)* What would happen to her? She didn't have anyone to rely on because ~~her mother~~ Mrs. del Sarto was the one that saved her when ~~her father~~ Dr. Richards died and now that ~~her mother~~ Mrs. del Sarto was dying she had run out of the trampolines waiting in case she jumped and fell from the top of the burning building.

Was it possible to drown in imaginary water? Her lungs were constricting in the worst way, and she was sure it was because of the water that was filling her brain, the fish swimming around in her stomach.

~~Her half-brother~~ Harry knew that she'd realized what he was waiting for her to get at. He nodded and half-heartedly said a word that was supposed to be reassuring. "Me."

The coffee was oil. Oil and water didn't mix, did they? The oil floated to the top, filling her brain, lighting her brain on fire. The water was on the bottom, the fish still swimming around, unknowing of the danger that there was fire in her mind that would slowly spread, melting the ice in her veins and killing all of the fish in her stomach and slowly roasting her skin to a crisp.

"You don't have to change your last name," he said, as if that made things better, as if he was giving her the permission to cling to its representation of the life she'd had in the two-bedroom apartment with ~~her father~~ Dr. Richards. He half-smiled, and it was a miracle that the expression on her face even looked remotely positive, because everything in her was bitter bitter bitter.

She would blame the coffee.

# THE LIVING ROOM
## ALISSA RICCARDELLI

There was a living room; do you remember the living room? There was a fish tank. There was your mother with a dishrag in the kitchen, and her pregnant belly, and the way she cut her finger on a knife in a soapy sink, she sucked the finger and said she was fine, it was fine, she was just fine. At the time the baby might have been kicking. She rubbed the sweater and under that the belly and under that the baby and told her, too, that she was fine.

Later, we'd listen to the water rushing through the pipes from the apartment above and their bathroom's constant flushings. We did flip cards between our fingers and snap them down onto the carpet in little games with numbers and pretty shapes, like spades. When the only sounds outside were faraway trucks or the distant snorings in the throats of your brothers, we'd tangle our tongues and touch each other on the hair and neck.

Oh my goodness, I did love you. I did love you.

# SHIT MY MOTHER GAVE ME
## DANNI GREEN

Kathleen says: *Danni and I were at the Mid-Manhattan Library writing down lists of ideas for our pair pieces when she came across the title "Shit My Mother Gave Me" in her notebook. Immediately, I knew I wanted to write something on this. We've been challenging each other to write outside of our genres, and I used this title as a launching pad for a poem, which is Danni's preferred form, while Danni chose to write a personal essay.*

*"Come now, and let us reason together, saith the Lord: though your sins are scarlet, they shall be white as snow: though they be red like crimson, they shall be as wool."*

—ISAIAH 1:18

I ran across the Manhattan Bridge. The summer day's heat was dulled by the coolness of night. I slugged my tired body down Jay Street to my house, and then a blonde woman in casual dress clothes stopped me. Her smile was even friendlier than her greeting. She handed me a million-dollar bill—obviously it was fake. The woman said that on the back of it was a million-dollar question. *Will you go to heaven?*

I'm always apprehensive about people on the street who want to preach to me about God and salvation. However, this time I forced myself to keep sarcasm and reproach from my voice. She asked me if I knew God. I told her I did and that I was raised in a Christian household.

Generally, at this point, people walk away once they acknowledge that they are talking to someone who knows the Good News. This woman did not. With delight all over her face, she shared with me that she was raised in the church too.

Her father was a minister, and so her family went to church weekly, she prayed nightly and celebrated Christian holidays, but she wasn't saved inwardly. I didn't want to listen to what she was saying. Her testimony too closely mirrored my walk with God.

This woman I didn't know was unknowingly speaking to me about the conflict I've had since I first learned to say Amen. I shared with her that my mother was always involved in our church, and the Word was never far from her lips. What she said next was something I was always too fearful to say aloud. She parted her lips and out came, "You know that you have to have a relationship with God. Your mother's faith won't get you into heaven." I got deathly silent. We got to Schermerhorn Street. The woman said she had to turn left to go home. She asked me my name. I said, "Danielle." I usually say Danni, but I felt it'd be a sin to give her a nickname. She introduced herself and said it was great to have met me. I held onto the worthless million-dollar bill. When I got to my house, I stored it at the bottom of the box that holds my journals. I never looked at it again, hoping that one day I'd be able to answer that question. It is still untouched under my bed, resting obliviously, waiting for me to dispel the ideas of Christ that my mother has given me. I always knew that having a personal connection with God gave a person entry into heaven, but I've seen the way my family — my mom in particular — has worshipped God and lost themselves in Him. Too many times I've sat in church and witnessed people try to sing hymns the loudest, recite scriptures the fastest, and pray the longest, therefore I rarely go. I feel so unwelcome, like everything is a joke. No one looks happy, just like they're checking off the requirements to be sanctified. I do *not* want to be like that. I believe that there is a god. I believe that that god had a son named Jesus who died for my sins. I believe that God loves me unconditionally and will forgive me unconditionally. But I'm scared to get close to God. I know that He has a plan for my life, but what if the direction He has for my life is different than mine? I ask myself that question every Easter, every Christmas, every time I listen to a gospel song or see women passing out pamphlets in train stations. I have a hard time believing that His plan surmounts any plan that I have for my life.

I'm afraid to pray. I haven't accepted Christ into my life the way I should. Every Christian I meet seems to have replaced their humanity with the Holy Bible. I wonder if what I want matters, if who I am matters, if God wants to know *me* or just wants me to worship Him as his servant?

I blame my mother for my struggle. Raising a child to have a Christian lifestyle does not give them salvation. I never had the chance for a desire to know God to grow in me naturally. I feel guilty and wrong for not being like her. Religion comes with a clear picture that I am not. Mother is that image, and I'm not sure that not being like her will be okay. I wish that by my own will I came to know of God. Maybe then I wouldn't feel like a heathen.

# SHIT MY MOTHER GAVE ME
## KATHLEEN SCHEINER

First of all, life.

Bows taped to my head so people would know I was a girl—
there's not a problem with that now.

All the Harry Potter books—after you read them.

And the habit of reading in the bathtub, which came from your mother, which maybe came from her mother.

A hairy, spider-like mole on my upper arm that scares people.

Green cat eyes—one bigger than the other.

A ten-year career in the Girl Scouts that I desperately did not want.

Five pounds of stale candy collected from all the holidays during one year.

You taped it up in a huge box and sent it to me when I moved to the East Coast.

My favorites—Smarties, marshmallow eggs, and Reese's peanut butter cups.

Sundresses made out of bedsheets.

Art, all of the ladies in your line were blessed with this gift, and the depression that runs hand and hand with it.

A swimming pool full of presents.

The silent treatment whenever I upset you. Nothing hurt worse than that.

My first ballet—*The Nutcracker*.

When I had a chance to work at the *Times-Picayune*, a postcard with a fortune-telling cat on it.

Scrawled on the back: "Madame Cat sees a bright future for you in New Orleans."

A vision of the Virgin Mary above my head while trying to cure my headaches with water from Lourdes.

And fifteen years later, a book on spells with candles—the inscription: "No black magic! Love, Mom."

My favorite memory—

A midnight phone call after I quit my first job to write, telling me, "The only thing I ever regretted are the things I didn't try."

## SITTING IN SILENCE WITH A FRIEND
### NORA GROSS

In seventh grade, my best friend and I had a habit of calling each other and sitting on the phone, for hours at a time sometimes, in silence. We never discussed why we did this, but I think we both knew—we were only children after all! Usually we did our homework, putting the phone (landlines only at that time) on speaker. Periodically, one of us would break the silence to share a story or ask a question, but mostly we just enjoyed the quiet company and the fact that if we listened closely, we could hear the faint sounds of someone else breathing or typing at the other end of Manhattan.

While this ritual faded when we entered high school and this friend and I have mostly lost touch, I have never forgotten the comforting feeling of sharing space with a good friend in silence. The coffee shop has become, for me, the new landline. I treasure the hours I get to spend sharing my table with a friend, each of us staring intently at our own laptop screens, wishing we had one more inch of elbow room or one less coffee cup taking up space, but unwilling to give up the closeness for those luxuries.

This happened just the other day and I realized that I was even more aware of our shared silence because we enjoyed it across—and in spite of—the wobble of a broken table. I discovered the frustrating beauty of sharing a wobbly table with a friend. We were united in misery, forced to move in unison. Without words, we knew to take turns creating false stability with an elbow or the palm of a hand pressed firmly into the edge of the table as if willing the legs to even out. Although we talked very little, each of us concentrating on our own work, I felt like we were intimately linked—and I was reminded of those quiet hours I used to spend on the phone with my best friend.

# THE SEARCH
## IDAMARIS PEREZ

Funny how an ordinary start of one's day can transform into something extraordinary. I observe through the crystal clean window of my dad's lime-green Toyota all of these Conch houses. I lay my head on the back of my car seat, as I sigh, bored of seeing an endless parade of wooden shingles and gabled roofs. Estamos aqui ya? "Areee weee threee yeet?" I ask my parents in an impatient, childish tone. Casi, casi. "Almost there," they respond in unison.

When it comes to conversing with my parents, Spanish is my customary language since they both were born and raised in the Dominican Republic. Que Viva La Republica Dominicana! "Long Live Dominican Republic!" screams that pitch voice in my head. I'm very patriotic about my beloved Dominican Republic—the jewel of the Caribbean Sea. I would always go to the Dominican Republic every summer without fail—until now. I'm annoyed about the fact that I have to go visit my great-grandma in Florida. I am not in the mood for it, but what can an 11-year-old girl possibly do other than obey her authorities. Besides, my great-grandma barely visits me and my family in New York. She doesn't care about us; why do my parents care to visit her?

Believe me, I'm not even a fanatic about architecture, but here I am admiring this house that my great-great-grandfather built with his own hands. My great-grandmother's house is not even a Conch house. It's a very long, wooden barn house. For some weird reason, the presence of this house makes me tingle with excitement, like it is inviting me to discover the wonders of my ancestors' past. I rush inside this beauty and see my great-grandmother; she has aged so much from the last time she came to visit us. She appears to be a hundred years old. Her cinnamon heart-shaped face screams tired with those three heavy wrinkles on her forehead and she already has a tiny hunchback. But her gleaming, hazel eyes reveal a youthful spirit. She starts commenting in Spanish how glad she is to see me, how I morphed into this beautiful, young Dominican princess, and that she missed me a lot.

Disinterested in her comments, I back off to explore the house; everything else, except her, seems interesting. I ascend a staircase that leads me into the attic, which is cluttered with antique, dusty items. I begin my search and find an album of ancestors and start gazing at these faces. Some of my ancestors were attractive, but some were not so good looking. While I flip through the pictures, a paper slips out of one of the pages. I pick up the old, dull paper, which is a map. "It's treasure hunt time!"

I follow the directions of the map until I encounter a sturdy mahogany trunk. Fortunately, it does not have a lock so I do not have to waste my time searching for the keys. I open it and, wow, I discover a pair of tattered books about Juan Bosch who was a Dominican scholar, political activist, and even president of Dominican Republic. "This is some fancy treasure," I quip sarcastically. "I should be in the Guinness Book of World Records for finding the dumbest treasure ever."

I feel the presence of somebody behind me; I turn my head impulsively and find my great-grandmother, staring sorrowfully yet nostalgically at the books. She turns her attention to me and caresses my shoulders. She begins to narrate for me her childhood story, that she and her sister were inseparable, sister soul mates. They were very attached, wore the same humble outfits too, and what they enjoyed doing the most was reading Juan Bosch's stories. Until a tragic fate befell them and left a footprint of pain in my great-grandma's heart. Her sister, in her teens, died tragically in a car accident, left with her head cracked wide open. My great-grandma was present for that car accident and saw her sister in that traumatic state. She says that the memory will always linger in her head. Luckily great-grandma survived with some cuts and bruises. After her sister's death, she decided to conceal the books inside the bunk because she couldn't cope with the painful memory. A fragment of her identity flew with her sister into heaven.

I try to stifle my tears, but the dam breaks and streams trickle down my cheeks. My great-grandma sheds a few tears too, but I know that she's mourning inside. I embrace my great-grandma tightly which pacifies her. *Gracias mi hija:* "Thank you my darling," she says. And we both leave our ancestor's room holding our hands together.

## MY SISSY
### WHITNEY JACOBY

My Sissy,
Smiling brightly as you watched me get dressed
I long for the years when I would catch you trying on my Chuck Taylors
Walking around the house pretending to be your big sister

My Sissy,
I was always jealous of your body
Staring at myself in the mirror for hours wishing away my fat
Not realizing your thinness came at a price

My Sissy,
Covering your bruised skin to hide how he treated you
Scared of what he would do if you told
Fearing for the lives of your family just as much as your own

My Sissy,
I can still see clearly your shaking hands

Courageous at the police station issuing a restraining order
Lost and leaning on your big sister
My Sissy,
My fists curl into a ball when I think of him
I fantasize of the ways I could hurt him
But no punishment could be great enough to undo what he took from you

My Sissy,
The pride I feel for you brings a smile to my face
You acted beyond your fourteen years
While I mourn the loss of your youth, I am rejuvenated by your strength

# MY BIG BROTHER
## SADE SWIFT

4 days and 3 nights wasn't enough to make up my lifetime of questions and wondering how you were and did you think of me.

I always used to wonder if we would have the same nose or the same eyes, make the same facial expressions.

4 days and 3 nights wasn't enough to explain our long staring contest, which were hidden conversations between you and me.

We have a sister that you've never met and at the same moment we thought we wish she was here, we knew we were thinking the same thing because we smiled and continued walking and you hugged me and told me, "We'll all be together soon."

You knew what to say and when to say it.

I don't think 4 days and 3 nights will ever be enough to make up for missed time.

I remember the first day you got here and it fascinated you to see your breath in the cold New York air.

For you it was a change in environment going from the hot orange state to the big apple.

But little did you know that to me it meant that you were real, that you were alive, that you were in front of me breathing the same air I did thinking the same thing I was and happy that finally after so many long conversations of anticipation the day had finally come.

I wanted to stop time then but I knew it was passing us by.

I hugged you for about five minutes and just by your hug I knew you would be around forever.

That you wouldn't be like everyone else and walk out when I needed you most.

That you wouldn't follow in the footsteps of the one person that brought us together.

When you said you cared I knew you meant it.

When you said you'd always be there I truly believed you.

And again all these conversations happened in our heads it was just a clear understanding only shared by us.

Snow made its way across your face two days later almost as if Mother Nature wanted you to stay a little longer, but she knew you were homesick so brought the sunshine back.

We had long conversations long before we met, but I knew that this time things would be different.

I didn't know if I would be able to hold an intellectual conversation with someone that knew what I was thinking.

At the age of ten I was convinced that you were real but I didn't picture you the way I saw you for 4 days and 3 nights.

You exceeded my expectations in great ways.

You write with your right hand and hold the pen the same way I do.

You lift your eyebrow when you're mad the same way I do.

You find humor in the smallest things and laugh until your belly hurts, just like I do.

Our laughs are so similar; it's like a mischievous, sneaky laugh that you would only understand if you were us.

Blood being thicker than water never made sense to me until I spent 4 days and 3 nights with you.

I didn't want your trip to come to an end and bringing you here I knew it would but not as fast as it did.

I will always hold on to the memories of the first time we met but I know there are many more memories to be shared.

I know there will be days that I'll call you in tears and tell you how much I miss you or how much someone has hurt me, and you'll tell me things will be ok and I'll be there soon.

I noticed that you have that protective instinct of the things you love just like I do and I knew that even though you never said it.

The best thing of this whole experience were the things that were never actually said but understood.

We stood on common ground 24/7 because somehow we knew what each other was thinking.

Aside from all the great things we shared for such a short period of time, I know that our time was well spent and I know that there are so many more things to do, so many more things to be explained but for now I'm glad that 4 days and 3 nights was enough to establish that I love you so much and I'm so glad to have a big brother like you!

Nathalie says: *"Turn it Down"* by Kaskade and *"Across the Universe"* by The Beatles are two of my favorite songs, so I wanted to create something using both. I read the lyrics and then this little story popped in my head. Welcome to my brain.

The rain's filling my cup. You're not here, and now my drink tastes weird.
I'm leaving, you're lying.

You turn up, umbrella in hand, with that smug look on your face.
"You gonna tell me why I waited here for you, for ten minutes in this rain?"
You're still looking at me like that. All cocky, knowing I'd be here, waiting.
You kissed me unexpectedly, and it felt like until that moment I was colorblind. Like I've lived in grayscale my entire life. After that kiss, I saw everything so much brighter, so much... better.
Especially your eyes. Your pupils dilated. With glimmers of excitement.
"I don't understand you." I don't understand this feeling.

You grab my hand, and we're off on another adventure in Wonderland.
The mirrors deceive us. Multiple illusions shine around us.
"Try to find which one I am," you say.
"I don't even know *who* you are."
I'm getting lost. There are three of you behind me, four in front of me, and two next to me.

"Come out, come out, wherever you are..." I sound cocky, huh? But you don't care because you know I still can't find you.
You try to tell me something, but it's muffled by The Beatles.
The music is blaring.
Sure the song is nice, but in a place like this, a hall full of mirrors, it just gets creepy.
More of your voice, but I can't hear you.
"What?" I still can't find you. Can they turn it down?

A whisper in my ear nearly flings me across the universe.
"I'm right here. Always right here." You say that now, but what about later?
You kiss me again, and waves of joy run through me.
"You make my heart beat loud."
"Really? Cause I can't hear it, it's really loud in here."
You turn my face, halfway in for a kiss, and I hold my breath. I don't know what to expect.
But I look again at you, and I see it.
I see our memories.
I see our adventures.

I see our love.
I can feel as our kiss lingers on our lips, then drifts.

I tried to keep on finding reasons why I felt this way.
But I didn't know what I was looking for.
And now I've found you, and I hope nothing changes that.
You are my world.
*Nothing's gonna change my world.*

# BEEN A LONG TIME THAT I'M WAITING
## AMANDA BERLIN

Amanda says: *This piece is dedicated to my infinitely patient beautiful soul of a husband; it's a remix of our wedding song, "Northern Sky" by Nick Drake.*

A car ride along a waving road
A vast black lake
Knuckles the ink-blot trees
Northern, southern, eastern and western skies collide
Pouring stars
Like rain
Down upon us

We speed up, hands clasped near the gearshift

Nick Drake on the stereo

This is it
This
This moment

*Been a long time that I'm waiting...*

So, I tell myself I can
Finally
Melt into it

I will myself to melt
To let go of the railing

The idea of melting
Doesn't land.
I am more of a turn-on-the-air-conditioner kind of gal
Wait for the big shift in degrees

The sign from above

Even when Love slammed open the door
And walked in like he owned the place
I didn't hear him

It was as though he tiptoed and whispered

I didn't pay him much mind

Love doesn't bang and clap
When he's around me

The temperature rises a couple degrees when Love's in the house
But, it's not like a thermal event
As they'd have you believe
It's his coffee-ring stain on the kitchen counter
It's thriving houseplants
Leaning into his care
It's a flat screen television
And electronics that don't break

*Been a long time that I'm waiting...*
For trumpets and lightening

What I was really looking for
Showed up as an acoustic guitar
And a steadily flickering candle

I had melted
Into "you and me"

The ease of it

There was no sign
In the absence of a sign,
We just kept driving

And as an "us," together, I'd arrived

You're crazy magic.
You're the moon and the meaning of the sea.
You're the possibility I hold in the palm of my hand.

You're my northern sky.

# ANTONIA + BASIE
## SUSAN BURTON

*Then do but say to me what I should do*
*That in your knowledge may by me be done,*
*And I am prest unto it.*

—Antonio to Bassanio, The Merchant of Venice

I was Antonia and she was Basie. Hers was a nickname for Elizabeth: a stretch. She had jazz-loving parents. "Basie is the improv; Elizabeth is the structure," she'd said. It was one of the weeks I was first friends with her. We were in her car. Even the way she shifted was elegant. She was known for the viola, but this was just as much her instrument.

"Mine is for Willa Cather," I'd said.

I wanted to write books, and she wanted to write songs. We'd both been christened with our destinies, which meant that our parents had once owned the powers of wizards. But were the spells they had cast good or bad?

We talked about things like this in her car, zooming around our mountain town, stopping at coffee shops. (She took cream; mine was black. I wanted her to be as delighted by my idiosyncrasies as I was with hers.)

"Porter called me," she said one day. Porter wasn't his real name; it was what she called him instead of Ryan Cole.

"And did you talk to him?" I said.

"I did," she said. "And I didn't hate him. It actually wasn't—bad."

A year ago, Basie and Porter had been serious. She had experience that I lacked. My major relationship of high school so far had been with a boy on whom I'd had an obsessive crush. I knew he hadn't been my boyfriend, I wasn't claiming that. But there had been something there. You couldn't name it but I believed it counted.

"I want to go see him," Basie said.

Porter was a year older than us. He was a piano genius, but he didn't get good grades so I wasn't sure if he was smart. After graduating last spring, he'd gone to a music conservatory in Massachusetts.

"Will Royal let you?" I said. Royal was her father. Basie called him by his first name, because it was hilarious. I did, too, even though I wasn't sure if I was supposed to. My father lived elsewhere. He wasn't in my daily life enough for me to have jokes about him.

"No," she said. "No, Royal would be very, very sad. But I'm going anyway," she announced. "I just need money."

"You know I would give it to you," I said. I had a job. My mother was single. I needed cash.

"Sweetie, would you?" she said. She looked away from the road, touched my wrist.

"Of course," I said.

Then we both got quiet.

I would give the money to Basie, not because I would do anything for her: that was the kind of cliché I hated. I would give it to her because I wanted to be a part of her life. I wanted my name in her song, and hers in my story.

# STRIPES
## MENNEN GORDON

Stripes were his favorite. He wore stripes on his shirt and stripes on his shoes. He would wear striped pants if his mother let him. In his bedroom his comforter was black and white striped. Those were his favorite colors, black and white. If he were to walk past a store with something striped in the window, he'd beg and wail until he got it.

His mother imagined it was his sister's fault. She used to read him stories she would write about prisoners in black and white uniforms. The prisoners would escape from their cells and lead successful lives in functioning society, inventing buttons that you didn't need to sew on, or finding a hundred dollar bill and investing in a stock that was steadily on the rise.

His mother always tried to fix everyone. She believed it was her birthright to fix the world around her, one rash decision at a time. That doesn't mean she was good at it. With an Amelia Bedelia-esque air about her, she misconstrued situations constantly, not realizing until it was far too late.

She was afraid that her poor son would want to become a prisoner, with a delusion of success coming from detainment. One day, while he was in school, she threw away all of his striped things and replaced them with a bright, solid orange.

# MY BLOODY HELL
## SUSSY LIZ

I have scars all over my face and body. Blood runs from my nose, and his hands leave me with strange bruises and terrible pain. All these aggressions come from the man who swore before God to take care of me, to love me and to protect me.

Louis was his name and people said he couldn't be better. He was muscular and tall, with pink lips, hazel eyes and a lovely voice. Though he worked in construction, he helped his father in the family store.

We met at the only park in San Francisco de Macoris. I was 17 then, a daddy's girl, and safe in my parents' overprotectiveness; he was three years older. The park was small, but beautiful with trees and flowers. We would often go there and walk in the sunshine.

Louis loved me then, and we married two years after we met. I wanted to become a teacher. But he insisted since I was his wife, I should stay home and take care of the house and him.

We were happy like that, and so madly in love. I couldn't wait until he got home from work to be with him and hear about his day. We planned to have a big family. He laughed about wanting a house full of kids—six or seven, at least—along with some cats and dogs. A full, happy house.

But, destiny had another plan for us.

"Honey, I'm expecting," I said, handing him the pregnancy test results.

He took me by the waist and held me up.

But this wasn't the first time I was pregnant. It was the third. One night my belly hurt, and as I took off the blanket, all I saw was blood. Blood coming from me! I woke him up with my weeping. He took me to the hospital and... and... all blanked out.

When I opened my eyes, I was lying on a stretcher and my husband and the doctor were there.

"I'm sorry. You have miscarried."

As I looked at Louis I saw a hint of hate in his eyes.

"Don't worry honey, we'll keep trying," I said.

But he let me know it was my fault. And maybe it was.

As the days went, he became more violent. He came home drunk, and I was afraid. But I understood him. His dreams were destroyed. So I sat beside him on the sofa.

"You know..."

"What do you want now?"

"We should think about adoption..."

Before I could even finish, he grabbed my hair with one hand, and with the other slapped my face so hard I fell down. Then he left. I stood up, packed some clothes and ran for my parents' house. The next morning, I told my mom the whole story. She was shocked. "This is still your house. Don't stand for nothing like that."

I heard a knock at the door. It was Louis. He brought flowers and chocolate. I let him in; we sat on the sofa. He told me how sorry he was and agreed that we should adopt. "My husband is back," I thought. He said I could stay for another day and think about what he told me.

But I wanted my life back. So I took my things and left happily.

As soon as we were home, and he had locked the door behind us, his face contorted with hate.

"How dare you leave me, I will kill you, you good for nothing!" Then he pressed his lips against mine.

———

After that, he would come home drunk often and attack me. He was once happy by my side, now he would take me by the hair and drag me around the house. Other times, after I had cleaned the house, he would throw baby formula all over.

Everything was falling apart, and I was a mess. I didn't dress like before, and, of course, I didn't go out with my friends anymore. I didn't tell my mom what was happening because I didn't want her to worry. Horror ran through my veins like blood.

To the outside world, he remained the brilliant man I had lost. Because of that, no one, not even my mom, asked if anything was wrong. Louis had closed every window through which I might have escaped.

How stupid I was.

One night he came home drunker than ever. He grabbed me by the hair and punched me on the face. Then he tied me to the table.

"So, you like my friend Ronald?"

"What are you talking about?"

"Somebody told me he came here!" He started punching me again.

"It was... a... lie!" I said between blows. "I am..." I couldn't even finish the sentence to tell him that I was pregnant again.

I saw him leave. I could barely open my eyes and every inch of my body hurt. I reached for the phone on the table, but I was still tied up. I almost couldn't reach it, but I mustered the last drop of energy and called 911, gave the address and... everything turned black.

# VERY INAPPROPRIATE BEDTIME STORIES
## RORY SATRAN

"More," said John, looking up at his sister Kathy.

It was always more, more, more.

When Kathy discovered that she had a rapt audience in her little brother (who was good for very little else), she began writing stories for him. It was extremely satisfying, like making soup for a grateful invalid. What started as a way to shut him up while their mother was at the grocery store became a *thing*. A thing that amused them for hours

He seemed to particularly enjoy crime stories at bedtime. For a five-year-old whose cultural tastes usually veered toward the fuzzy animal and train story genres, he loved cops and robbers. Particularly robbers. The kind that stole a piece of bread from a marketplace and were sentenced to life imprisonment.

The prisoners Kathy described took on a life of their own. Amaryllis Crawford, a wrongly accused woman on death row, was a recurring character and particular favorite. Once night, Kathy's mom walked by while she was describing Amaryllis being beaten in an interrogation cell. When she protested, John told her to go to jail.

# A LOVE NOTE
## SHYANNE MARIA FIGUEROA BENNETT

Written on a napkin shoved
in my coat pocket
when I had not noticed
scribbled wiry little letters:

You are my wobbly table
Like a wobbly table
With uneven table legs
wedged with books
that fail to achieve
the purpose intended

To be lovably flawed.

# ON HEART BONE SKIN
## AMANDA ORENSTEIN

Sitting on the steps
Of Sacre-Coeur
Dark of night
Kneeling into my heart, it
Beats in sync with all the others
A pulsing mass expands retracts
With each glow of glittering light
From down below the city site

White domes of marble colored bone
Encase hard candy glass
Moonlit from the past
Ribs stretched wide, contain the
Very vault of life
Solid as a stone, it holds
Our soul in a delicate throne

Palm to palm, arm to arm
Feel the breeze upon your breath
It skims across the ivory flesh
Senses heightened to the core
To wish for this and nothing more

# JUST FRIENDS
## ALEXANDRA MANGUAL

Alexandra-Lily says: *This piece was inspired by the novel I am working on. In the novel the main character dedicated a song to his best friend, and this is the description of what the song means to him.*

I see her every day. She's my best friend, and I'm keeping the biggest secret from her. I can't tell her. It would ruin our whole friendship, because I know she doesn't feel the same way.

*"There she goes again, the girl I'm in love with. It's cool we're just friends."*

We went to the same high school. The day she walked into the building, I was awestruck. I knew then that I wanted her in my life. She bumped into me and I helped her find her classes. After school I walked her to her dorm. She was in the boarding school program, while I just went home every day, not having to worry about keeping my grades perfect to stay here. I continued to wish she was mine, but she barely spoke to me in school. Halfway through the semester she was transferred into my music class. Finally, I had my chance. She saw me sitting alone; she smiled and sat next to me. Since then I walked her to every class and our friendship began.

*"We walk the halls at school, we know it's casual. It's cool we're just..."*

Everywhere we went, people asked if we were together; my parents really liked her and my younger brother and sister adored her. It was always obvious that we belonged together. I tried everything; I just wanted her to fall in love with me like so many fans had so easily. At that time I was really only famous in California. She didn't seem to care about it, though. She was so accepting when I canceled plans due to a gig. I guess my fame just never got to her, just like me.

*"Everyone knows it's meant to be, falling in love just you and me."*

I knew I would never stop trying. We belong together and everyone can see that but her. I just know we're going to be together one day; I don't care what needs to be done. I don't care about Joe; I want to call her mine, forever.

*"Till the end of time, till I'm on her mind it'll happen."*

# GIRL IN THE BATHROOM
## JESSICA PISHKO

Jessica says: *This piece is a remix of my mentee's writing, which is inspired by these lyrics from a Jonas Brother's song "Just Friends." While I wasn't familiar with the song before, I was able to think about how it felt to be young and (in my case) confused about love.*

"There she goes again, the girl I'm in love with..."

No one ever sang those words to me, although I suppose somewhere deep inside I wished a boy would. Actually, that's not true at all. While I pined for love in theory, in reality, I was more afraid of being noticed than I was of being loveless. I was the girl who ran into the bathroom when the boy she liked asked her to dance at a terrible middle school dance – the party was beach-themed, I remember, and we all wore shorts and flowered leis. When he asked me to dance, I ran into the bathroom, already crying from my perceived humiliation. I forgot his name, but I remember his terrible jokes and the way he cheated on a history test, hiding the answers under his desk, just where I could tantalizingly see them, but the teacher could not.

"We walk the halls at school/ We know it's casual it's cool..."

As a freshman in high school, I went to a dance called a snowball dance. It starts with one couple dancing, then that couple has to split up and ask two other people to dance, and on and on. There was a guy I had always thought was nice. He was pale, almost as pale as I was, and when he asked me to dance, he blushed as red as a strawberry up to the roots of his blonde hair. I was sitting on the steps, not expecting to be asked. I was happy to be next to my friend for company. My friend was beautiful, or so I thought. She had long blond hair, the kind people call corn silk, and was slender and athletic. I was skinny and gawky, all elbows and knees. He asked me to dance, and I thought he had made a mistake. But, he hadn't, he was asking me and not my beautiful friend. I wanted to run to the bathroom again, I wanted to go somewhere else so nobody would see how awkward I felt. I was afraid that if I spoke to him, he would know that I was nothing special. My beautiful friend pushed me forward. "She says yes."

"Everyone knows it's meant to be/ Falling in love, just you and me."

# #WHOWEARE

Mentee Christina Butan has a secret strategy for getting through something scary. She glances at a silver ring she wears that's inscribed with the words, "Remember who you are and suddenly she finds her voice, and her courage."

The women whose works centered around notions of identity in this anthology remembered who they are, whether defined by language, family, home, gender, crimes committed in kindergarten or even by the way they see themselves, reflected in a surface, or by another person. This takes a measure of bravery.

Poet and professor Idra Novey, who led a Found Poetry Craft Talk for our writers, was moved by these words to share her own:

> "The Brazilian writer Clarice Lispector wrote, 'if it has to be said, it has to be said,' and the works of the promising writers showcased here say it. They know great writing is not about delivering what's palatable, but delivering the unsaid truth. In 'Punctuation Members,' Lucy Tan writes, 'don't let the dash/leave you so certain.' Writing about identity means writing about uncertainty, about surprising oneself as much as the reader. But to write honestly about the self also requires great boldness, the courage to speak of one's experience in all its contradictions and without apology, to write, as Meg Cassidy says, 'in my own voice, strong and clear.'"

Brave, then, to take on this scary act of introspection. But every woman who was bold enough to share her words here took a look at her own invisible ring and was reminded: Remember who you are. And she did.

— *Amy DiLuna*
2012 Mentor and Anthology Committee Member

# ROSE & FRIDA
## PRISCILLA GUO

ROSE

I.

Her name was Rose but she never bloomed.
she had eyes like pieces of stars
            but then the people came and made it night.

II.

When she was seven,
the doctor came and said
many things and many tests,
but my mother knew when he said
            she was developmentally. Delayed.

III.

School called her slow
            as though she were in a race
            And she just couldn't finish.
Nobody would wait for her in the middle.

IV.

People called her a retard.
            She asked me one day
                    "What's a retard?"
I smiled and said a nice person.
She smiled back and went on coloring her pages.

V.

That was her name.
            And she would thank them for it.
He snickers: "Retard."
And she would look right back and say: "Thank you, sir."
And I hope to god he remembers the smile on her face.

VI.

My mother would make her banana pudding, just for her.
That was her favorite.
            She would hold out a spoon to her daughter's mouth
And quietly sob.
People called her the mother of the retard.

VII.

They never knew she was my sister.
            I walked the long way home from school.

I laughed when they made jokes about her.
I secretly cried in the bathroom stalls when they weren't there.
She was my secret.

VIII.
I was her shame.
     She died last month, aneurysm.
At school, they say there was nothing quite right
with her mind.
I cry in the bathroom, where no one can hear me
say her name, Rose.
because it was too precious for them.

FRIDA
I. Sizzle.
A ladle dribbles out
     the thick batter of corn and flour
which hits the grill
like
     step after
          step
of her mother's feet
of her heavy feet.
of feet that leave the day at 10 PM
after an early morning before the rooster
     took his breath.
And her parents called to her
     "Frida."
     "Frida."
     "Frida."
to set up the corn pancake booth
     and stop lagging behind,
          worker bee.

II. Her hands switched
     between heavy textbooks
on colonial America and the
     steam and sweat
that hung on her palms.
No one wanted to hold
her hands
in line at school.
Rough like a rag, they said.
     Rough like a rag.

III. Madre says they are my
      "Las manos del sol"
      hands of the sun.
      hard-working hands.
      "my hands, mihija."

IV. My suns burn bright with me.
They hold me back tight
      like white wraps around the insane
The oil from the grill spitters
 spatters on her skin
 Tss! Tss!
Her hands can't feel it though
      She can only feel the weight of her feet
On the pavement.
Her heels burning
      while only her hands can take the heat.

V. She went to school
      when she was little.
Her teacher called her name out:
      "Fry-da" she said.
Wrong. Wrong. She walked up
to collect her homework sheets.
She held out her hands and
      "Oh dear." the teacher said.
She stood confused, like
      someone had taken her by the arm
soon her lips sewed her voice
and her eyes broke the dam
      and when she looked down
all she could see were hands that burned her eyes to look at.
Rough rags. rags.
      Like an animal
with bare and bloody knuckles
      with rows of oil scars
with uncut gnarled finger nails.

VI. They named me Frida
because they wanted me to be at peace
with myself
      and the world.
At one point, I stopped going to school
      Because I wanted peace
But I think it's my destiny to keep working

keep pushing
until death calms me down.
For mi familia
    to feed their empty stomachs
    with these suns of mine.

VII. When she was 30,
and she had a daughter of her own,
she would sing her songs about the
beautiful princesses with the beautiful eyes and the hair sparkled next to their eyes.
And she looked at her daughter's hand
    and her eyes broke the dam.

# II. BAILE DE IDIOMAS [LANGUAGE DANCE]
## SOPHIA CHAN

### I. 나를, MYSELF, Y 我

I. 안녕하세요, 저는 Sophia 입니다. I learned English and 中文 together while growing up. As a child, though, I had no interest in languages and had found 中文 school very bothersome. However, I was interested in the 日本の club in middle school and have continued my Japanese studies in the 日本の club at my high school right now. When I saw a few 한국어 dramas, I grew very interested in the 한국어 language and culture. I started studying Korean on my own and I realized mi pasión para estudiar idiomas nuevas and am currently aspiring to learn Français y Italiano as well. Usually people think in one language, but I throw around different dialects, and sometimes languages seem to even be having a conversation in my head. I was never really interested in learning about my background, but now that I find myself so infatuated by a foreign culture, I wonder if I should have some pride for my own. In a way I feel like I am a connecting point for all of the cultures I have been exposed to, but I don't have a clear standing and am still in the stage of organizing myself.

II.

ni hao
你好。囧

annyeonghaseyo
안녕하세요! ㅇㅂㅇ

Hi. :)

¡Hola! ñ_ñ

zhai zuo sum ma
在做什麼?

jiguem mwo haeyo
지금 뭐 해요?

Just staying low. . __ .

Si, si.

wo yi jin gao shu ni
我已經告訴你 —

nol-i      gaja
놀이 가자!

I don't want to fall.

¡Cualquier cosa que quieren es bueno!

wo bu yao
我不要.

wae yo     jebal    a
왜요?? 제발, 아? ㅠㅅㅠ

Aww. );

¡Dios mío, vamos a alegrar esta cara preciosa!

ni men yao zuo sum ma jui zuo ba
你們要做什麼 就做吧。

ya-ho    u-ri   mal no-eul-kka-yo
야호! 우리 말 놓을까요?

# GAELIC GREETING
## SIOBHAN BURKE

*Dia is Muire dhuit, ardmháister. Tá failte romhat.*
*Hello, headmaster. Welcome.*
The mháister (sounds like vaw-shter)
Didn't exactly foster
Warmth and kindness.

We greeted him
With an air akin
To servants bowing down to a Your Highness.
*Dee-is mu-rah guit*
We quipped
(Though "quip" fails to suggest it was laborious).
We rose from the trenches
Of those clattering benches,
Our voices joined in unconvincing chorus.
Just shy of ten years old
We told
Of rote respect through inattentive posture.

The sodden air, his thinning hair,
His in-the-doorway-standing-there,
A prelude to our daily prayer
(I'm Jewish; no one seems to care)
*Taw fawlta roh.* May we sit down now, mháister?

# HYPNOSIS FOR PREGNANCY
## LATOYA JORDAN

LaToya says: *The last line of my piece is from a poem written by my mentee, Joanne, at the Found Poetry Workshop.*

We are in a special place, my unborn child and I. That unnamed intersection between two worlds: Dreams and Reality. My baby holds my index finger; she is cradled in my arms as I walk on the uncharted beach, exploring the landscape. We hear a woman's voice. She talks to us; "Get to know each other," she says. Tell each other secrets. She is our guide in this our first meeting as mother and child. The woman's voice is not from the trees or sand. Not from the gentle waves kissing the earth. Not from the inside of the conch shell I put my ear to. Her voice surrounds us; she is the sun, warm and enveloping. I sit on the sand, staring at the baby in my arms. My baby. I don't know what to say. Will I be a good mother? What should be your first words to your baby the first time you meet? My little one squeezes my hand as if to comfort me and says, It's an adventure, I promise.

# I THINK IN POETRY
## LASHANDA ANAKWAH

I've become this still watching person
Deep in thought, staring into space—daydreaming
drifting away.
Someone catches my eye.
A knowing half-smile
I communicate with my eyes,
Caught me
I can only imagine what they're thinking,
about the girl who's always half-there
I've been drifting up, up and away.
Ms. Lewkowicz is watching me from the side
With a concerned grimace on her brow
and eyes and lips.
I don't know how I manage
to always get the window seat.

The sun is hitting the red brick building just right
and it's hypnotizing.
The trees are reaching to me—this close
but never close enough.
But I like it—when everything around me echoes
and can't quite reach me.
when I am staring at the air between the spaces.
when I am thinking in poetry.

It's frightening as well.
One day I might drift too far
away
lost—in grand ideas and abstract thoughts
my feet may never touch the ground,
I may never be fully there.
There there, not there in physicality.
Jokes and people, places and things.
Really living and laughing and interacting.
Caught up in the moment, not drifting in it.
There there.

# PUNCTUATION MEMBERS
## LUCY TAN

Lucy says: *Emily and I are both poets. During one of our pair meetings, we wrote poems that personified punctuation marks as our family members.*

Beware of the walking exclamation mark—
spot her flare-headed rush around
the house, into your room, as she
scolds you for the petty things,
the pennies you drop, the
invisible footsteps you leave.

Avoid the period—
the stop to emotions, flow of thoughts,
of words, of heart ramblings.
Leave him to be a dot in the cold backyard,
where you'll see the glowing circle
at the end of his cigarette butt.

Let the ellipsis bury himself—
in unwashed clothing, computer games
as he puts the story on hold no
matter how you urge him to brush
his own dust off, remnants of
gathered time piled high.

Listen to the slash—
as he shuffles his way across
concrete sidewalks. Hear his footsteps

slide noisily into the driveway every
night, post-bus-rides through the
forward hills of our neighborhood.

Let the semicolon reason with herself—
as she provides the conclusions,
the results, the judgments.
See how the salt crystals trail
from her hand; listen to the
pauses taken to taste the soup.

And lastly, don't let the dash
leave you so certain—
separated by her presence, the

second part of the sentence
is something you'll never
expect from the first.

# FAMILY
## EMILY HAZEL

How differently we punctuate ourselves,
fitting our separate personalities
into this paragraph of related thoughts.

My sister is an exclamation point:
easily excitable, often loud; emphatic,
demanding justice and fun for all.
She calls our attention
to otherwise minor announcements
and celebrates everything—
Earth Day, Election Day, Cinco de Mayo—
bringing the party to Brooklyn!

My brother is, without a doubt, the period.
For him, everything is definitive.
There is an unbudging matter-of-factness
to his statements of opinion, instruction, belief—
an illusion of certainty he likes to create
to convince us that a single sentence
can contain the whole world.

My mother is a question mark—
naming herself "relentlessly analytical,"
could she see things any other way?
Pressing us into hard thinking,

higher living, she is always hungry
to learn, her persistent quest
bending back on itself,
balancing on one round truth.

My father is a comma, working hard
but embracing the pause that refreshes
while my mother motors on, refusing to rest

until her sentence is complete.
He is the softer one, the flexible boundary
instead of the hard slap of a full stop;
the peacemaker, gently separating
meanings in a tangle.

And I am the middle child
of a comma and a question mark,
the ever open-ended ellipsis.
Composed of three periods, my triplets
suggest the possibility of multiple conclusions.
Sifting through fragments and glimpses
until I discover connections,
I am the queen of tangents,
the bridge in the abridgment:
adjectives, phrases, whole pages even,
can hide between my dots.
The revisionist and the indecisionist,
I am always searching for
the words that come next...

# THE BEST CHAO IN THE WORLD
## MY-THUAN TRAN

My-Thuan says: *One of the first pieces my mentee Priscilla showed me was a haibun poem about a family meal that had a lot of imagery about eating jellyfish (yum!). I liked how the haibun mixed prose and haiku. I'd never written a haibun before and wanted to "remix" a piece about a dish my own family eats.*

My dad cooked only one dish when I was growing up, over and over. It was the only time he commanded the kitchen that usually bustled with five women and their complicated concoctions.

His dish was simple. Three ingredients: a chicken, an onion, roasted grains of rice. Simmered in a pot with water until the grains blossomed and the chicken released a light broth. Tasted to perfection with dashes of fish sauce that soothed the grains and served with a pinch of fresh cilantro and scallions. Chao ga. To describe it in English makes it sound unappetizing.

My dad e-mails my sister who lives nearby him, "Come home to eat the best chao in the world!" I live far away now, so I can't come eat the best chao in the world.

The city I live in pulses constantly. But when I feel like I need to find a bit of quiet, I buy a chicken, some rice and an onion and watch the dish unfold as the commotion from the city melts away.

Watch the grains blossom
As my apartment fills up
With the scent of home

# WAKING UP
## FANTA CAMARA + MEG CASSIDY

Meg says: *Everyone experiences unique things when waking up. Some mornings are filled with lovely memories, smells, and sounds—while some are much more jarring, like a way-too-early alarm. Fanta and I lived in very different places before moving to NYC; we examined how awaking, both day-to-day, and over the course of growing up, shaped us.*

### FANTA IN GUINEA
In Guinea at 6 AM the noisy train passes with a loud whistle. And the singing sounds of chickens "cocorico" are signs in the morning there for waking up. I knew these sounds, and I love them.

The atmosphere in the Guinea mornings feels very cloudy and smells fresh and everywhere in the town looks smoky until 7:30 AM. This habit of nature is always the same, every day, in Guinea.

### MEG IN WISCONSIN
Awaking to a rural Wisconsin sunrise is still the most peaceful thing I can imagine. Even on school days, there was a calm that surrounded the house like the fog lying low over the hay fields. At least for an hour or so. Then my mom's soft singing in the kitchen would grow louder until she'd finally call up to us: *Time for the Rising and the Shining!* I never knew what that phrase came from, but it was not my favorite thing to hear. Nor was finding out that we were having millet for breakfast—again. Still, I never remember feeling rushed or stressed, because mornings there were tranquil, slow, and sacred.

### MEG IN NEW YORK
Here, of course, I'm sure many of you, like me, feel quite the opposite. Could mornings be any more hectic? Just once, I would love to wake up *before* my alarm assaults me. Or the little red light on my cell phone always gets me too, blinking out of the corner of my eye, daring me to ignore checking how many work emails have come in...while I dreamt of millet mornings in Wisconsin.

## Fanta in New York

While in New York I can stay sleeping until 7 AM without noticing anything—no trains, no chickens. Here, I have to program my alarm to wake me wake me wake me.

However the weather also is a sign for waking up in New York City, and it's always different. During wintertime the air is frozen, while in spring it is warm, and in summer even the sunlight can wake me up.

Likewise, the different qualities of Guinea and New York always make me compare them, which can make me sad. It might surprise you, but I think Guinea was noisier, and sometimes in the morning many animals like sheep, goats, and cows get spread everywhere in the town and wake up many lazy people. In New York, animals are not really visible on the road or at home to wake people up, but they have their own separate places to live. The different ways that people wake up in both parts shows that life in New York is more modernized than Guinea because of the way people's lives in it are organized.

These different ways of waking bring me a lot of memories and make me nostalgic because whenever I think about Guinea, I feel like I really left something behind. I think of my friends and family there because waking up and looking at their faces every day made me very grateful and thankful to God.

## EMOTION
### FLORA LI

### To My Dear Memory

It's heavy, lousy and ugly for other people.
It's light, awesome and pretty for me.
I've carried it since I was born.
I'm alone, it's with me. I'm in a group of people, it's with me.
It brought me sadness, anger, pain, even death.
Many people told me I should "take it down."
But I say, "No."
Because I know, without it, I would never know
what's love, what's life and what's me.
I treasure you, my dear memory.

### Run

I run,
The shrub rips into my skin, the wound bleeds,
My heart jumps quickly.
But, I run—

For the sun—
For the love—
For the liberty.


## Tired of a Relationship

They are in a relationship many years.
He never says he wants her to be his wife and she never talks about it.
One day she's cooking, he's smoking and he says,—"I'm tired of this life with you."
She's quiet, turns back to the stove and lets the tears drop down.
A pair of arms comes around her—he says,—"How about we get married?"


## Phone Number

"Please leave your message to xxx..."
"Son, why you always speak English and I don't understand?
Mammy just want to tell you,—"I'm thinking of you."


## Marathon

The sun was pretty
their bodies sweating
cups of water were caught quickly
and the water fell down on the street.
Step by step, one by one, the shadows were *farther and farther,*
We jumped, we yelled,—"Let's go, sweetie!"


## An Observer in NYC

New York is a city.
It has a huge population.
Has the most beautiful night scenery in the whole world.
Towers stand straight and tall and look at the Hudson River.

New York is a history.
Over 200 years old, the subway runs through the underground.
The corner of the renovated building has an imprint—name, date, of original.
The Church bell rings every day on time.
The page of a Bible turns into yellow, which sends out the smell of old.

New York is a dream.
The center of the economic world is here.
Everything comes and goes—time, money and people.
In the office, the cup of coffee is always cool until its owner finds out.

Seems like they work harder to get closer to their dream.

In the street, a person brushes against a person.

But, the step never stops.

The music from the street artist is in the air.

The people, including the street artist, are following their dream.

## CONEY ISLAND IN WINTER

I walk from the subway, few people walk on the streets.

All the stores are closed. They will open again in the summer.

The poster on the wall is basked by the sunshine. It's fading.

The world is so quiet. My ears only can listen to the voices of the breeze and the sea waves.

I raise my head—the sea gulls fly freely in the sky, the color of sunset shoots into my eyes as if in a Fairyland.

I keep walking on the beach. The seawater kisses my feet.

I leave my footprint on the soft sand.

Here, such a paradise.

## NOTORIOUS
## KRISTEN DEMALINE

Kristen says: *My mentee Brianna's scene, drafted in the Crime Fiction workshop, hinged on the confession of her killer, who said: "I did something." Running in the Cleveland neighborhood where I grew up, I suddenly remembered a confession of my own, and this brief piece of memoir was born.*

I did something.

I'm not sure I remember the confession. I sat in the principal's office, legs and pigtails dangling.

After only a few weeks, I got to walk to school by myself without my mom pushing my little brother alongside in the stroller. At first, I'd get there 15 minutes early. I loved school so much.

I had a secret identity, though. My imagination ran wild, and after a few weeks, I took more time heading to school. The pay phone in front of the lamp store on the corner was tall enough that I had to stand on tiptoe. I remember cradling the receiver against my head. Dialing everyone.

One day during morning announcements, Principal Lazer warned that the police were looking for a student who'd been prank-calling from a pay phone in the morning. I knew that was *my* pay phone. A thrill surged up my spine.

Kindergarten permanently lost any allure. What does a secret agent need with finger paints and Lincoln Logs?

A week or so later, I was on the pay phone when my dad drove by on his way to work.

Busted.

There were visits to the psychologist, tests of all kinds, and another visit to the principal's office. My parents sentenced me to Catholic school, where I'd immediately be promoted to the first grade. No friends. On the lam.

No one asked the questions I needed, my calls unanswered.

Thirty years later, I ran past my grimy, rusting pay phone as Christmas snow fell.

My spine tingled.

## SMILE
## AMANDA NERVAIS

Kate says: *My piece was inspired by they poem "Smile," by Mandy Nervais, and our outing to the Metropolitan Museum of Art. Mandy's quote, which she used as a postscript to her poem serves as an epigraph to my piece.*

The smile that sometimes pops on my face. . . doesn't feel quite right.
It doesn't seem really appropriate at the given times it appears,
like to be smiling at the boy who just asked me to the dance as a joke,
or smiling at the girl who just admitted she took my umbrella,
or smiling at the joke everyone's laughing at that secretly is about me... and I'm aware it's about me.
Don't misunderstand.
Being declared a five-star premium member of the "Nobody cares about you, please fall off *my* planet and die" union doesn't bring me joy,
and smiling the truth away isn't actually my way of facing it.
Am I afraid of the truth behind their words? No. . .
I smile just for the simple fact that I *can* keep smiling, I am still alive.
I may not be able to walk up five flights of stairs without stopping once,
make pancakes for breakfast without redecorating my kitchen floor,
or remember to lock both locks when I go outside,
but if there's one thing I can do better than anything else
it's smile.

*"I was smiling yesterday, I am smiling today and I will smile tomorrow. Simply because life is too short to cry for anything."*

—SANTOSH KALWAR

# SMILE II
## KATE JACOBS

We meet at the museum on a rainy Friday evening. She wanted to see the European art and we wandered rooms of paintings—Madonna and Childs, Impressionist countrysides, Dutch Masters. She stops most often in front of dramatically lit pictures of women in large dresses with mysterious smiles.

We talk about the pieces, but there's not much to say. She takes pictures with her phone. I think about how each painting might have a story behind it. What is the woman thinking? What is her relationship with the painter? What is she hiding behind her smile? Or what is she trying to show with her mysterious look? What would she think of all of us walking past her portrait, trying to imagine her life?

In many parts of the world, people don't smile for pictures. When I lived in Eastern Europe, people often marveled at my big grin. "Why, you're positively laughing," one friend remarked about my driver's license. Perhaps it's because Americans are a determinedly optimistic bunch. Our national narrative is defined by success and progress and the confident belief that the pursuit of happiness is our birthright. Other countries find unity in national suffering and the strength of survival. They hold their smiles beneath the surface, ready to give, but needing to be earned by more than the flash of a camera.

If eyes are the windows to the soul, then smiles are the language of the heart. Women have known this for centuries. I think the women who sat for those painters, the women in their corsets and silk and jewels, knew something about both steeling and opening their hearts. They knew that a smile could protect them from the world and express the individuality of their own spirit. They call to us on wet, cold winter nights to warm ourselves with a smile. There is no yesterday, there is no tomorrow, there is only this moment and this fleeting expression of self-love.

# REFLECTION
## ALICIA MALDONADO

Who is she?

The girl that I am looking at in the mirror.

The one that is having a staring contest withat me, but blinks when I blink.

She copies every silly face I make at her.

Her eyes are deep dark brown, but she wishes she had those blue eyes that when you look at them you become overwhelmed with beauty.

Who is she?

Her long curly light brown hair sometimes covers her face when she becomes shy.

This girl has the chubbiest cheeks you have ever seen, but she is disgusted by them as if they were a horrible disease.

Who is she?

She looks at me and I feel loneliness and sorrow.

She talks, but no one understands how she feels.

Her mouth is open, but nothing is coming out.

When she screams in a crowded room no one even looks her way.

This is how this mysterious girl lives.

So who is she?

Why is she so insecure about her body, her face, her thin light brown curly hair?

Why is she only noticing her insecurities and not how beautiful she actually is?

Why does she always look at the glass half empty and not half full?

Who is she?

She won't face the fact that she is loved by many.

She won't believe that she is a sensitive girl and that it is better to have a beautiful heart then a cruel and miserable one.

Who is she, you ask?

Well, she is me.

I look in the mirror and see another person looking back.

I do not see the person that everyone else sees.

I do not see someone I am sure I know.

I realize though that I am strong and powerful.

I am beautiful and confident.

My deep dark brown eyes finally do see how loved I am by my family and friends.

When I see my curvaceous body in the mirror I will never again question how gorgeous I truly am.

I have goals I want to reach.

I have places I want to see.

This is the girl I am and forever will be.

Not that girl in the mirror who I see.

I am me and I accept everything that makes this young lady that I see before me.

So again I repeat this for anyone who dares not see me for me.

My name is Alicia Elizabeth Maldonado.

The life I have originates from Puerto Rico and Italy.

I am the reflection of my mother, and I have the confidence of my father.

This is me and I am happy to call myself a beautiful, smart, creative young lady and not the reflection in my mirror.

# I AM A WOMAN
## CHANTAREYA PAREDES

I am a woman.

My mind revolves around the thoughts of those

who live and plot to see me lose.

My body is composed up of pleasure,

created for man, to be used by man, to be hurt by man,

all for man.

And who would have ever known

that the pattern never stops at one generation.

It's a rotting plague of depression that continues to break away whatever resolve

to live happily, that I may have or had.

My title was not properly given,

because my status is that of a child,

who only gets a reward of laying on the bed,

while the punishment of possible anger

is getting beaten by the hands which provide you with a home.

And I don't want to cry because they will not empathize.

The tears are stains that follow me around,

only proving to me that I can't handle what I have found.

She asked "why does the caged bird sing?"

and I want to tell her it's because she's a girl and since she can't spell out anything

other than what a lady would say, she has to disguise all of her disgust

behind pretty little notes that no one cares enough about to translate.

My soul is dirty laundry.

Only cleansed by machines.

I find comfort in the stability of the way that it spins me,

around and around,

until I am drunk on hallucinating.

I am at peace when the soap slides across my skin,

washing away the filth that I am forced to live with,

brushing clean the bruises that have nothing to do with my physical,

but has tormented and remixed the dreams of real love.

And when I am in that dryer, I close my eyes and long for death,

because sooner or later, I will be taken out, and folded back to my primped and press

And once again I will be touched by hands

that don't deserve to feel my cloth, or skin.

If I could label my life as a status,

then I would download the dislike button and complain about it.

Because only then would I be allowed to create the expression of my thoughts like salt and pepper.

And who would have known that when I said no one is supposed to be here that the words would flow through my fingers like melted ice in the summer?

I should have known better than to allow someone who wants superwoman,
come to a house who only houses little women.
And don't act like I can only have you because if I need to then me and my little kitty cat will go,
because you weren't man enough to take me as I am.
And get it through your head that before there was us, there was me, myself and I, and I can remix that into U.N.I.T.Y so that you understand that without you I am still alright.
I am a woman.
My mind is made up of emotions that followed me throughout the lessons that I have learned.
My body is composed up of a four-page letter that describes my problems and triumphs, torn from a book titled "Everything Is Everything."
My soul is the basis of all that is real,
carrying on the pride of girls who feel.
Of girls who win.
Of girls who live.
Of girls who make it.
Of girls who turn into women.
Of girls who are women.
I am a woman.

# THE VOICE
## MEG CASSIDY

And so it strikes again. One moment, you're striding tall and purposefully across busy avenues, sipping an iced coffee while running a dozen errands on a 30-minute lunch break in Midtown, when it hits you like a hijacked MTA bus going 50 MPH down Madison—that voice. What set it off this time?

Was it the glimpse you caught of yourself in the pristine windows of Saks: ponytail slightly askew, bangs a bit too frizzed out (as they always were in middle school when the voice found you the first time?) Was it the dream last night about the missed deadline that is actually still a week away? Or the fact that even though your phone has gone off every single minute today, Mr. Let's-do-this-again-soon from Wednesday still hasn't responded to the quirky text you sent without really thinking about it this morning—of a Buddhist monk, waiting for the subway on a busy platform. If only you could have traded places with him for a day.

You scan yourself again, asking what body part does this voice arise from so unannounced? Head, overthinking things as usual? Heart, expecting another tough break before it even happens? Lungs, aching with the stress some days of never taking a deep enough breath because you always feel you're not doing enough, never doing enough. Who do you think you are walking down the street like that? It asks. Put your head down.

You recognize this voice almost better than your own, although you're better at quelling it now; like the calls of an ex that can be forgotten within minutes. But you still can't predict what allows it to reach you, or why it took hold so firmly, muting your own voice in 6th grade. No longer allowing you to be the loud-mouthed tomboy you were up till then, let alone try to speak up in class. So teachers had to get to know you through writing, some even begging in their comments: "That voice you have on paper—use it in class!" And so it's been a lifelong struggle—ignoring the voice that seeks to define you, finding the courage to make your own thoughts heard over it.

Walking back to the office, while taking deep breaths of thanksgiving and peace, you reach the publisher's boardroom for a very important meeting. Sitting down with colleagues, agents, and editors, the meeting starts at 2pm on the dot, and soon after, I say in my own voice, strong and clear: "I have an idea."

# YOU ARE NOT A DICTIONARY
## TAYSHA CLARK

The Bible says to love my neighbor as I love myself,
But there is an impenetrable field through which I cannot pass
You are not my neighbor, but a stranger,
In my world, that is synonymous with danger.
That is, that I am a danger to you...
An imminent threat.
A gun fully loaded with a thousand bullets,
Against that which is rival to equality.
In the Garden of Eden, we are the same
But this land is not paradise, do not fall into that trap.
We are the children of a hierarchal structure,
Slaves to the belief that my milky complexion is an index of perfection
And the dark of your skin and the impurity of your soul is a blemish to the race.
We are enemy soldiers without a war, perhaps the incarnation of the cold war,
Because how can I fight a war in a battlefield that is foreign to me,
An imagined turf where real individuals are casualties.
You live in my neighborhood but we are not neighbors
Because I was taught to love my neighbors, yet I hate thee
A foreign concept not worth unraveling...
In your face are the contours of an exotic land not worth traveling to.
The rejection of all color.
The lack of melanin in my skin

Seems to indicate that I am free of sin

And since I am free of sin, I do not hate my neighbor

I hate a stranger

Blood does not flow through my veins, in my lexicon does not exist the word "pain"

My heart does not palpitate ever so slowly within the confines of my chest

I am a robotic police, and you the criminal that I am dictated to arrest

My story is fiction.

Yet since you're different, YOU ARE AN AUTOBIOGRAPHY

You are my walking mirror image

Yet understanding you or loving you is an unfathomable notion

Because you hate me for a mere quality, an unchangeable part of my genes.

I cannot know you

Because you've stripped me of my humanity

And made me equal to a word in the dictionary

Because my skin is the definition of me?

You do not know me or where I come from

My God is not your God

And my story is a collection of unique authors while yours is an anthology of the same

individual, simply with different names

And you are newly fallen snow,

Before it has been trekked on and a memoir of someone's past

With footsteps that don't last

Long enough to tell a story.

I am an aberration to your nation,

God's blunder in the story of creation.

I am put down because I am not the same as you,

And if I am your brother or sister, I am the deformed child

An error since conception subject to rejection

So even though we belong to the same human race, my pain is not your own and my story

cannot be read on your face

So I must hate you

My natural foe, the cause of all my woes

I fight this war alone

And you will be a casualty

In my revolution against the tyranny

Created by your inherent skin and sexuality

You are not me, nor my brother nor sister nor neighbor

And I cannot love that which I do not understand...that which I do not know

I am bereft of emotions towards you...you complex entity.

In this food chain, I am prey to society's ignorance,

The slave of years of misunderstanding.

# THE INVISIBLE RACE—BEING YOUNG, BLACK + UNDER ATTACK NYIESHA SHOWERS

Nyiesha says: *I took a line from my mentor's novel and used it in a narrative poem.*

The sounds of our neighbors crying out to their loved ones, their enemies, and their
Gods, fanned through the country.
When they heard of the tragedy, some couldn't believe it.
It's 2012, how could such a thing still be happening?
And to who? To me.
I am a person of a people that has been shamed.
I walk with my head high but still feel low and insecure because
I'm blamed
For my name, the color of my skin, all of which I was given and did not create.
Living in a world filled with hate,
To love myself is an overstatement.
This is the sad reality that no one wants to face
So I represent the invisible faces of an invisible race
With no emotions, no feelings and no safe place
To rest my worried and occupied mind
And to walk blindly with bliss is what my people have become accustomed to.
So the fact that we can interracially date
And escape death,
We are blinded by the illusions of integration and unity
To think that this society could ever be true to us is a dream.

The truth is I couldn't even get to see 18.
The milestone of adulthood will never be familiar to me
Because I was shot to my death
Just for being me.
But who determines who I am, if not me?
Society.
If I'm a gentleman, I must be gay.
But if I'm rude I get no play.
If I like to read, I'm a nerd.
But if not, I'm just on the corner smoking herb.
If I talk about politics and use standard English, I'm acting "white"
But If I use slang, I'm ghetto.
If I'm from the hood, I'm on welfare
But if not, I'm siddity.
If I'm a young black male, they tell me all I can do is play basketball.
But If I'm a young white male the
possibilities are endless.

So can you see how this society has me restless?
I'm constantly on edge, even in my own neighborhood.
Because If I'm wearing a hoodie and walking to the store,
I must be a criminal and up to no good
Because I'm young black and from the hood.
There's something wrong with this,
Sad part is some people don't think so.
They agree because society uses their media to paint a stereotypical image of me.
So it's possible for Zimmerman to get away with murder.
Because I'm young and black and up to no good,
Because I got suspended from school for smoking weed,
My life is irrelevant and someone taking it is okay.
This is the world I live in. My name is Trayvon Martin.

# I AM
# SULEYMA CUELLAR

Jennifer says: "We Are" is a remix from Suleyma's original piece "I am." There are many gifts that I have gotten from Suleyma during this mentoring experience. One of the gifts that I have "remixed" into my own work is Suleyma's courage. She has been completely unafraid in her writing and expression. She takes chances in her work and challenges herself to try new material and even different genres from romantic poetry to science fiction. Her poem "I am" is one of my favorite pieces that she has shared because it is written with such honesty. Suleyma has the ability to question life and life's circumstances while still remaining open to hope. It also is a piece where Suleyma imagines what I might write back to her in the poem which inspired me to use this same writing technique in creating "We are."

I am Suleyma/ I am Jennifer
I am Mexican/ I am American
I have seen so much poverty/ I have seen so much lost
My parents/ My family
My image judged/ My image secure
I am 17 years old/ I don't tell my age:)
I want to understand/ I want to teach
I have faith to strengthen me/ I have hope to help
Little chances/ Big decisions
Not a lot of opportunities/ No time to be wrong
I lay awake, frightened for the future/ I lay awake, from the
blessed memories

These are my worst hours/ These are my best hours
My dreams/ My hopes
My goals for a better future/ My goals for tomorrow
Carries me through/ Carries me through
Carries us through

## WE ARE
### JENNIFER BACON

I am Jennifer (a mentor)
I am Suleyma (a mentee)
We are each other's teachers and learners
We are made of our lived experiences, dreams and imaginations
This piece is a symbol of worlds and visions that connected and the futures we have envisioned

These writings are born of our work together
The serious, reflective, and funny
Together we are the hope that carries us through

## ELLISONIAN
### PATRICIA LESPINASSE

Patricia says: *I chose to remix my mentee Nyiesha's poem, "Naked," by using the first two words of the first two lines in her poem.*

I preach Ralph Ellison
I am the Invisible
Haitian-Woman
walking through
life
with a pen
marking
my blues

in red
on
the also and also
of
white paper
speaking on the lower
frequencies
frequently
and
seeing around
corners
desperately
seeking
Truth
in the beginning
of
the end.

## NOTHING BETTER THAN A WOMAN... A TRUE WOMAN RUBY FELIZ

Nothing better than a woman.
A woman who respects herself,
and everyone else.
A woman who knows when to stay,
when to change her way,
but will never give herself away.
A true woman.

Nothing better than a woman.
A woman who's no bigger than an elf,
but stands up for herself.
A woman who speaks her mind,
without feeling left behind,
or denied by mankind.
A true woman.

Nothing better than a woman.
A woman who knows what she's got,
and doesn't need a man to tell her she's hot.

A woman who has the brains,
to refrain,
or step up her game.
A true woman.

Nothing better than a woman.
A woman who's brisk,
and isn't afraid to take a risk.
A woman who's got the nerves,
to stay preserved,
and settle for nothing less than what she deserves.
A true woman.

Nothing better than a woman.
A woman who's full of passion,
and shows it with her actions.
A woman who knows how to treat a man,
even if parting is part of his plan.

———

When the situation is at hand,
remember there's nothing better than a woman,
who doesn't forget where she began,
and what made her a woman.
A true woman.

# HIP-HOP IS MY EVERYTHING
## NAJAYA ROYAL

Anuja says: *We knew we wanted to incorporate music into our pieces, and so we first turned to lyrics in search of inspiration. In this process, Najaya remembered the story of a stranger she had crossed paths with, and it was from this that her poem was born. In remixing her piece, I envisioned this same woman and tried to tell her story from a different point of view. The reader will see a clear connection between these two pieces, both in the language and in the woman's story.*

"Life check 1,2,1,2
I endure in a world that's a concrete zoo

Lyrics are my gravity
Hip-hop is my everything"

I speak of my love for hip-hop
As though it were a person
Attempting to scrub away my memories
But Bounty paper towels cannot tackle my story
Years of misled dreams and hidden secrets
Gold-plated hoop earrings and a smile
Deceiving those who worry about me
Talking for attention
Loving without affection
The only thing I feel is hip-hop

Mos Def's "Brown Sugar" keeps me from sinking to the bottom of the sea
His lyrics are the only thing that truly know me
Feel me
Nas said hip-hop's dying
So what will happen to me
Will my gold hoops fade to reveal my life's artificiality

Hip is my heartbeat
Keeping me alive
Or, is it eating me alive
You see, I'm starting to lose myself
Fade out like the end of a song
I wake up to silent mornings
A new stranger in the mirror

Hop has dropped
And so has my world
My smile has vanished
And here I lie
Forgotten with hip-hop
Ms. Soul without her namesake

# A MUSICAL JOURNEY
## ANUJA MADAR

A hip-hop beat pulsed through her veins
Imprisoning her with each of its 16 bars
Low notes scratched the surface
But high notes tore deep into flesh
Sending the walls she had carefully built

Brick by brick
Crumbling to her feet

The odds were stacked against her
Tried to suffocate her song
Similes, metaphors and clichés
Starts and stops
At times a different narrative
But always the same plot

She scrubbed violently
Tried to change the course of her melody
Turn destruction into glory
Change the ending of her story

With weary hands
A shattered heart
She surveyed what remained
Her life's mistakes
Now shriveled eraser shavings
Gone with one simple breath

She faced a blank page
Fresh and ready
Waiting for a new tune to unfold
But like a chorus
Her past life's lyrics returned
Kept pace with her new beat
Forever guiding her story

# RED
## MAYURI CHANDRA

The truth is, I really liked her. Like, really liked her, without even knowing her. Even though she ran with a different group. Even though she was white. I have plenty of white girlfriends, don't get me wrong. But for some reason, I just always felt like she and I were kindred spirits. I always admired how her frizzy red hair was sort of unruly, just like mine. And she chewed on her pens, just like I did. We had the same teal blue hoodie and I always tried to time wearing mine when I thought she'd wear hers. I heard she got into Duke. That somehow seems like the right place for her. Maybe she'll be a cheerleader there too. Every now and then I catch her looking at me too, across the cafeteria or when she's walking by my locker with her gaggle of girlfriends. I bet she's thinking we should be friends, we should have been friends. Once I caught a glimpse of her iPod playing and it was "Part of Me" by Katy Perry—which just happens to be my own number-one-most-played song. When I imagine us together, touching each other's kinky hair, I imagine it to that song.

# ENTANGLED IN DARKNESS
## GEORGIA SOARES

Karen says: *My piece was inspired by my mentee Georgia's essay, "Entangled in Darkness."*

Sometimes darkness welcomes me, and I approach it slowly, not to hide or run away from reality, but to think freely. Since I was little, I heard that over-thinking was not a good practice, because it could fill me with doubts. However, the danger of over-thinking was never strong enough to stop me, once my heart's desire to find answers spoke louder than my caution.

So I give darkness a chance. I turn off the lights in my room, walk to bed and tuck myself in. This time, however, I do not close my eyes and I do not try to sleep. I face the dark, demanding explanations. Where does it come from, and where do I come from? What is this life all about? What am I supposed to learn? Should I neglect the dark and only appreciate the light? Or am I living life the wrong way? To neglect darkness is to neglect myself, I ponder. Maybe if I do not question the dark, I will not question myself. And why not question?

I keep my eyes open for an interminable amount of time, not stressing about the exhaustion I'll feel tomorrow if I don't fall into slumber. After all, I want to discover what I am missing out on, every time I give in to a dreamy world of sleep. Even then, the world continues to exist, the air continues to circulate slowly, the sun and the moon hold their usual sacred spots. And is it possible that I no longer belong to this world, while I sleep and rove in my dreams?

My eyes, still open and staring at nothing, feel lost in the midst of the infinite dark. But what seems to be nothing slowly reveals itself as an ocean of mysteries. And I catch myself raising the usual questions brought by the tide: from where do we come, where do we go? I don't know, and to not know troubles me. If I could only extract from this dark hollow some soothing and calming answers, I would certainly live with a less excruciating hunger for discoveries.

Time goes by, and my questions remain nervously alive. No answers I receive; I'm afloat in this ocean of darkness, wondering about this world, and this life, and where we all come from, and what's the point and... and what else? Because I know there is more, though I cannot know beyond the more. A greater sense of familiarity eventually settles in the room as my eyes adjust to the dark, but I still bear my doubts, my curiosity. Darkness embraces me and leads me to lose my own self.

Questions are not answered directly, but the sense of familiarity grows. Meanwhile I do not shut my eyes, I do not deprive myself of life's infinity. For each unsettling thought and hungry doubt, the dark responds with a sense of warmth and companionship. There is no reply, but the darkness listens quietly and patiently. And for tonight, that seems enough.

# LIGHT+DARK
## KAREN KAWAGUCHI

We all have darkness in our lives—fine gradations of gray slowly deepening to black. A scary diagnosis, getting fired, a lover's betrayal, losing a friend, a sister's suicide. Darkness can arrive unexpectedly. It's often completely random. Few of us deserve bad things to happen to us.

What surprises me is how people strive to find the light. Darkness may fall randomly, but the striving to find light is intentional, persistent, courageous. We seek light with no assurance that it's achievable. And even if we attain the light, it can vanish at any moment. The desire for light is based on faith or hope or some kind of DNA-based tenacity. A life force that drives us toward new love, new homes, new jobs, new friends, creating art, feeling joy.

But for some, no amount of striving can erase the blackness of despair, illness, catastrophes. I don't know why the light evaded my sister's grasp, while I continue to reach for it and often bask in the pleasure of its golden rays.

Some people are suffused with light—we can see it in their shining eyes, feel it in the kindness of their hands and words.

But others are vessels for darkness. They cling to darkness because it's familiar, it's safe. Pain, anger, and bitterness are old friends. Darkness shields them from the prickly warmth of life.

The convergence of light and dark. Those transitional moments when our lives are changing, for better or for worse. Shadows recede and give way to light. Or shadows intensify and devour light. The moments we long for. The moments we fear.

# THE END OF FISH
## HILARY LEICHTER

Even when the fish were gone, people still went fishing. Fathers took their sons to the edges of lakes and women waded in waist deep in tall boots. The waters were calm and we pierced them with wires and long lines, held up the oceans with our rods. The end of fish came quickly, and we fished to think about the ends of other things. Mother thought about the end of trees, the end of birds, the end of marriages. I thought about the end of the school year, the summer stretching out before me like my reflection in the pond. Bait was no longer necessary, but sometimes I'd feed a worm to a wave. An offering, or a request.

No one put messages in bottles, not anymore. The water was deep and empty. It hugged the continents on the map in my room, a blue abandoned cloud. I wondered what would become of all that lonely space. Mother said the world was surrounded by an old, flooded house, and so we took our fishing poles and went to knock on its doors.

# #ATACROSSROADS

Merriam Webster defines crossroad as "a crucial point." We come to our own crossroads at different times and via separate roads, armed with diverse outlooks and distinct experiences. Some of us arrive alone, others with a band of fellow voyagers and the luckiest ones with a full team of supporters.

But make no mistake—at some point, we all find ourselves there. Sometimes we're dropped into a strange new world by sudden heartbreak. Other times we're blindsided by a distressing injustice. At some of the hardest times, we're our own worst enemies, troubled by the rumblings and ruminations that spring from our insecurities and fears. The crossroads is a confusing place, one where it's nearly impossible to differentiate between up and down, real emotions and fleeting panic, what we want and what the world wants of us.

So what to do, as writers and as women, when we find ourselves at one of these points?

Sojourna Collier, a fellow writer, educator and multimedia producer, offers this simple yet meaningful directive: we write. Having kept a journal her entire life, she often looks back on her own experiences at the crossroads to find lessons to guide her today—in writing, in relationships, and in life. Sojourna emphasizes the catharsis that comes with writing about these challenges—the heartbreaks, the betrayals, the inequalities, the disappointments— because it's that release that gives us needed perspective and empowers us to keep moving. Or, as Sojourna more eloquently put it, because it can "show us the answers between the lines and allow us to have a conversation with the universe."

Writing is a relatively simple tool for navigating the crossroads. But it is also one that can bring liberation, peace and solutions. And as the work that follows shows, it can bring amazing writing.

— JILLIAN GALLAGHER
2012 MENTOR AND
ANTHOLOGY COMMITTEE MEMBER

g

# DRINK UNTIL FULL
## JOANNE LIN

Take the crooked teeth,
soft dimples in his cheek.
Take the dry cracked hands,
beauty mark under her eye.
Take the shape their bodies make,
the scent their breaths create.
Take it all and
drink until full.
Drink until your heart
sinks from heavy sighs.

Empty
Shadows line
the inside of his skull.
The creeping black engulfs
the whiteness of his bones.
Thick air clings to
his rotting body.
The heart is silent, but the
constant cry of
bitter emptiness.
The cry wakes me from
dreams to silence.

# REFLECTIONS ON A SCHOOL PICTURE
## KATE TREBUSS

Strange art,
Photography—
Science
of desirable and detestable bodies.

Framed,
Arrested by the camera's steely eye, you found yourself
Initiated, with/out consent, into the School of Law and Order.

A flash,
And your warm flesh exploded into a blizzard of pixels,
Your face metabolized and transcribed,
Was encoded, serialized, categorized.

You were seared to a vast corpus of images
That together reframe a nation's differences in terms of

this girl's size and
that boy's color;
this girl's sad eyes, and
that boy's swagger.

In your school photograph,
Your gaze is unflinching—
The shot suppresses a carefully cultivated reflex to glance away to avoid being seen
By someone who might look in the eyes of a black boy
And feel justified in killing him.

Your school photograph,
Though a certificate of your presence,
Lies
When it claims that your body was viewed no differently
From other bodies
Outside the scrupulous democracy of glossy 3 x 4 snapshots.

I look at your photograph
And am filled with Rage
By this living image of a dead boy,
Who tasted rainbows
Only moments before he found himself choking on the appalling redness of his own blood.

I find myself pierced by the catastrophe of your indexicality—
Breathless
As I realize
That your death is here foretold:
He is going to die: this will be and has been.

It is not the beauty or wholesomeness of your face
That moves me—

(For I will not forgive the world for its need to see you so young, so handsome, so luminous
In order to feel sorrow and anger in response to the
Outrageous decisions
That rendered you expendable,
Weightless on the scales of Justice)

Rather,
It is the resistant resonance of your voice, as it renders obscene
Attempts to explain your senseless death,
That animates me.

Will you be heard,
I wonder,
Though meaning and memory congeal,
Slick like oil,
Around your waggish smile.

## IMBASIYA
### AMY FELDMAN

Hiring the taxi driver seemed like a good idea at the time. Hiring him to drive us the 610 miles from Aswan to Cairo meant we wouldn't have to suffer through another 19-hour, un-air-conditioned train ride, with men selling live chickens in the aisles. We'd had tea with the taxi driver and met his family, and he'd proudly shown us his new porcelain toilet, a sign of his recent rise to the middle class.

In retrospect it seems so obviously a bad idea, the geographic equivalent of hailing a New York City cab to go to Wilmington, North Carolina. Of course, something happened. Of course, something went wrong.

First the car stalled and then stopped, stuck in the middle of the road in the middle of nowhere. Our driver insisted we pay: His car wouldn't work, so the journey was finished. We told him no, no, no, no, we would pay when we got to Cairo.

Then there was a bump, a thump, a noise that was not what we wanted to hear. In the middle of nowhere, with sand all around, we had been hit by another taxi.

Our two taxi drivers were yelling at each other. I couldn't understand, but I knew enough to be worried. We were two young foreign women wearing jeans and no head scarves in the middle of nowhere. No one knew where we were and we had no way of telling anyone where we were.

We got out of the car. I remember thinking that we could become an international incident, and that as Americans, perhaps, this lent us some safety. We went to the trunk to get our luggage. Our taxi driver slammed the trunk closed.

A swarm of young men with machine guns came running out to see what had happened. The police or the army, or perhaps that day they were one and the same in that village, which turned out to be Bani Suwayf, nearly 200 miles from Cairo. Bani Suwayf is one of the poorest regions in Egypt, known for its cement factories and cotton mills, I later discovered, and, as was obvious at the time, foreign women traveling alone in jeans and no head scarves were not particularly welcomed there.

I had learned one word in Arabic for emergency situations like this: *Imbasiya*. I still don't know if this is the real Arabic word for embassy, or if it was some word my friend who was studying Arabic made up, but I repeated it over and over again. *Imbasiya*.

For hours, as we sat in an empty room and I refused to sign the papers in beautiful scrawls that I could not read—the charges against us—I repeated: *Imbasiya*.

It was my talisman, my shield, for I believed that despite my atrocious pronunciation and despite perhaps not even using the word right, that if I could just make myself understood that I was American then I would be safe. Years later, perhaps longer than I ought to have, I continued to believe this to be true.

# A GRAIN OF SAND EN *EL DESIERTO DE TU CORAZON* YODALIN PERALTA

As I enter the door shadows cover my eyes
and blurry becomes my new best friend.

As much as I fear, the more I like his words.
Powerful and hurtful.

My heart breaks as a mirror does.
Never thought that seven years of bad luck
could lean in my heart.
But I became the most known widow
in the dark shadow of the night.

*Inmensamente sola, inmensamente juntos,*
*simplemente triste, simplemente oscuro.*

(Immensely lonely, immensely together
Just sad, just darkness.)

*Nada, dentro, en el todo del afuera,*
*corazón triste, corazón contento,*
*no hace ninguna diferencia cuando se vacía por dentro*
(Nothing in, on the whole of the outside
A sad heart, a happy heart
it doesn't make a difference when empty inside.)

*Dolor sin razon, amor no cuerdo,*
*Puede que piense que duele menos perderte,*
*pero sigo tratando de encontrarte, el dueño de mi corazon.*

(Pain without a reason, love is insane,
It might hurt less to lose you again,
but I am still trying to find you, the owner of my heart.)

*Inmenso, simple, profundo, oculto.*
*Que soy, sino, un granito de arena,*
*en el amor, desierto de tu Corazon.*

(Huge, flat, deep, hidden.
I am but a grain of sand in love,
a desert of your heart.)

Staring at a black screen waiting for your arrival
but you never came.
Knowing that I was only a figment from your past
And that this was really the end of everything.

You told me you loved me with all your heart,
I should have known from the very start
That our love would come to a bitter end.

I wanted to hold and care for you every night but I couldn't.
I can't stop thinking of your face,
how I love it and how soft and sweet it seems.
I can't stop thinking of your voice,
as cute as the body that possesses it.

I can't feel this feeling any more.
My temperature raises and emotions explode.

No matter what I do I can't stop thinking of you
and every night shadows try to erase this feeling
but it's stronger than me and weaker then darkness.
I can't forget you as much as I try
you are stuck on my heart like a tattoo.

I wanted to feel you beside me
I want to feel that you love me and remember me
I wanted to hold and care for you every night
But now I can feel you behind me.

# THE PERFECT MORNING
## KARMA DOLKAR

Dreaming in the morning summer of July,
I felt the arrival of my long awaited samurai.
When the cool wind rushed through the window,
A sensation of beautiful feeling had a flow.

It invaded my sleep,
And made me forget that for you, I always weep.
It simply took away all my exhaustion,
And answered all my unanswered questions.
Filling me in with the strong sense of acceptance,
And slowly it dispersed my anger and vengeance.

An acceptance from that special someone,
Yet, the absent image of everyone.
Am I lost in your thoughts?
If not, why am I collecting your love dots?
Seems like you intentionally stole my heart,
Gifted me with this perfect morning, full of color—you played the part.

# SWEET AUNT KANNY
## FANTA CAMARA

During those cool spring days, when I went on vacation to your house, I expected you to be on my side. And also, to be supportive so our relationship could be solidified, since I'd never met you before in my life, but my mother had and she is very thankful to your parents. So this expectation is familiar for any teenager for their precious break time. I remember how excited I was to hear that I'd be spending my spring break with you and your family.

There was always this reason that made so excited. This was that my mom always told only positive stories about you. She always told me about how nice and fun it was to spend her whole childhood with your parents and yourself, Aunt Kanny, and she would hardly spend a day without talking about you. Guess what? That's the exact sweet aunt I wanted to know, so I would listen with interest to my mom's conversations whenever she shared her memories about you.

Unfortunately, sometimes the things that human beings propose on one hand, God disposes of on the other. My expectation of meeting you was proven otherwise when I came into your world. My vacation to your house was a hell and not once at the time did

I think of the paradise I had imagined it being. I was so lonely and lost in your wide world without anybody's concern or interest to bring me into their own smaller world. Not only did you leave me all alone in the house while you went out with your children, I had to clean up all the messes after both the children and yourself; I cooked every day while you planned dinners in restaurants, was in charge of doing everyone else's laundry in the house, and I had to watch the house after you'd leave like some sort of guardian.

I didn't have anyone to stay with or even talk to. There was no one to guide me into town or plan any fun for my break times. You disappointed me. As long days were passing one after another, I felt how hard you were trying to push me down. However, it was impossible because of my braveness and courage. These things helped me to put myself together and forget my fear against you. They also taught me how to spend my days in the house without letting you notice how frustrated I was with you and your family. So now, thinking about you makes me feel horrible. However, knowing you opened my mind to the world where I'll use it to analyze wrong, good, right, important things in my life. Which is that I got more experience in life. I can take care of myself wherever I go now, and know how to deal with these situations. There will always be people like you in life. I also learned that in the future, things will be different in different places, and I have to get used to always changing.

Maybe it was my fault, that I didn't show or explain to you that I needed someone to stay with, to share my feelings with. That I needed support. I'm sorry, but if you were interested in my visit or at least had a concern about my feelings, Aunt Kanny, you will now.

I want to tell you that I erased you in heart but not in memory because I'll remember you whenever something horrible happens to me for the rest of my life. But I don't want the same horrible things that you did to me to happen to anyone in the future, because according to the philosophers, "bad things happen to bad people and good things happen to good people." So I hope you understand this and stop being so evil. I'm keeping my life in a new world without you, and I hope that you too will keep going in yours, and I wish that with God's help, you'll change.

# THE AMBITION TO EXHALE
## BRE'ANN NEWSOME

I may not have much money or expensive clothes in my closet
I may not have many electronics or extensive dollar signs in my pocket
But what I do have is ambition and a handful of courage
And I'm willing to do whatever it takes until it works

My mother doesn't own a car or a Prada purse
And I may not have much worth in my last name
But I've seen worse

And I've been called worse
Been expected to achieve lower
But I refuse to stop running until this race is over

All the other kids may have jewelry and jeans identified by the brand
But I have a quarter in my pocket
Two pennies in my left hand
They all may doubt me
And nor does anyone see
The greatness that has been endowed and is so deeply rooted within me

I am greatness
I am phenomenal
I am the tallest mountain among these brown-bricked buildings you see
I write
I speak
But I am the best by far at being me

My dad doesn't live with me
And nor does my brother
Yeah, she's flawed
But you've got me wrong if you think I'd want another

They may have seen me trip
Slip and stumble
Tear, blink twice
Curse, heard me mumble
But I promise you they will never see me cry or fall
I have a point to prove
To myself, my competition, their mothers and all

I may not ever be rich
But I wouldn't mind being middle class in a condo
Don't need to own a company
But a small business, fine, make it mine pronto

I have the longest history of never going too far
If you look into my background, you get a hint of why I'm trying so hard
So hard just to find an open ear
I have the kind of luck that if I knock on someone's door
All of a sudden no one's there

But I don't care if I get turned down
I will find someone else who will listen
Rain, snow, hail, I don't care
I will fight and thump and knock down doors until I find someone there

Whether you all like it or not I will prevail
And when you see, you ALL see
I will scream, cry, smile

And then exhale

# DANCE TO THE CONCRETE BLUES
## TATYANA ALEXANDER

Jillian says: *I chose one of my favorite lines from my mentee Tatyana's piece, and flipped it backwards to begin my own poem.*

Little jazz man don't be afraid of the dark.

Whistle until your steps match your heartbeat.
Beat your way from the men whom the streets raped then hold hostage.
Snap your fingers to the flicking of the needles that endanger the stray animals in the concrete jungle.

Jiggle your hips to the echo of the weapon that rips apart a soul from its life.

Little jazz man don't be afraid if you're lost.

Shuffle your feet past the barriers of unsolved sins with no forgiveness.
Forgive the man who's forcing his body upon the promiscuous woman in the alley, his virus can't be contained any longer.

Rock your head mimicking the chills sent up the spines of the homeless.
Don't block out ANYTHING; the world is your blues.

Little jazz man don't be afraid to go home.

Jump into the open fist that your father smashes across your blemishless face.
Face the mirror not to pity yourself, instead
Remember this moment you became a man.

Little jazz man don't be afraid of yourself.

Dive out the world of the concrete blues.
Keep dancing until you grow out of the Jungle.

Bow to your new home.

# BATTLE WITH THE BEAST
## JILLIAN GALLAGHER

Forgiveness, no.
Sins unsolved, barriers past.
They weigh, and push, until the epic break.

Contentment, no.
Wrongs unrighted, chances lost.
They eat, and pry, until only the deadness remains.

Progress, no.
Beauty unnoticed, smiles missed.
They hover, and drift, but never land.

Peacefulness, no.
Pain remembered, pleasure dimmed.
They rise, and flow, then recede to come again.

Slumber, no.
Rest forgotten, lens swelled shut.
They whisper, and lure, but never open their arms.

Reassurance, no.
Hope ignored, faith remiss.
It all surfaces in the battle with the beast.

# HAIR CANCER, AN UNFOUNDED FEAR [EXCERPT] PRISCILLA GUO

Priscilla says: *Everyone has a story associated with hair — whether you try to maintain your mane or get rid of it. We've written two pieces that reflect our trials and tribulations with the dead cells on our head.*

Since I was little, I was afraid I had a variety of ailments ranging from early death by chicken pox to hair cancer. It all started at the vague period of time when you become a person, when you start to have real fears. All that time I was happily moving around on the swing, it was at this point that I started to think: what would happen if I fell? And at that time, there was a series of things going around children more than just the average cold. Here is where you contract cooties, the source of all paranoia and alienation. Cooties is an infectious disease, spread through bodily contact with the opposite sex. It was this disease that caused the 1929 Stock Market Crash. Paranoia is infectious. It catches like wildfire. You never know when it will strike you or how. It never goes away. It is sort of like cancer.

Cancer has always appeared in my mind as a very large, angry, skittering crab poking one to death. For example, if one had lymphatic cancer, I imagined that crab inching around their lymph and continuously saying: "Haha!" And as all sensible people know, this crab had a moustache and a vaguely French/Spanish accent saying: "Haha!"

I blame most of this irrational fear on schooling. In health class, we watched a horrid video on the consequences of smoking. You would think that the video wouldn't get graphic, seeing as we were only 13, but nooo, PBS had to go there. The man in question had smoked since he was 15, and he was talking to us with no throat, no fingertips, no hair, no tongue, and no lips. The large crab had chopped them off with his claws. It terrified the crap out of us. On Wikipedia, if you search cancer, you will get to see what a large invasive ductal carcinoma in a mastectomy specimen looks like. Basically, a giant ham with a large purple brain tumor growing out the side of it like it's waiting to pop out with a "gotcha" phrase.

I don't smoke, but I did start to lose my hair. It wasn't obvious hair loss, to the point of George Costanza from Seinfeld, but there were strands falling out. Little by little. Then I started getting really scared. There was one thing in common with all cancer patients: they had no hair. Absence of hair wasn't a bad thing, but it also wasn't something Bosley's Hair Transplants could fix. The angry crab was not going away.

A few strands here and there and before I knew it, I was going to be the poster child for hair cancer. I never thought hair was such a great thing. Some people have too much (we deem them as furry); some, too little. Some people want straight hair, curly hair, weaves, extensions, colored hair, or not-graying hair. I looked in the mirror, and I wondered what I was going to look like with no hair. Nobody on the Disney Channel is bald. Natalie Portman had pulled it off but hey, she was Natalie Portman.

I decided if I was going to go bald, I would go bald on my own accord!

I mean, it's just sad watching the progression of balding in Prince William's scalp in paparazzi pictures. I didn't want to be a deathly skinny kid with stringent clumps of hair still attached to my shrunken skull.

I decided I needed to shave my head.

# A SERVING OF MAYA AND EGGS ON TOP
## MY-THUAN TRAN

No matter what I did to my hair, the frizz could not be tamed. Half of my hair would crinkle bizarrely into mini-curls that angrily shot out from the outer layer. I brushed and blow-dried aggressively and slathered on multiple hair glosses and gels, but that only did so much.

I was about to begin 8th grade and was determined to unlock the secret to perfect hair. I decided that having great hair was critical to having a great 8th grade year. It would magically help me become popular, make boys like me, and detract from the tangle of braces in my mouth.

At the supermarket as my mom shopped, I would rifle through beauty magazines with headlines that screamed out "Secrets to perfect hair!" and "Bombshell hair in 4 easy steps!" Most of the hair products the beauty magazines recommended were too expensive for my allowance. At 13, I couldn't afford a $100 hair iron and a $40 bottle of hair gloss the size of my thumb.

One day, I came across an article called "Homemade recipes for incredibly smooth, gorgeous hair!" where one girl described a concoction made of egg yolk and mayonnaise. She claimed that the fatty acids in the mayonnaise and egg would serve as a kind of super-hydrating conditioner. I could not wait to try it out. Perhaps the secret to my hair woes was right in my refrigerator!

Right when I got home, I grabbed a bowl and mixed together an egg yolk and a half-cup of mayonnaise with a fork. The end result smelled a lot like salad dressing, but I didn't care. I took it to the bathroom and slathered it onto my hair.

I thought my hair looked pretty good after it dried. There were still a few flyaways, but most of the frizz was tamed. I was ecstatic.

For years, I used this concoction on my hair. Looking back, it is pretty disgusting, but I was convinced it was the secret I was looking for.

I also ended up having a pretty good 8th grade year. I wasn't ever one of the most popular girls, but I had a good group of friends. And there were boys who thought I was cool and cute. The braces came off that year as well.

I can't remember when I stopped using the mayo egg conditioner. Maybe it was when I found other hair techniques that worked. Or maybe it was after I gained a few more years of wisdom and realized that hair and looks were something on the surface—and not worth putting food products in your hair.

# STOP SHACKLING PREGNANT PRISONERS!
## ALEX BERG

*One of this year's GWN writing workshops studied journalism. This piece is an excerpt from a story originally published in* The Daily Beast *in September, 2011.*

From the moment her daughter was born, Kellie Phelan, 37, felt like an embarrassment. It wasn't that she'd hid her pregnancy from her family, or even that she spent part of it behind bars at Rikers Island. Rather, Phelan was mortified by the metal cuff that bound her leg to her bed during labor at New York's Elmhurst Hospital—the same cuff that shackled her swollen ankles together during the ambulance ride over.

Phelan's experience is not unique. In 36 states, it is legal to shackle pregnant inmates during labor and not uncommon to cuff a woman's limbs to a hospital bed until delivery. Due to health risks to both mother and child, however, a growing number of states are banning the practice with anti-shackling bills.

This year alone, 16 states introduced bills that would restrict the use of restraints on pregnant prisoners at varying points perinatally. Of those states, Hawaii, Idaho, Rhode Island, and Nevada passed bills to join the ranks of 10 others that, at the very least, ban shackling during labor (a ban already exists in federal prisons). And, most recently, a woman in Tennessee was awarded $200,000 after she sued the state for being shackled when she went into labor shortly after she was arrested for driving without a license.

According to Malika Saada Saar, founder and executive director of the Rebecca Project for Human Rights, little data exists on babies born to incarcerated mothers—yet the Women's Prison Association reported that 4 percent of women in state prisons and 3 percent of women in federal prisons were pregnant when they were jailed in 2004. Since 1980, the number of incarcerated women in the U.S. has increased eightfold, from 12,300 to more than 180,000, according to the ACLU.

Phelan counts herself among the women locked up as a result of America's war on drugs, which is largely responsible for the spike in female prisoners. "When I was seven months pregnant, every day [it was] crack cocaine. I was smoking crack. From the second she was conceived, I put her through hell," Phelan said of her daughter, Savannah Grace, who is now 4 years old.

Shackling refers to the use of restraints anywhere on a pregnant prisoner's body, from binding her hands and feet to chaining her abdomen. Pregnant prisoners' arms and legs are usually shackled with metal handcuffs during transportation, then cuffed directly to their hospital bed by an arm and a leg in the delivery room. The American Congress of Obstetricians and Gynecologists, the American Medical Association, and the United Nations have condemned the practice, citing the serious health risks posed to mother and infant.

When Rachel Sutton, 28, was transported from Ohio to New York while six months pregnant in 2009, both her hands and feet were cuffed for the duration of the five-and-a-half-hour trip. During a stop at a gas station, one hand was uncuffed while Sutton used the bathroom. "I could barely walk," Sutton, who was incarcerated for criminal sales of a controlled substance, told *The Daily Beast*. "They had to keep stopping because I was out of breath, first of all, because I was huge and I couldn't even really walk in shackles because they were so small."

# THE NO-LIVES
## DEMETRIA IRWIN

Not low-lives
No-lives

The fiery glow of brown brilliance
Suffocated under morgue make-up
Confined in silk and wood and tears
Their possibilities, though countless and limitless
Evaporated in the squeal of the coffin hinges closing
For the last time

Felled by bullets and fists from
Neighbors
Cops
Classmates and a
Delusional racist with a superman complex
(Might have been more than one of those)

Murderers who killed because
The no-lives looked nothing like them
And it scared them

Murderers who killed because
The no-lives looked just like them
And it scared them

Derrion Albert had no senior prom
Ayanna Jordan had no teenage crushes
Delric Miller IV had no first steps
Trayvon Martin had no high school graduation
Ramarley Graham had no 21st birthday

Give me a city and I'll give you a name
Of a no-life in your area

A dream deferred?
A dream not dreamt
Not enough life yet to imagine a better one
A real life
A long life
A life that matters

This dark skin is
A threat to some people
Imposing

Scary
Intimidating
That's a powerful thing

Imagine all of those no-lives as powerful lives
Joyful, dynamic lives

The next time you see someone
Blessed with this powerful, dark skin
Don't shoot or punch or run or clutch your purse

Smile at the beauty
Affirm the humanity
And most of all
Breathe
And let that person do the same

# A TASTE
## SARAI ARROYO

### PROLOGUE: A LITTLE TASTE

Why did I jump into the ocean for two fallen red coins? I don't think my conscience would ever give me the answer.

But the experience was so, *exhilarating*. Yet terrifying to the point that I resisted the powerful urge to swim back to the surface after swimming about six feet down. Why had I jumped into a bottomless pit of water without as much as an oxygen tank? Perhaps common sense eluded me at the time. However, my unyielding stubbornness refused to let Tia Helena convince everyone I was irresponsible. I wasn't incapable of guarding former Captain Rosario's (stolen) red coins blocked—I dove into the cold mass of blue to retrieve them. That counts for something.

I had been doing a damn good job at guarding them—really, I had only been sitting in my room reading *Treasure Island* and sneaking a glance every two minutes at the coins which lay on a small velvet cushion. Why did Tia Helena not use what was left of her common sense to lock them away? The answer eludes me too. I didn't even sprint to the dining room and back for a much-needed cheeseburger, fearing that my diabolical second cousins Carmen and Paco would construct a foolproof plan to frame me for their crimes on *Tito81* and blacken my name more than it already was. No matter how many times I calmly picked apart how manipulative and pathetic they were, I only seemed to encourage the relentless pair's attempts to have everyone onboard hate me.

They were so lucky I was not allowed to bring my taser onboard without a license.

But now as I think of it, I would've preferred my cousins any day than the guy who broke into my room, unannounced and armed. Jim had just made a deal with the strange Tarzan man* when suddenly the door of my room met the wooden floor with a bang loud enough to send my heart into a series of panic dances. This was followed by the yells of my aggravated neighbors. Next the blurred silhouette of a man sprinting inside the room and overturning the velvet pillow on the dresser; then his flight out the room where the door once stood.

It took the wail of an infant in the next room to snap me back into reality and start running after him.

My frayed mind struggled to remember the man who had taken the coins and thrown them overboard. However the salt water all around me invaded my ears and eyes, preventing any bit of comprehensive thought towards my current situation. My heart beat at a fast rate; every inch of skin had turned into gooseflesh and tingled with adrenaline with every yard I swam down. The coins were thankfully dropping at a slow rate by now, but I did lose sight of them every few feet or so due to my unprotected eyes, but I managed to remember to chase the small blurry red circles.

That's when I began to feel it, the fire slowly, but painfully, growing in my lungs. I never thought I could hold my breath for so long—I wasn't even sure how far down I swam, but the area around me began to dim so I'd say pretty far. Where were those coins?

Ah-ha! My damaged radar didn't fail me yet. Only about five feet away from my reach were the coins, still moving at a glacial pace. All I had to do was conjure up some adrenaline and—

Something circular and white caught the corner of my eye, but when I snapped my head in its direction, not pausing in my swimming, all I saw was the continuous mass of dark blue. A foreboding sensation began to attack my heart, almost into near-cardiac arrest as I reached for the coins and held them securely in my stiff hand.

Almost immediately a giant white fish appeared before my eyes and my heart practically escaped from my mouth to somewhere safe.

———

She hadn't looked menacing; at least she wasn't a man. Men were *monsters.*

It was the most astounding human it had ever laid eyes upon however. Brown hair billowed all about along with her dark clothing, green eyes so big and terrified they looked ready to pop out and fall to the bottom of the ocean.

The girl's eyes had glazed over.

*But what have they done for me to deserve this fresh meat?*

He knew his jaws would ache for hours afterwards; nevertheless the white fish swallowed her whole and swam to the surface where it spat her out.

———

*To be continued...*

---

*Jim, protagonist of *Treasure Island*, while on an island with his crew encounters a man claiming to have been one of Captain Fitzgerald's crewmates and promises Jim riches if he gets him off the island.

Heather says: *This piece of found poetry is inspired by a mystery that Andreina and I have been working on since the crime/mystery writing workshop, which is excerpted above.*

The perfect moment had come. My father was in my baby sister's room reading her a bedtime story. I snuck across the hallway to my father's bedroom and started searching for my PS3 game. He took it from me yesterday because my annoying teacher called saying that I was being rude to her. All I actually did was state my opinion in class and apparently she took it the wrong way.

When mom was alive, she never took any games away from me. She used to sit down and talk to me. But all that changed when she died. Two years ago she gave birth to my sister Melissa. A few days later, my mother was injected with an overdose of medication by a nurse named Rachel. But my father and I never saw that nurse and the police didn't find any employment records on Rachel. There was no evidence left behind. I miss my mother. I lost her when I was 11. The police never found who killed my mother.

———

I started searching for the game by his desk, in the draws, everywhere. I needed that game. I was determined to beat Michael's high score. The phone rang, and I knew my father was coming to pick it up. I heard his footsteps approaching, and I ran into closet and left the door cracked.

My father came in the room and picked up the phone.

"Hello."

"Yes, this is Richard. With whom am I speaking with?" His voice began to tremble.

"Alma? It's you! What do you want?!" There was a long pause.

"You...you were the nurse who killed Jessica? You knew I loved her! Is that why you did it? You evil witch! The police will arrest you and you'll spend your life in prison!" My father was furious.

"Why should I be afraid? You won't harm us anymore, justice will be served. And don't you dare come near us." He hung up.

Alma? Was she the nurse who murdered my mom? Why was she calling? Tears started running down my face. My father picked up my mother's photo from his nightstand and said, "Jessica, don't worry, justice will be served." After that I noticed him wiping tears off his face. He got up and went back to Melissa's room. As soon as he left, I came out of the closet and snuck to my room down the hall.

I felt overwhelmed; I didn't know how to react. I got into my bed before my father came in to wish me goodnight and turn off the light. I stared at the ceiling thinking about the memories I had with my mom as I fell asleep.

———

The next day my father woke me up to drive me to school. Since we lived in the suburbs, it took us about 30 minutes to get to school. We were almost there when I saw him become worried. I had never seen his face like that. He kept staring at the rearview mirror. I turned around to turn look to Melissa; she was giggling, talking to her teddy bear. All of a sudden a car bumped us from behind and my father lost control.

———

I opened my eyes and I saw my father sitting lifeless in the driver's seat. His was blood everywhere. I couldn't move my right leg, my arms were all scratched up and I had a huge headache. Everything was blurry. I turned to look for my sister and I saw a woman with short brown hair. I thought she was going to help us but instead, she took Melissa and I heard her say, "This is what you get Richard for not wanting me in your life." She left so fast. I tried to stop her, but I couldn't. My legs didn't allow me to. I started screaming until I lost consciousness.

# A REMIX OF BEYOND WHAT I KNOW
## HEATHER M. GRAHAM

Yesterday
was alive,
But all that changed
Melissa
injected
an overdose
But
I never saw that
and the police didn't find any
evidence left behind.
I miss her.
I was killed.

———

I started searching
I needed that
The phone rang and I picked up.
"Hello."

"Yes?" His voice began to tremble.

"Alma?" There was a long pause.
"Spend your furious, don't you dare come"

He hung up.
Tears started running down my face.
mother's photo said, "Don't worry"

I noticed Melissa's room and snuck down the hall.

I felt overwhelmed;
I stared at the ceiling thinking about memories as I fell asleep.

―――

We lived in the suburbs, it took us about 30 minutes to get school. We were almost there.

I had never seen the rearview mirror. I turned around to turn Melissa. She was giggling; a car bumped us, and my father lost control.

―――

I opened my eyes, my arms were scratched up. I had a huge headache. Everything was blurry. I turned to look for Melissa and I heard her say, "Stop" but I couldn't. I started screaming until I lost consciousness.

# UNTITLED
## IRIS TORRES

Iris says: *At first, I felt a little odd with someone "remixing" my work. I had never done anything like it before, and I was skeptical as to how it worked. After my mentor Heather and I swapped our pieces to be remixed, I found that it was really fun and enjoyable! I enjoyed the fact that I could take her words and make something else, something completely my own with what she had written. I had done some erasing on her work, blacking it out and finding a way to string the sentences together without adding anything new to it. It was also interesting to see how she took my words and interpreted them in her own way. Now I enjoy remixing others' works because it's a chance for you to take something original and make it into something totally different.*

My friend Ashleigh and I were both 17, wild, unstoppable. Ash was a good girl, a talented honor student who played violin, flute, and trumpet. Her life came tumbling down the day Seth died.

I sat at home in my room, listening to "Haru Haru" a song by my favorite Korean band. Ashleigh came in, her face no longer radiated with her uncanny happiness.

"Ash?" I paused the music and removed my headphones as I waited for her response. She looked at me with a blank stare. I walked over to her and like the last leaves of autumn she zoomed down the stairway and out the door. No point in catching up to a track star.

Three hours later I got a call from Ashleigh's mom saying that Seth was found dead this afternoon and she hadn't seen Ashleigh since. I told her I hadn't seen her either, even though she had come by hours earlier. I knew where she was. I knew where to find her. I slipped on my coat, grabbed my headphones and slipped out my window to avoid any confrontation with my sister.

I found Ashleigh sitting under Old Bridge vandalized with graffiti. Her knees pulled up to her chest, her eyes staring idly into the polluted bank in front of her. I said nothing to her as I sat beside her and slipped my arm around her. She cried for hours.

Six weeks after Seth died we tagged his name into the same bridge she sat under.

We never spoke of Seth again.

She smoked to numb the pain. I began smoking at around the same time she did so I could escape my hellish life. Ash knew what she as running from. As for me, I didn't know what or who I was running from. All I knew was I was supposed to run from something. Some people think getting high is stupid, but they don't understand the feeling. When I'm high, my fights are less annoying. One time I got so high, I was shouting words that sounded like Yiddish.

When I'm stoned, I can see the beauty in her large green eyes and her straight blond hair half up in a bun and half down. She thrusts her body onto her bed and the coils in the springs moan. Ash takes in a deep breath and breathes heavily. Her shaky hands reach for the joint resting in my hands.

I see a unicorn sit on top of Ashleigh's shoulders, then it jumps off and it gallops out the window and into the cold. I burst out in hysteria and so does Ashleigh. My mind is playing tricks on me, I'm 10,000% sure. I'm falling to darkness. My arms and legs are flailing around, but I refuse to scream. I continue to fall down miles of pure darkness. Next thing I know, I'm swimming in a black gulf. No offense to those poor ducks who died that day of the BP spill, but I know how you feel, or felt rather: helpless.

I never felt so confused, so lost. Even when stoned I could tell every little detail about myself. But now I didn't even feel like I was in the right body, let alone the right state of mind.

Jennifer says: *My poem, "even smaller," is an erasure poem made from erasing words from Yesenia's poem "August."*

White walls kiss each corner of the dull room.
The only sound I hear besides my breathing is the humming of the computer screen
to my right.
Shining metal objects invade my peripheral vision as I try to count to ten
hoping this day will come to a quicker end,
but I know directly overhead the clock ticks to eight thirty AM.
His balding head rises from between my legs
and his mouth moves,
giving birth to words I wish my ears
never knew how to listen to.
"You are actually farther along than you
seem to believe. You are fifteen weeks."
The weight of his words contradicts his nonchalant attitude
causing my thoughts to collide with each other.
I follow his hand gestures as the rest of his words fall mute.
I walk back to the dressing room as he points to my clothes
and closes the door behind him.
His blue scrubs walk on to another girl with the same fate.
I inhale and exhale quickly with each breath more intense
as the situation begins to settle in.
I hear a loud scream and slowly realize
it's my voice rising in the hospitalized air.
A nurse comes in holding my arms trying to calm me down.
But just as my heart pounds in my chest,
I know there's an even smaller one pounding
methodically along with mine
"What am I supposed to do with another life growing inside of me?"

# EVEN SMALLER
## JENNIFER TENCH

kiss each corner
hear my breathing
metal vision
a quicker end
the clock ticks

my legs
and his mouth
words I never knew

collide with each other
his hand points and closes
on to another girl

with each breath
I slowly realize
my voice rising
my arms trying

as my heart pounds
even smaller

# THE BRIDGE
## MONICA CHIN + ELAINE STUART-SHAH

Monica and Elaine say: *For our piece we experimented with different points of view. We decided on one setting in which two lives were intertwined: a car accident on a winter night on the Verrazano Bridge. Monica wrote from the perspective of a twelve-year-old in a car of teenagers, and I wrote from the perspective of a single mother driving her two kids.*

### MONICA CHIN
When I open my eyes, the side of my head feels warm and a bit wet despite the blistering cold wind pelting me. I don't remember opening the window. It's not open. The glass is ragged like those Appalachian Mountains I saw in Mrs. Pinkerton's history class.

My head hurts like crazy! Did I drink too much eggnog or has Paul's reckless driving really got us into trouble this time?

My ears ring, just one of the effects of a hangover? I see Michelle waking up next to me; there is blood dripping from her nose. I see Paul screaming as he pulls at his leg beneath the steering wheel. But I hear nothing, only feel the vibrations in my eardrums... That blasting ringing in my ear will not stop!

Dancing red and blue colors reflect against the rearview mirrors of mom's car. I don't understand, what happened? Did Paul total the car again? Sound is coming back now. I can hear the distant cries and groans coming from Michelle. Paul grunts as he tries to pull his foot free now. I see his bloody skin scraped off his knee. I feel like I'm going to throw up.

The stench reeks and firemen now are speaking to us, holding a saw like a weapon not a rescue tool. They ask us if we are all right. Of course we're not all right, how could we be?

My eyes close and I fall into a deep pit. The sounds of the police sirens and the saw start fading away. It is nice, cool and peaceful now. But then I feel something. It burns, fire licking the back of my scalp. I start to hear noises, a clamor of noises now. My heart pounds so hard, pounds like an Indian drum with animal skin pulled too tight. It aches as if it is awakening from a winter slumber. My eyes jerk open. My chest inflates like a balloon too full of air, but I don't mind; I'm breathing.

A brilliant white light shines into my eyes, but it is only the paramedic. As it dims, I see a little pale face through the window of the car next to me.

———

Elaine Stuart-Shah
One minute I feel the steering wheel firm in my hands and the next I'm floating, suspended like the sheet of concrete beneath us, slicing through the sky.

Jaime's voice brings me back.

"Mom?" he whimpers, but it sounds tinny and distant as if he's speaking over a bad phone connection rather than the back seat. I open my eyes, and one by one objects come into focus, like those paint-by-numbers art projects he's always doing: my white knuckles, the steering wheel, the dashboard, the windshield—wipers smearing heavy snowflakes—and beyond, the soaring spires of the bridge. I read something once about its construction, about the fearless men who strung those cables, and the families who were displaced when its towers were planted in their front yard.

"Mom!" It hits me that the strange quality in Jaime's voice is panic.

"Yes, honey." I swallow hard as I realize I can't move my head. "It's alright. I'm here. Everything's ok." I try to relax my talon-like grip on the steering wheel, but it's like my brain can't communicate with my body. As if the circuitry is stunned.

I train my eyes on the rearview mirror and the sight of the tops of two car seats steadies me. I think back to the frustration of installing them and the daily, tear-filled struggle to get Jaime and Sammy to sit in them, and I'm so overcome with gratitude for such a trivial annoyance that it takes a second for the next thought to register:

Why isn't the baby crying?

# #TRANSFORMINGINTO

When I was about 10 years old, I began to get impatient with change: I wanted it to stop. While my friends were eager to grow up, I fantasized about stasis. I was waiting for life to arrive at some sort of standstill, settle into a lull, so that I might pause and take stock of what was going on—my evershifting surroundings, my evolving self, transforming too quickly for me to comprehend.

Of course, as I would come to learn, we can't conveniently put a halt to change. But through writing, we can make some sense of its endless unfurling, as the pieces in this chapter attest. Putting words on the page, we can reclaim moments that seem to have slipped from our grasp, grapple with the grey area of moving from something we know into something we don't. We can look backwards, pinpoint those pivotal shifts (maybe we couldn't see them at the time) from who we were into who we are. We can jump ahead, envisioning what's to come. When we tire of ourselves, we can reshape our realities by imagining new worlds or stepping momentarily into the lives of others.

As uncomfortable as change can be, it can also be freeing. Vanessa Grigoriadis, who spoke at Girls Write Now's Journalism Profiles Workshop in March, recalls a liberating turn in her path as a writer:

> "My biggest moment of transformation was when I stopped trying to impress others with vocabulary or abstract ideas, and started tuning into what pleased my own ear. If you can't amuse yourself on the page, you can't expect to entertain anyone else. This happened when I was about 25 years old and made drastic changes in my writing. A few years later, I began to try to push myself by writing extremely fast. I found that the faster I wrote, the more I loosened up, and the better the stories became."

Speeding up, slowing down, we transform into and out of and into again, never quite there, always arriving.

— SIOBHAN BURKE
2012 MENTOR AND
ANTHOLOGY COMMITTEE MEMBER

# ABUELO'S PORCH
## MARCELA GRILLO

*Coqui, coqui.* Close my eyes and listen closely. I can hear. The singsong voice of the Coqui frog. Lulls me to sleep. In the morning, I sip *café con leche*. The black and white tiles of Abuelo's porch are warm under my feet. Tall coconut trees stretch into the sky over the horizon. The air smells of fresh leaves and of animals who run. Of breadfruit and mangoes and *platanos*. Abuelo's calloused hands reach up and he plucks a coconut down from the tree. Sticks a straw inside, and without a word, hands it to me. I know to take the coconut and sip directly from it. The sweet taste floods over my tongue.

Even when there is no more juice left to sip, I can still feel the tang of the coconut on the bottom of my teeth. Abuelo and I sit next to each other, my legs swinging, and every so often a film of dust sprinkles onto the bottom of my toes.

I see cars drive by. The passengers wave their hands out the car windows, yelling *hello* or an exaggerated shout of sorts that I cannot understand.

"Abuelo," I ask, turning my head to the right. I admire everything from his white cotton sleeve shirt to the way he crosses his knees. I try to mimic him but fail. "Who are all those people driving by?"

Abuelo's thin lips curve into something like a smile as he wipes a bit of coconut juice from his upper lips. "Sometimes I wish I didn't know them," he says. "But they are my friends."

I simply nod and wonder how Abuelo has so many friends when the tinted glass hides their faces.

We pass the rest of the evening watching the sun descend into the mountain's embrace. I sit on Abuelo's porch, and I know I cannot be touched.

When night falls and the roads turn into unknown paths, I pad into my room and run under the scratchy blanket. The thunder claps like an angry command, once, twice, three times.

As if he knows, Abuelo comes into the room and sits beside me. He smiles down gently and whispers that I shouldn't be scared. His hands pat my forehead before he leaves again, closing the door behind him with a soft thump, although it seems louder with all the lights out.

That's when I think I hear the front door slam. *Who is there?* I try to look for the time and then remember I don't have my own watch. I love Abuelo's watch though. I hope he'll let me have it one day. My toes tingle underneath the blankets, and before thinking twice I escape, my toes twitching against the now-cold floor.

The door handle is grey and dented, but my hand fits around it perfectly. I open the door only slightly and hope not to get caught. I see the outline of Abuelo's thin, gray hair as he stands firmly on two feet. He is blocking another man's path. I try to get a better look and stand on my tippy toes. The strange man wears a red bandana and a shirt with sleeves that are cut. His eyes are a beady dark brown. He only has two fingers. It is Samuel— Abuelo used to always invite him over for drinks.

"*Go,*" I hear him tell the man. I can see the glint of a machete hiding behind Abuelo's back. It is the same machete he always tells me to leave hidden underneath his cracked flowerpot. The one that sits on Abuelo's porch, waiting.

# SILENT WATCHERS
## SHYANNE MELENDEZ

Sara says: *These poems were written by taking a line from another work and repeating it as a recurring line in our own pieces. The lines were borrowed from two contemporary books of poems by young women poets, both published this year. Shyanne used a piece from Heather Christle's "What is Amazing" and I used a line from Stacy Gnall's "Self-Portrait As Thousand Furs." The poems were written during a pair meeting, and then we each brought them home and worked on revisions on our own.*

I inhale deeply, to hide the fact that death lingers, wrapping around me like a dress I never purchased. Oh all the sorrows I've whispered to leaves.

When I walk through the yard holding my breath, I am careful to not awaken the watchers. Oh all the sorrows I've whispered to leaves.

Sometimes I close my eyes and imagine life without you: Miserable. Dry. Burdensome. Who do I tell these thoughts to? Oh all the sorrows I've whispered to leaves.

Sometimes I lay down in the leaves, cross my arms on my chest and envision the cause of a demise all my own. A death that I own, one I cannot escape from. Though I wouldn't share it, in fear that my demise would scare those around. So a quiet fantasy, a myth created solely in my mind, remains there until it becomes reality. Oh all the sorrows I've whispered to leaves.

Fallen leaves are worth speaking to. There's no chance of them suddenly hearing me. Whispering to a tree allows reply.

A reply I'd rather not find. The heavens can keep their shrugs of disbelief as I allow life to pass by. Their sighs of disappointment. No I'd rather a reply of no existence.

*Oh all the Sorrows I've whispered to leaves.*


# SELF-PORTRAIT AS ELEPHANT
## SARA FEMENELLA

To have slipped into that primitive skin
To mourn, to harbor, to heave decades
Against a tusked genus, to thick tongue the harsh
The drought, the dust and suffrage
To hieroglyph and the mystery of it, to other language

To have slipped into that primitive skin, heart
Quickening at the thirst, to memory in the bones
The deep, deep, to stagger up in morning splendor
I elephant this sad world and what dies
Out there in the thieving thousands

To have slipped into that primitive skin, to be
Beautiful in my own destruction, my beauty is destructive
A cold heart after all, I elephant, having or pertaining
To melancholy, ie: nostalgia

To depend everything on the dream
Of elephant, on the thick skinned
On the heavy gait and the confidence in moving
See me elephant ink by ink across a white page
See how sorry I am not

# THE BIRTHDAY THAT NEVER HAPPENED
## WENDY LEE

The orange-and-pomegranate salad was dressed. The chickpea stew was simmering on the stove and the Ethiopian pancakes to go with them were warming in the oven. The chocolate cake, although it was cracked in the middle, lay frosted and ready on the counter for the birthday candles. But the birthday girl had not arrived yet.

Z., T., and I were waiting in the living room of my apartment for A., the fourth person in our writing group. We had met through an ad on Craigslist a few months earlier and had become friends, sharing evenings of talking and movies as well as our writing. When A. revealed that her birthday was coming up soon, I volunteered to throw a dinner party in her honor. I wasn't doing it completely out of the goodness of my heart. I wanted to prove to myself that, at 25, I was finally an adult, meaning that I was capable of having people over for a dinner of good food and conversation.

Since A. was a vegan, I bought a cookbook called *The Voluptuous Vegan,* as well as wine glasses, which to me were the ultimate sign of sophistication. I'd scattered scented candles around my apartment, which was the kind I'd imagined living in when I moved to New York City—a brownstone with hardwood floors and bookcases that reached to the ceilings—except for the fact that I had a 60-year-old roommate.

It was 9:00 and A. still hadn't shown up. The food was growing cold, so Z., T., and I reluctantly ate it. The salad was full of intense citrus flavors, the chocolate cake gooey and rich. But, of course, without the guest of honor it didn't feel like a celebration. Later, we discovered that A. had been sitting and crying in the lobby of my building the whole time, calling our different cell phones, which we'd left in my bedroom, because the buzzer was broken. A. was so upset that she left the writing group. T. also departed within the month, probably bored from being the only boy. I never used that vegan cookbook or the wine glasses again. But, ten years later, even though we don't talk much about our writing anymore, Z. is my closest friend in New York City. And I've come to realize that being an adult doesn't mean having the right glassware or being able to throw a dinner party, but making and keeping good friends.

# THE DREAM OF ALL THE RIGHT WORDS
## KAYTLIN CARLO

Kaytlin says: *My piece is a remix poem of my mentor's work, "The Dream of the Eruption During Which I am Visited by Your Ghost and You Save Me." It was based off of an exercise in the Found Poetry Workshop.*

Your soft whispers trickle against my eardrum, and I can hear you loud and clear now. Whispers holding the words of everything I could not say but the strip around my mouth isn't there and it still stings when I try to form my mouth into the most perfect shape. I try to soothe this angry mountain, and while I stand there pointing a finger towards the sky blaming it for my dilemmas, I still have four more fingers pointing back at me. I can still remember the soft kisses that made me feel like a child, that made my heart melt and fall into my ribcages like jungle bars at a playground. The relations that made me forget what pain was and whom anger was related to. My body begins to tremble as I hear all the right words in all the wrong places, blowing life into that little cup where a pool of roe lays. I manage one final gasp of air before I awake, and you're gone.

# THE DREAM OF THE ERUPTION DURING WHICH I AM VISITED BY YOUR GHOST AND YOU SAVE ME COLLEEN BARRY

some drone in my sadness spirit has brought me to the bottom of the mountain, some new blue sin, some conifers rubbing rough and quiet needles together, some revelation as i find you rowing a white boat in the mountain lake in rags all silver and milky, all frustrated with being brave like some dog i promised i would sit in place of, your back hunched so gorgeously, a sliver of wing of muscle, like the tender aching stretches of my lungs, they are numbered, i can count them, everything has to do with so many things i want to whisper in your ear before i die, for example

the word cumulonimbus, which is a beautiful rain-bearing heap and about the snakes i caught when i was six and how before i go on long runs i bend at the waist so that i snap in half, so that i make of my body the most imperfect crescent moon, but i can't even get close to you as the mountain begins to spout angry, the reflection of it in the lake like a great witness to love, constantly moving but always in the same place, it is there and it is not there, and it reminds me of that tiny cup where my thighs dip to meet my hips, i can imagine when i think of it that the only substance it could hold is a pool of someone's breath and then the mountain got angrier faster louder a fever pitch so i pounded my chest i shouted go ahead breathe a fire into me go ahead burn me a painting burn me a poem burn me back into love and you turned,

ash you said and you covered me with the red-striped blanket you said our lives got buried under filled the sky you said this great and terrible bellowing is rare and terrifying coming only once every 100 years and the mountain is sick you said and you rowed to the shore you kissed my hip you burned the boat you burned the trees you burned away you never came back.

##  WILD ROOM
## GINA DIFRISCO

I wonder about the mystery of my room, as I lie flat on the floor. I always end up face flat on the ground after tripping over bags and books, clothes and cords. Banging into storage cubes and my computer chair. My room is packed with stuff and everything is drenched in the scent of orange perfume. At times, it feels as though my many stuffed animals are coming to life when I'm not around, touching and moving my things so they are all in my way. My stuffed animals are everywhere. They're spontaneously generating stuffed animals. I thought scientists proved inanimate objects could not reproduce. Yet, somehow, these stuffed animals have disproved this natural law.

Every day I have to clear a space on my bed for me to sleep. Still, these crazy stuffed toys seem to love taking over both my bed and the second bed that's here for anyone who stays the night, where my mom leaves clothes that need to be put away after being washed. Somehow both are always covered with stuffed animals that never seem to stay still. Things go missing when the animals move. The animals move again and the things that went missing are found and new things disappear. Whenever I reach for the second bed, I must brace myself—to maybe find something lost or to lose something found.

I leave for a moment to go get some water. WAIT!! Now the walls are painted? I was only gone for a minute! How did the walls get painted so fast, and when no one was at home? Well, not all the walls are painted, but still—how the hell did it happen? Was it the stuffed animals again? Red and blue are now splashed across parts of the original off-white walls. From the corner of my eye, I swear I see one of my Hello Kitty dolls creep out of sight. My things appear and disappear and now I find the walls changing colors? I must be crazy. If I told this to anyone, who would believe me, really? The problems never end. Neither does the disorder. Just last week I found a corner of my room that had somehow been filled with yarn in every color. Pink, black, yellow, orange, brown, just to name a few. It all seemed to have materialized from thin air.

I am continuously trying to find a way out of this weird situation. Cleaning up, organizing things, packing up the stuffed animals so they don't appear randomly. Much to my horror it doesn't help, and I must face a rainbow colored labyrinth of never vanishing inanimate creatures. Where on earth do they come from? How can I get rid of them, is perhaps the better question. Still, I am never one to give up. Or at least I'm never the first to give up.

Thinking that it's time to call it quits because all is lost, I come across a fancy teddy bear I didn't realize I even had. It is a simple brown bear in a simple holiday sweater—the only sanity that seems to be in this place.

To my surprise, this bear has somehow escaped the toxic smell of cheap orange perfume. The mess of its fellow stuffed animals. The clothes sitting in a disastrous pile, adding to all the other disorders. He got away and now is free. Good that one of us made it.

# BLINDED EYES
## TEMA REGIST

Lynn says: *I decided to remix Tema's poem, so I made an erasure using Blinded Eyes as the source text.*

The wheels that twist and turn
as they crash into sewer-filled water,
the blue sky smothered by gray-filled clouds,
a drowsy feeling surrounding me.

Suddenly, jealousy and anger strike,
my ex-boyfriend and his new girlfriend
in sight,
tension builds as I pass by them

until I reach the end of the hall.
Calmness settles in as I get myself together.
The water seeps into my shoes as I exit school.
Cold air hits my body.

A huge splash of water
plants itself on me
as busses and cars pass by.
Tears saturate my eyeballs until

they are forced to roll down my cheeks.
Could this day get any worse?

But then, jubilant sounds begin to punctuate my ears,
the sweet melodies of birds chirping.

A shiny object blinds me, the sun rises
from between the dark gray clouds
and my tears are gone.
Suddenly, my cheeks turn a rosy red color.

I begin smiling from ear to ear.
Suddenly, the flowers around me
start to look extra beautiful,
the sentimental words uttered leave me

gloating,
relieved,
happy,
joyful.

Thoughts run through my head,
and my hands no longer seem heavy.
What did he say?
He said, "It's over." I smile.

A new beginning.

## WHILE THINKING ABOUT THE WAR ON WOMEN, I WRITE THIS POEM LYNN MELNICK

Wheels twist,
they crash the clouds,
surrounding anger.

My water, my air, my body.

My eyeballs forced to roll down this day.
Worse? Then, jubilant: begin to punctuate my ears.

The sweet shiny between,
the dark gone suddenly rosy,
suddenly gloating.

My head, my hands, no longer
over.

# OUTSIDE LOOKING IN
## EMILY SARITA

ACT I, SCENE 3

INT. NEWSPAPER HEADQUARTERS-1955- DAY

*ANNELISE walks into a large office space. Several desks separated by pillars and thin partitions are lined-up in neat rows. The walls are covered with framed newspaper articles and awards. A woman in her late twenties, ANNELISE, confidently swings her briefcase with every step she takes. Her long brown, wavy hairy is pulled into a soft bun, and her lips are red. She wears a pressed slim-fit navy blue dress that accentuates her tall frame, and her tan high heels are slightly worn out, but well cared for. Papers are being shuffled and men quickly compose themselves as she walks down the aisle.*

*Men run to their desks and one spills coffee, while the others stand there stiffly.*

ANNELISE: (walks over to MAN #1) I suggest you clean that up.

MAN #1: Well, aren't you going to clean that up for me?

MAN #2: (*laughing*) She works in an office now; she probably expects us to clean it up.

*The rest of the men in the room chuckle.*

ANNELISE: I don't suppose you talk to your mother with that insulting mouth of yours.

MAN #1: I don't suppose my mother works in an office when she clearly belongs at home, now does she?

ANNELISE: If she did, she probably would have done a better job than you.
(*walks away*)

*MAN #1 stands there, shocked*

ANNELISE walks down the hallway, dark hair swinging back and forth. She comes across a wooden door with a plaque that reads SAMUEL NORTHINGTON, editor-in-chief. She knocks lightly and enters the room. A tall, pale older man with salt and pepper hair holds a phone in one hand and tries to hold a pen in the other. He has bags under his pale blue eyes. He coughs constantly due to his illness, and his eyes light up as he sees her.

SAMUEL: Annelise, there you are! Good morning!

ANNELISE: Good morning, sir. (*grabs the pen and the note pad and waits intently for instructions.*)

SAMUEL: There are many things that we need to cover today. For starters, I want to you to write the next feature story article. I know your capabilities as a writer, and you are ready. You have given me my best story ideas, and if we are totally honest with each other—you've practically written them for me since I've been sick.

ANNELISE: (*shocked*) Me?

SAMUEL: Yes, you. I don't suppose you know another woman named Annelise? (*smiles*) For starters, the deadline is this Friday, and there are no men capable of writing a decent article. I will be gone first thing tomorrow morning for another doctor's appointment and who knows when I will be back.

ANNELISE: Sir, I am flattered, but if I published a piece under my own name, it will be a problem for this company.

SAMUEL: Don't worry, darling. You will figure something out. (*looks at the time*) Well, I have to go, Annelise. Duties call. (*about to leave, but turns around*) Oh, I almost forgot! Make sure that no one knows that you're in charge. It would make these hooligans mistreat you even more.

ANNELISE: Bu-

SAMUEL: Good luck! (*Walks out*)

*ANNELISE is left alone in the room and is obviously flustered. She goes back to her desk and fidgets with her coffee cup, excited and nervous. She glances around the room, nervously, making sure that no one is looking at her and slowly brings out her typewriter. Her fingers graze the keys, and she finally places all her fingers on the typewriter and begins to type slowly and carefully, but after a couple of paragraphs, she began to feel comfortable and her typing quickens.*

*Hours pass by as she continues to type. People leave the office one by one. The sun rises as she finishes her last word and gathers her article.*

*ANNELISE places the article on Samuel's desk. As the light fades, the name of the article can be seen.*

ANNELISE: "Women Creators of Men: Women Should Have Higher Positions in Jobs Instead of the Opposite Sex," by ANNELISE MCGUIRE.

# NEWSPAPER GIRL
## JANA BRANSON

ACT I, SCENE I

INT. Newspaper Headquarters-Present- Night

*Lights come up on a small, cubicle-filled office floor. Half of the fluorescent lights are off, and the other half burn brightly without flickering. The cubicles look dated, but not antique. They are low-walled, half sized, with space for eyes to see above them, but not to see workspaces below.*

*Three characters are visible: ANNELISE, MAN #1, and MAN #2. ANNELISE is beautiful, from her wavy, dark-brown hair, to her well-tanned and muscular legs, visible and crossed to one side of her office chair. She holds her temples in her hands, leaning purposefully forward towards the flat screen she reads from. Although the majority of the lights are off, and it's clearly late at night, a cup of coffee steams next to ANNELISE's mousepad.*

*MAN #1 is reclined casually in his office chair, which sits too low to the ground for a person his height. He grips a "stress-ball" and looks idly at the ceiling, occasionally tossing the ball into the air, aiming as straight as he can. His computer screen is blank, and he periodically looks expectantly at his cell phone, sitting on the desk. A half-eaten tray of chicken pad thai sits near his phone, with chopsticks hanging off the rim.*

*MAN #2 is reading a stack of clips. He looks like he could be an editor, in his blue-plaid button-up shirt and grey slacks, but he sits in the same cubicle row as the rest of the staff's desks, desks occupied this evening or otherwise. He looks to be working methodically, but not urgently.*

MAN #2: *(over his shoulder, to no one)* I don't think any of my clips fit the resume I'm putting together.

ANNELISE: *(blinking, then turning in MAN #2's direction)* Isn't the "TRIPLE HOOKER HOMICIDE" story due in thirty minutes?

MAN #2: I've got the meat finished. I just need to proof it once more. I'm trying to get my clipbook ready for next week when the reorganization interviews start.

*(The SAN JOSE MERCURY NEWS is preparing to be folded into Bay Area News Group, and the news department is re-interviewing for the five newsroom positions that will remain, of the twenty previous. This marks the second round of layoffs in the past year.)*

ANNELISE: Either way, keep the headline. We want to make sure that people click-through to the subscriber-only section.

MAN #1: So the first paragraph needs to be good, and that's it?

ANNELISE: I'm trying to finish my pieces for Features, Food, Gardening and obit, and Sam's out this week, so I'm covering his movie critic piece of *Mall Cop*. Just get your piece in on time—that's all I ask.

MAN #1: *(Ironically)* Right—on time is all you ask.

MAN #2: *(Unironically)* It'll be done.

# UNSPOKEN PROMISES
## YANIBEL VERAS

Ashley says: *Yanibel often points out that I try to see the positive in her writing, even if its tone is dark and tragic. So when she submitted this serious piece about unspoken promises, I decided to remix it into a lighter love poem.*

She met him when she was just ten years old. They were both hiding behind a bush across from her house when she heard someone whisper, "Psst, what are you doing?"

Amber quickly turned around to see a young boy squatting behind her. The boy was about her age and had short black hair and a light complexion that complemented his piercing brown eyes.

"What are you doing?" the boy repeated.

"Nothing," Amber responded and turned back around to spy on the other kids playing across the street.

"Then why you hiding?" he asked.

"None of your business!"

Amber stood up and threw a water balloon at the kids. SPLAT! The girls began screaming, as they got soaked and ran away. The boy laughed.

"My name is Troy," he said, as he moved in closer.

"I'm Amber."

*7 years later*

"Amber, are you listening to me?" Troy yelled. "You have to stop fighting with the other girls just because they're annoying or you're going to get in trouble. Amber? Amber! AMBER!!"

"WHAT?" she screamed back. A group of kids turned around and stared.

"What are you looking at?" Amber yelled louder. "Mind your own business!" Troy pulled her to the side of the courtyard.

"You have got to stop acting like that or you're going to get kicked out of school again," Troy said. Amber turned as red as the brick wall behind them and warned Troy to stop acting like her father.

"Fine, do whatever you want," Troy barked at her, "but if your father finds out you have been fighting with the other girls again, you'll be in for it."

"That's not going to happen," she yelled back, "because you won't tell on me. Right, Troy? Right, Troy?" she yelled louder.

Troy looked at her with the same piercing glare she saw in the bushes seven years prior. "You know I will do anything to protect you, Amber," he said, "I don't want anything to ever happen to you."

*1 month later*

Amber got invited to her first party and accepted the invitation, even though Troy tried to convince her it was a bad idea. There were always fights at the parties in this particular neighborhood, but Amber decided to go anyway. Troy then decided he had to come along in order to make sure nothing happened to her.

Amber was dancing with one of the guys and everything was fine until he started to get forceful. Amber kept rejecting him and that's when he hit her. Amber quickly pulled her arm from his grip and punched him in the face. He was shocked. He tightened his fingers into a fist and just as he was about to swing back, Troy got in the middle and knocked the guy down with one swoop of his right-hook. He grabbed Amber's hand and warned her that this guy was a gang member so they needed to get out of there immediately. They turned to run; but it was too late.

"Amber duck!!" Troy screamed. Before she could move, Troy jumped in front of her. "BANG!" Amber felt the weight of Troy come crashing backwards onto her. She fell to the floor with Troy in her arms. In the background she heard what seemed like faint whispers of people screaming. "You shot him! You shot him! We have to get out of here!" She ignored all of the chaos going on around her and remained focused on the blood trickling down from Troy's bullet wound.

"No!" Amber screamed. "Troy you can't die on me! You have to hold on!"

"It's okay, Amber," he said, "I'm a fighter."

"I can't lose you," she cried.

Just as they heard sirens, Troy gave Amber one last smile. "Promise to always be who you are and follow all of your dreams." Amber just kept crying. "Promise me, Amber." She was crying even harder now. "Promise me..."

*5 years later*

"Congratulations on your new rank as a Captain, Amber," said a fellow police officer as he extended out his hand. "Now, let's go celebrate!"

"Thanks, Dave, but I have someone I want to go see."

"Well, congrats again. You deserve it."

Amber got into her police car and drove to the cemetery where Troy was buried. She kneeled down in front of his grave and began to speak. "I've kept my promise, Troy. I have continued to stay who I am and follow my biggest dreams." Amber gently placed a few handpicked flowers across the letters of his engraved name.

"I've loved you since we were ten, Troy, and someday we'll be together again."

# UNSPOKEN PROMISES
## ASHLEY ROSE HOWARD

A promise is a pledge made to keep
Like a vow of love that goes skin deep

For better are for worse, to this I hold dear
Until the day your love became my biggest fear

My heart always knew it was right, but still it felt so wrong
Many times I tried to tell you, then in one moment you were gone

We were so young, only ten
Yet, still I knew then

My love for you was unspoken
Our connection broken

Just when I thought I had enough courage to give you my heart
You got in the middle and ended any chance of a start

I know you said you'd always protect me
But holding your body in my arms is now the last thing I see

I still cry at night knowing I never got the chance to say I love you
But I made you a promise, and this I'll hold true

Be who I am and go for my dreams, that's what you said
It's still so surreal to admit you are dead

I've loved you since we were ten
And I know we'll be together again

I know this even when I feel most weak
Because to keep our promise, we don't have to speak

# R.I.P. BIRTHDAY CAKE
## CINDY CABAN

Each year on January 5th, my birthday, my parents used to buy me the same cake because it was the only desert that would fulfill my everlasting wish. It was a chocolate vanilla ice-cream cake with pirouette cookies wrapped around the side, and each year I devoured it like an animal. I've never asked for another kind of cake because after five years of having the same one, I thought of it as tradition. Though, when my family or friends came over to sing me happy birthday, they would nag me about how I was so predictable because I didn't try a different cake. Their complaints didn't bother me because besides my parents, the cake was the only other thing that was always there for me on my birthday. What did they know? Most of these people would just show up for the free food or because they felt it was an obligation. The cake, on the other hand, would always be right beside me, not changing its character one bit.

Then, the day I turned fifteen, I remember sitting down while waiting for my cake to arrive. As my parents walked into the dining room, they sang me happy birthday but I was completely shocked to see that my very own special cake wasn't in front of me. Instead, there was a strawberry cake looking at me with its beady eyes and taunting me because I didn't get what I had originally wanted. After they finished singing, I just stood there silently, my eyes blurry from what I had just seen. I didn't even want to blow my candles out, so I asked my mom and dad what happened to my cake. They both looked at each other as if waiting for the other one to break the news to me. My mother responded by telling me that the bakery where they usually bought the cake had been closed down. Now, I know it was just a cake, but I was devastated. The cake that I had gotten since I was five years old, basically, died on my fifteenth birthday. It would no longer exist or have the opportunity to visit my stomach. It was also gone in such short notice. I wasn't able to give it a proper goodbye, similar to the way most things leave our lives.

Now every time it's my birthday, I feel a tinge of sadness because this cake was a part of my life. It wasn't something that I just ate, but it had become a person in my mind's eye. I felt like I lost someone dear to me that day, who would never be able to sing happy birthday to my taste buds ever again. It was also a realization for me that things will begin to change as you get older. Nothing remains the same, in the way that people always leave, your innocence about life gets darkened by the world's madness, and your youth becomes trampled by society's expectations. And that's a part of life; having to transform into an older figure while watching your life steer into different roads right before your delicate yet twisted mind.

#TRANSFORMINGINTO

# LOST + FOUND
## NAKISHA WILLIAMS

She gave it away initially, hoping
that he would treasure it and care for it as if it was his own prized possession
but he was reckless.
He played with it for awhile and then broke it.
washed his hands of the pieces and walked away
when he was done.

And so the search began for the parts.
But where to start?
She was puzzled.

She called her mother for help
After all, that was who gave it to her in the first place
but a strange voice told her to try again
She left a message, marked urgent, and continued on.

Her friends couldn't help
as they were on their own hunts
with maps that led to here and there and nowhere.
She found herself lost following their directions.

She stole a few from strangers
but her thieving hands felt the consequences
when theirs became too heavy to hold.
It was all too much to carry,
so she gave theirs back and moved on.

She searched high and low, far and wide
light turned to dark many times over
and every time she went looking somewhere new
she came up empty.

"Will I ever get it back!?" she screamed out
as the single expression rolling down her cheek
opened up the flood gates, sweeping her away
as she nearly drowned.

Weary and cold she decided to surrender
She quit and willed herself home.
THE END
But then...

Her plan to rest from the exhausting journey, forever,
was thwarted when she went to the medicine cabinet

eyes darting past the unrecognizable face in the mirror
and caught on a something sticking to her sleeve.

She snorted with laughter at the realization that was still
simply too complicated to fully grasp.
She picked it off piece by piece
and began to put the puzzle pieces together.

The phone rang, and startled her
If it's not one thing it's your mother
and there was hers, anxious to reach her
as it had been days since she had called for help.

"Where have you been sweet daughter?"
She thought back on her journey,
marveled at how far she'd gone in her search.

"You are wise to guard it," mother said.
"But you'll never really lose your heart. And if your mind
or the world, plays tricks and you forget where it is,
follow the beat, march, and you will remember again soon enough."

# A TRUE LOVE FOR NATURE
## AVA NADEL

*Jessi says: I created an erasure poem from Ava's essay. She edited it and we collaboratively attempted to use a new form to derive similar meaning.*

"How's everyone doing back there?!" Doug yelled. "We're good," we called back. Some of us panted, others mumbled. The rest said nothing. We had another two miles until we reached Alder Lake. Caroline had an infected bliste,r and my leg was burning from stinging nettle. It was day four. This was supposed to be the hardest day out of the entire week. Joy.

Upon signing up for the Counselor-in-Training program at Frost Valley YMCA, the camp where I'd spent the past four·summers of my adolescence, I knew I would have to complete a week-long hike in the Catskill Mountains. I was unaware of what was awaiting me. Thorns, rain, iodine tablets, carrying moldy canisters of spaghetti. But also: the rush of flinging myself into a serene lake and standing atop a fire tower.

On the first afternoon of the hike, I pulled my hair into a tight bun, laced up my hiking boots, and applied sunscreen. My group devoured four trays of pizza during lunch, filled up our Nalgenes and headed back to Biscuit, our lodge, to soak up some sun till the bus arrived.

Stepping off the white mini-bus, I knew there was no turning back. I hoisted the pack on my shoulders as a strong wave of nausea rippled through me. Our trip coordinator, Doug, said we had only 1-½ miles to hike until we got to our lean-to. *Hmm. Not bad.* I started to think that it would be like this every day. I fooled myself. The next morning would be the first real day. As I breakfasted on steamed Quaker oats, which tasted like mushy saltines with honey, I couldn't tell if I was excited, or nervous.

That night, we didn't have a designated camp spot, but a camping area. We settled in a spot covered with pine needles, uprooted branches, and a huge uprooted tree. (The boys in our group said, "it makes a perfect pooping spot!" Mhm, TMI.) Dinner was spaghetti and tomato sauce with the mozzarella cheese we used on our pita pizzas, since we had a two-gallon bag of it. We made too much for dinner and the excess was put in our spare containers for lunch and after that, the remains turned to mold.

Day 4. The day we dreaded the most. Two? Three mountains? And five miles of hiking. The coordinator, Doug, actually said his day four as a Counselor-in-Training was nine miles long, so we should stop complaining. Leaving our campsite that morning, we were faced with a steep, narrow hill, and we trekked. My hand was covered in stinging nettle marks and my legs were covered in scratches from thorn bushes. We got to our resting spot, drenched in sweat, ripped off our packs and sat on the moist, leafy ground. We looked up at the sign above us: "Alder Lake: 2.9 miles." We were speechless. My friend Emma cried out to Sarah, our other coordinator, "Are you kidding me?! I am *so* sure we hiked more than two miles and now we have to hike *three* to get to the lake?!!?" We were fuming. We had had enough, but we couldn't stop. Hours later we saw the clearing. We tossed our shoes and shirts on the ground. We sprinted in and let our bodies infuse into the water. Relief.

The next two days flew by. We swam in another lake. It didn't give us the rush that Alder Lake had, but the sight was breathtaking, like a perfectly Photoshopped photograph. One night, Doug gave us bandanas. As a group, we had to decide who would get which bandanna based on how the color associated with each person's personality. It was a moving movement. There was no quarreling or favoring and each of us felt the rewarding sense of teamwork.

Two rainy nights passed and it was the last day. On our way back to the bus stop, we traveled up to the fire tower. It was striking; I was 400 feet higher in the air than I had ever been. The hills rolled endlessly, and the clouds were almost touchable. I was surrounded by people who cared for each other. THIS WAS TRUE HAPPINESS.

Half an hour after the fire tower visit, we reached the bus stop. I hadn't showered in a week, and had no earrings or eyeliner. We rejoiced in smelly hugs, threw off our packs and collapsed to the ground in relief. Our head coordinator emerged with four boxes of pizza, and we dove forward. The hot, zesty sauce burned my chapped lips, but I didn't care. Riding back to camp was about an hour and yes, the bus reeked of twelve putrid teenagers and their two fantastic yet awfully smelly coordinators. We rode back into the Valley and stepped off the bus. I looked around myself in disbelief. I didn't have anything on me: no jewelry, no money to my name but I had everything I needed.

Six days. 30 miles. Six mountains and an appreciation for nature to last eternity.

# THE HIKE
## JESSI HEMPEL

"How's everyone there?!" Doug yelled.
We panted, mumbled.
Two miles until Alder Lake.
Infected blister, heat wave. DAY FOUR.
Hardest.
Joy.

Frost Valley YMCA. My home
Four summers.
Adolescence, a long hike.
Unaware of thorns, moldy spaghetti.
The rush of standing atop fire tower,
Serene lakes.

The first afternoon: hair buns, hiking boots, sunscreen.
Pizza lunch, Nalgenes

I hoisted pack over shoulders
Strong nausea rippled through me. 1-½ mi
Hike until Lean-Two. Not
bad. You're probably thinking
I thought this every day.
Fooled myself.
Morning would be real
Eating steamed Quaker oats
like mushy saltines. Couldn't tell if I

Or nervous.
Camp spot. Perfect.
Clustered.

DAY FOUR. Fives miles.
Leaving morning, we were steep,
Narrow hills, though
covering my legs in sweat.
And sat on ground. We looked at a
sign above us: 2.9 miles. "Are you kidding?!!?"
Fuming.

We swam at Alder
sight was something.
Same night,
Bandanas, given

Movement.
We were on our bus stop,
The fire I experienced. The air
Endless cloud
Surrounded true happiness,
Smelly hugs, packs and relief.
Teenagers.
Awfully smelly.

Six days. 30 miles. Six mountains
Nature to last eternity.

# ALLEY POND
## SHANNON DANIELS

On Sundays, he ditched his yet-to-do homework and never-silent cell phone to hike up to the highest point of Alley Pond Park. To Brian, it was the only real park in the city, an almost magical place that somehow escaped tourists' radars. Usually, he visited it on dreary afternoons when things weren't quite right: days when the weather was too rainy for swimming, when his friends were too busy for a pickup basketball game, or when the girl he wanted to take to the movies said no – again. Somehow, every churn of the cycle of dullish-average-days brought him back to the great big, almost-made-to-be-a-chair rock at the top of the park and left him sitting there alone watching cars fly under the highway beneath him.

Today would have been no different if it hadn't been for Bradley, his rash-spoiled-thoughtless younger brother. He had just received his permit and tried to be nonchalant when he asked to borrow Brian's car: a too-awe-inspiring-for-words-sleek-black Lexus Mom and Dad had given him because college was only three months away.

When he returned home, Brian saw his brother walk guiltily up the steps to their front door, his baby being towed right behind, completely and utterly totaled. He was still learning, Bradley explained, and he didn't *mean* to crash the car, he had just, well, forgotten to put the car into park.

Brian locked eyes with his brother. His lips tried to form the words of every thought that came to mind, from *How could you be so stupid?* to *I thought I could trust you*, but between them was only a silence that made their tongues too swollen to speak. It was an almost-moment, one of those brief pockets of time where a couple of words, a gesture, or a step can change everything. In an almost-moment, the floor threatens to tilt from the weight cradled in your arms. Brian had never dealt with these moments easily; he wasn't just angry, nor was he just sad. One word never grounded his emotions in all of their wholeness. He wanted to hyphenate every word imaginable just so he could articulate a sliver of what he felt inside.

Bradley furrowed his brow and cleared his throat, but by that time Brian was already out the door and headed for the only place where he could find solace.

What Bradley had done was just unforgivable. He could never get anything right, and never did anything for the right reasons. When Brian joined the neighborhood little league baseball team, Bradley just *had* to join, too. But no matter how many laps he ran in the park or how many hours he spent at batting practice, he could never catch fly balls faster than Brian or hit nearly as many home runs. After one particularly rough game, Bradley threw his bat on the ground and never picked it up again. Brian was convinced that Bradley had given up the struggle of trying to be like him.

But, when Brian signed up for AP Calculus and snagged an impressive internship with a research company, his younger brother suddenly gained a liking for math. He signed up for the same class, knowing well that he couldn't handle it. Even though Bradley rarely spoke to him, it didn't take long for Brian to realize his brother had dug himself inside a hole and was silently begging for his help to return to steady ground. Brian turned away.

He had just gotten to the top of Alley Pond Park when a rustle came from the tangle of trees behind him. He gripped his stony chair, and his knuckles grew white. No one knew about this place; it had to be a wild animal.

"Don't worry," a voice echoed, "it's just me."

Bradley pushed back a tree branch and revealed a face wearing a type of sorrow Brian had never seen before.

"What are you doing here? Did you follow me?" Brian eased back into his chair. Bradley sat next to him on the grass.

"Well, I wanted to say..." He took a deep breath and closed his eyes. "Look, I know that no apology is going to make you forgive me, and I understand that."

A long pause.

"But I want us to talk again. Like we used to." The plum-colored-pockets under his eyes said everything. "Like I wanted us to."

Another rustle and a squeak sounded from the bushes. They looked at each other. Bradley got up first. He pulled back a dark green curtain of weeping willows and uncovered a small, golden puppy.

It was another almost-moment. Brian was the older brother, the one who needed to make a decision and fast, and—

The thoughts hadn't even finished forming in his mind when Bradley scooped up the dog and said firmly, "We need to help him."

Brian was speechless yet again. All of Bradley's desperate attempts of finding steady footing were outweighed by this instinctive, real decision.

They headed home, and along the winding paths of Alley Pond Park, Brian was ready to understand this feeling, of course, not a one-word feeling, but something he recognized as a willingness to forgive. With this, Brian could take the first step. He would learn how to climb too.

## NAMES
### RACHEL COHEN

*Dear Ms. Lewkowicz,*

*I enjoy your articles and I've wondered if you're by chance related to Joe Lewkowicz? He was a high school classmate of mine at Foreman in Chicago.*

*Sincerely,*

TOM GRABOWSKI

Beth averaged one of those emails every six months or so. Where in Poland is your family from? Which church did you go to? She would politely reply, "Sorry, I don't think we're related."

Beth's father's father was indeed Polish, but Peter Lewkowicz married Anna Murray, a Scottish Methodist. They had a boy and two girls, and their son—Beth's dad—married a Cuban Jew. Beth grew up getting presents on both Christmas and Hanukkah, with no baby Jesus or singing the Hebrew prayers while lighting the candles. Her grandfather had died when Beth was six; pierogi and kielbasa were never family traditions. Peter was an only child, and his relatives apparently weren't too pleased about the Methodist. The only Lewkowiczs she knew were her grandmother and her dad; if there were any others out there who shared the floppy ears she clearly inherited from Grampa, Beth wasn't aware. Her mother hadn't changed her name, and her sister—much to Beth's and their mom's horror—had changed hers when she married Rob Deriya. It's one thing, Beth thought, to turn in Lewkowicz for Smith under the argument of easier spelling and pronunciation. But Deriya was just as bad and sounded uncomfortably like diarrhea.

"The worst sin you can commit is spelling a subject's name wrong." So intoned the professor on Day 1 of her introductory journalism class freshman year. The ridiculous hyperbole served its purpose; daydreaming students snapped to attention. As the victim of years of Lewkowitzs and Lukowiczs, Beth took the advice as a bit of an epiphany.

Her journalism career might have ended unceremoniously the summer before her senior year had she left an interview seconds earlier. Beth had been assigned a classic intern story: the two local high school students who started their own business. The editor's email mentioned the two names.

Marcus Jackson and Matt Riley. She was stuffing her notepad into her purse when she overheard the freelance photographer talking to the kids as they posed for a portrait.

"R-E-I-L-L-Y?"

"No, R-I-L-E-Y."

She looked up, puzzled. The voice was Marcus'. Were they pulling a prank on the photog, each telling him the other's name? Beth had taken a step toward the three when her brain processed it. Upon arriving, she had never confirmed who was who. Just assumed unconsciously that Matt Riley was the white kid and Marcus Jackson the black kid. On her way out, Beth stopped by the school's main office and asked to see the yearbook— mumbling something about the photog needing it. Under the J's, there he was: the kid with shaggy blond hair. She crossed out all the Matts in her notepad and replaced them with Marcuses and the Marcuses with Matts. Her editor complimented her the next day on the nice details in what could have been a mundane story.

# MY EVEREST
## TOBI ELKIN

Larissa says: *I was inspired by my mentor Tobi's original prose poem to create a new poem—something heartfelt, honest and revealing. Using Tobi's line "Like a current, you were always on" as a starting place, I decided to reflect on an experience that dominated my thoughts but never actually developed in reality.*

You once told me
"I don't exist."
That sounded strange since you dominated most of my waking thoughts, real or imagined
Like a current, you were always on.

I remember you telling me
"All my life, I coulda, woulda, shoulda, then couldn't."
Though I would never know exactly what you meant by it,

You only became more real to me after you said it.
I wondered whether your confiding in me was a sign of intimacy
Or merely a drunken lapse in judgment.

"You've never met anyone like me,"
I ventured in a moment of earnest self-possession.
When you heard me say it, you smiled faintly.

Growing more emboldened by a series of serves and returns, I said,
"Devour me whole and leave nothing but a tiny skeleton."
I angled for a visceral impact,
You threw up a wall of silence instead.
Addicted to my one-sided desire,
My heart turned any morsel thrown its way into a sign of affection.

"I don't have time for complicated social engagements," you said,
Aiming to decimate my vision of our pairing.
Thereafter, you became a challenge that could be scaled with determination.
I likened you to Everest,
A long, slow ascent filled with pitfalls and casualties.

You once told me
"I'm here in spirit, always."
A spirit sans presence,
Someone who was never really there.

But you told me you didn't exist.
Incredibly disingenuous, I thought.

You remain an ineffable mysterious island
A person I kind of used to know
A world withheld
Uncharted
Extant.

# DEAD ON ARRIVAL
## LARISSA HERON

"What's your name, again?"
He asked for maybe the hundredth time.
I didn't think much of it then
Though in retrospect, maybe I should have.

I remember he'd always say "hi" in the hallway
And then he stopped.
He'd talk to me as a friend, but I wished for a little more
I secretly hoped he felt the same way.

As the weeks rushed by,
The idea of him grew larger in my mind.
Like a current, he was always on.
He was never far from my thoughts.

A year later,
A friend confirmed what I'd hoped for.
But it was too late:
Too much time had passed, and with it, the moment.

"It's all the things left unsaid that [return to] haunt us the most," I once read.
If only I'd expressed myself,
Perhaps I wouldn't feel so laden with regret.

# #OTHER WORLDS

> "When I was a teenager, I was miserable and lonely, and felt completely trapped by the realities of the world I was stuck in. I escaped into stories, where people like me got to go on adventures, make lifelong friendships, fall in love, travel through outer space or work magical miracles. Be brave, be wild, be happy—all the things I wasn't and feared I would never be."

This is what author Robin Wasserman, who led a Girls Write Now Crime Fiction Craft Talk, had to saying regarding books that take the reader to "other worlds." In the following pieces, women writers allow us to escape into alternate worlds or realities, while also forcing us to reflect upon our own world and ourselves. In Robin's words:

> "There's an element of reading that's all about searching for ourselves—recognizing ourselves in strange, unexpected places doing strange unexpected things, discovering things that we didn't even know we knew or believed, finding ourselves, without even quite realizing we were lost. The best books are mirrors, of our worlds and ourselves, alternate universes that reflect a twisted version of the truth."

—WHITNEY JACOBY
2012 MENTOR AND ANTHOLOGY COMMITTEE MEMBER

# GASWORK HEART STOP
## KATHRYN JAGAI

#OTHERWORLDS

Therese says: *Kat and I were inspired by the November Found Poetry Workshop, particularly the examples of erasure poems where found text is used to create poetry by removing or blacking out a selection of the author's original words. For the anthology, we thought it would be fun to take excerpts from each other's novels—our favorite form of writing—and to remix them by creating erasure poems. Kat and I gave each other chapters of our novels—Kat's* Monochromacy *and my* Dear Dirty Dublin—*and had fun with each other's texts, erasing words and creating new meaning and turns of phrase out of what remained. Some of the short phrases in my poem are absolutely Kat's own, but I tried to butcher the writing enough so that the creation is mine but Kat's original meaning shines through. It was kind of ridiculously fun.*

Annihilation come quick—factories report a sea of uncertainty.
Can I give you ten years
to drift into the sea? The ghost of
the architect draws up the Royal blackguard
the king, small and cold, glistening purple under stars.

Only half there—the story
drifting somewhere icy cold—now, into the underground.
Down into the gasworks. An elaborate ritual
at peace with God. The heart—drained of all life
the tick-tick-tock, bereft.

Turn it off.

The Blessed Virgin—fucked. The dirge—beautiful Misery.
They are Enemies, Sponsoring the gloom—
the squalid spectacle of memory. Lights flash;
the Highwayman, the butcher, the last supper, the Devil—
swinging naked from a chandelier.

Save your life! You know my secret—
I'm only here to pay my respects.
Do you know where you are?
The Edge. Excellent. Selling his soul. The Devil laughs.

Jesus with a butter knife,
posh and correct. I forgot, Our Lady,
are you my mother? Devil, I can't tell—
do you still pray? God, Mary,
a dream—are you lying? I swear it.
I wouldn't know them.

The coffin, love. Goodbye.

# BRAT PRINCE AMBULANCE
## THERESE COX

The windshield realized that it must be the car horn:
She was not dead yet.
Tandem tongues untangled their meaning
And burning dark flickered in the distance.

Her ribcage closed against her shoulder,
Twins collected the other.
Sniping, shrieking: "This is not hell."

She had gone sober, the drummer played chaperone.
The brat prince ambulance swerved into the sky.
He'd been awake, a one-night-stand,
Tipsy and speeding as she twitched to the windshield.
The greenish web beneath her could radiate hieroglyphs.
Shifting her body, they took her eyes.
The passenger crumpled, unsure.

An EMT was crawling;
He wasn't old enough to drive.
Another month, a litany of mutters,
A man was murmuring things she winced away.

Behind him, the Menace.
White distance refrained.
Prosthetic Miss, can you hear her stethoscope?

# FLOATING CASTLE, HIDDEN CLOUD
## BEGINA ARMSTRONG

Begina says: *On one of our mentoring outings, Jackie and I went to see the movie* Pina *and we decided to write pieces in response to our experience. We ended up both creating poems, which was funny because it was like a telepathic thing going on. The pieces are very similar in a distant kind of way, where one was about a specific dance that was in the movie and the other was simply inspired by the dances overall.*

Tinted windowpanes shade my eyes from outside tragedies
Gilded and gloss covered footprints taunt me to leave this place
Someone else has done it before me

Probably a ghost because gold shoes wouldn't chip off leaving sunny residue on
perfection
Cheaply made roads are outside
Taunting me, however, I am not frugal enough to care
If I could waltz past the guards holding my fantasies captive
And my mileage is retained between iron fences
And locked away by trenches of monsters
I am trapped in a fantasy of someone else
By who, I don't know
Who keeps me here
Bribing me to stay with them
I do not accept this lie
I am kept from my home
Which is not here
And how I wish to break free
Flying, soaring, and climbing to great heights
Envious of eagles, mourned by ants
I am however wingless
Flightless
So maybe that's why I stay
This prison flies for me
However I am kept away from all civilization
Making this the worst dream ever
Kept here by who
My sanity
To save my imaginary palace stuck
Between dream and a sudden awakening
Then living lucidly among the celestial creatures
This is what I need
But I forget how to feel anything but joy
So I'll be bored of this fake
Floating dreams I have and let them go
This day I dread with eyes wide open
Staring through the windowpane

# LA PRIMA VEZ
## JACKIE CLARK

Just as tempestuous as the labor
The guttural elbows
The labored breathing
Every opening is like this in some way
The combination of surprise and despair
The realization that one must carry on
Even after the fall, the winter, the summer, the spring
Signing our way through the seasons
Across mountain ridges and deserts
Everyone you have ever loved lined up like ghosts behind you
Mimicking your movements
The memory of your movements alive in their arms
It's repetition full of catapult
The sky above the bridge
A series of chairs under it
How we arrange the room is how the room is arranged
I will be outside standing under the Metro all day
Or I will be standing in the Café Müller
I will be trying to hold you in my arms and failing
Or you will be trying to hold me in your arms and failing
We will try to forgo the holding
The weight of our persons
Gathering our embrace after each disappointment
But the ides of March will appear and rearrange us
Will always expect one of us to bear the weight
With the chairs scattered all around it is easier to walk with our eyes closed
Guided by a single hand stretching out to nothing
There will always be a sense of darkness
You take this train
I take that train
Sandstorms and rainstorms
The water retiring with the moon
Beauty as an image of our disrepair
The caterwauls of trumpets moving further and further away
Yet there is always a movement that will soften our expectations
Our glass house, with as many windows as we need

# UNDERGROUND
## ERIKA ALFARO

Erika says: *This piece is inspired by the journey I made when I moved with my family from El Salvador to the United States. I adapted my personal experience to the context of overpopulation and its effects on the world.*

Everything would've been different if my family had not won the lottery nine years ago. We were selected to live underground because the earth's population had exceeded 16 billion people, causing a lot of pressure on the environment. The U.S. government designed a plan in which each year twelve young families from every country are randomly picked via a lottery system to relocate seventy thousand feet underground for 15 years. My family was among the first settlers when the program was launched eight years ago.

I was only three when we moved. I don't remember anything about the surface. I constantly badger my mom to tell me stories of how it is up there and show me the few photos she was able to bring with her. "Here is where we would picnic together on the weekends," she'd say, showing me a picture of a green floor, furry creatures, and wooden plants "See this?" she always said, "that's the tree we'd sit under, and it was the biggest one of all." I would always stare at the picture in disbelief that I was there at some point. The blue sky and the cotton white clouds were not just a hologram. The sunlight was real too. Underground, the environmental lights were programmed to change every twelve hours to recreate the sunrise and sunset. But we knew that was just an illusion. The surface was like a planet in a totally different galaxy to mine. I could not wait to visit it. And that moment was fast approaching.

On the morning of the journey, my fourth grade class boarded a metallic capsule, which was the only mode of transport. It traveled through a tunnel for about ten hours. Each one carried a backpack filled with water and food for the day. Our chaperones were Mr. Rusell and Mrs. Kim. When the doors closed my heart started beating really fast as the excitement and fear bubbled up. I was sweating; my hands were cold; my legs were shaking. I had never left home for so long. What if I never saw my parents again?

A week ahead of the trip, our bodies were conditioned to what we would experience on the surface. We were exposed to temperatures of twenty to ninety degrees Fahrenheit and to wind currents of forty miles per hour. We were taught to always wear sunscreen in order to keep our skin protected. At first I had headaches because of all those changes, but by the end of the week I felt fine. Mr. Rusell warned us that we might experience water or ice falling out of nowhere or skin bumps that he called "bug bites," but he said not to worry because our visit was temporary.

As we approached the surface, Mrs. Kim gave us more instructions. She said that we should always stay with the group. We weren't to talk to anyone and if we did, we would be sent back immediately. She also gave us each a bottle of sunscreen. It would protect our skin since we had never been exposed to real sunlight. When the capsule stopped, I felt my heart stop too.

The doors opened and there were three men in black waiting for us. As they exchanged some words with Mr. Rusell and Mrs. Kim, I peered out. The place looked like a big busy transportation center. Everyone carried huge suitcases, and they all seemed to be in a rush. People walked at a quick pace and some pushed through the crowd without apologizing. No one paid attention to us. I had never seen so many people in just one place. There was no room to walk. We went down the stairs and at the end there were two big glass doors. We saw an incredibly bright light shining through. The doors opened right along with my mouth and everyone else's.

I could barely open my eyes because the light was so intense. I felt something I had never felt before. Mrs. Kim explained that is was the wind or breeze. It felt like tiny hands caressing my skin. Then I looked up and saw the sky, but it wasn't as blue as in the photographs. It was almost gray like the air. It was difficult to breath sometimes.

From there we were then taken to a place called "Zoo." Mr. Rusell explained that we would see many kinds of animals and a variety of plants, so we had to be careful not to touch anything. We saw an animal with an extremely long neck and a yellowish brown coat called giraffe. We also saw animals that fly called birds. They had colorful feathers and they made a very high-pitched noise.

All of a sudden I felt a drop of water slide down my cheek. At first I thought I was crying but I didn't feel sad. I didn't know where it came from. Then everyone else felt it too. Many more drops started falling, drenching my clothes. Everyone started running for cover from the rain including my classmates. I stood still feeling the water and the light and the wind. I knew this was the place where I belonged. It was something I had missed for so long and was not willing to go back to the dark. This world was made for me, too. With its imperfections and benefits, I wanted it all.

# HONOR
## JOSLEEN WILSON

Lumbering buses disgorge brightly clothed tourists, excited, cameras for eyes. Been planning this trip for months. The air is clear, no acrid motes clinging to their nose hairs. Whenever I travel outside the City, people ask me what this place looks like. Tell me they want to make a big trip to see it for themselves. They're dismayed when I say I've never been, never will go. No killing fields for me.

But walk a little way with me, just around the corner from where I live. See the two-storied firehouse? Its big doors standing open, the shiny red hook & ladder inside, like local firehouses everywhere? Big red letters over the door identify it: Engine Co. 22, Ladder Co. 13, 10th Battalion. Underneath, three large plaques hang, one under the other. On each plaque are three framed smiling faces:

Martin, Thomas C., Michael,

Vincent, Thomas S., Gregory,

Walter, Dennis, Thomas H.

Nine all together. They are wearing their big fireman's helmets that they used to let the neighborhood kids try on. Even after all these years, sprays of flowers appear on the Elysian sidewalk in front of the firehouse, little notes with their names on them, attached with ribbon.

## A WARRIOR'S TALE
### TUHFA BEGUM

In Elysian Fields, the heroes await,
Hands outstretched with goblets
Waiting to be filled with the nectar of the Gods.
And the world below them is wrapped in silence.
The sky weeps tears; the battle has come to an end.
Footsteps, heartbeats; I'd forgotten how they sound.
Why is my land soaked in rivers of blood?
Will the Phoenix burned to ashes come back to roam?
Will this war ever end with the sound of a cry,
A child scarcely asking why?
Glory it may be for those who kill the most,
But is it worth the price to pay
For nothing but the ghost
Of a country that once was the triumph of the world?
Count the bodies of innocence rotting on the floor.
These are the stories of war, waiting to be told.

## PROJECT MILLENNIUM
### CHANDRA HUGHES + CLAUDIA PARSONS

Claudia says: *We wrote this piece together during our first meeting of the year—it's the first scene of a radio play that Chandra plans to record with her friends acting the parts.*

JASON: It's time, Greta. Time to go back to work. This is an important year, you know.

GRETA: Yeah, I know. Every year is important, brother.

JASON: It is. And you know our father is counting on you.

GRETA: *(mumbling)* Like he has, every year before. Yeah, yeah, I know.

JASON: What was that? I don't want to hear any more of your complaining. You know we have a job to do and you've just got to do it.

GRETA: Whether I complain or not, it doesn't matter. The only importance is the outcome, isn't that right?

JASON: Exactly. You know we have to do what's best for the country. Your father has always done what's best, and that's more important than you and me and everybody else. Now, for your orders...

GRETA: Of course it's more important than us or anyone. I mean, it's the president we're talking about. He *always* comes first.

JASON: Of course he does. So, we've identified several suspects on campus, and you will need to focus on getting to know them. I'll give you the dossiers on them later. You've done this before, so it shouldn't be too hard.

GRETA: No, of course I *haven't!* Why don't you go over the rules again?

JASON: Come on, Greta. Don't be difficult. You know we need to know everything they're thinking. You might not think there's anything wrong with what they're thinking, but you aren't in a position to know. Every little detail we pass on to the experts, and they'll know what's important. So don't start trying to protect people just because you think we don't need to know everything.

GRETA: Yes, your majesty, whatever the king wishes.

JASON: I've had enough of your sarcasm. Our father is the democratically elected president of this country. I won't have you talking about him like that.

GRETA: Of course I wouldn't. *(mumbling)* Who knows what he would do to me if I did.

JASON: *(more kindly now)* Greta, come on. I know you don't mean to be like this. Dad knows it's tough for you, but he relies on you. You're the only one who's had the implant. We need you to find out what people are thinking. There are dangerous subversives everywhere; we have to stop them.

GRETA: You know brother, I've done this every single year. Ever since I was six. I'm aware of what I need to do. You don't have to tell me over and over.

JASON: Good. Now, the first suspect is David Hampton. I think you've come across him before, right?

GRETA: Of course. Halle Jones knows everybody in the school. Don't you worry, boss.

JASON: Right. David hasn't demonstrated any subversive activity yet, but his parents were radicals at the height of the trouble. It's likely that they corrupted him, so we need to watch him closely. He's in the science program, but he's working in a safe area. He doesn't know anything about The Project, but we need to make sure it stays that way. He could be dangerous.

GRETA: Likely? *(laughs)* Aren't you being a little too judgmental?

JASON: No, Greta, this is serious stuff. We are protecting our country. You can't be too careful with people like the Hamptons.

GRETA: So, in other words, you're saying if someone committed a murder, we should suspect their family and friends, because who knows, maybe that person "corrupted" the people around him?

JASON: Of course. These deviants are capable of anything. Especially when it comes to their children. They will have been brainwashing David from a young age. We can't trust him.

GRETA: *(sighs)* In that case, I could just commit a crime today; then you would be suspected, as well as our father. *(smirks)*

JASON: You always have to argue back, don't you Greta? Really—when are you going to grow up and take this seriously?

GRETA: Argue back? Grow up? Are you kidding me? I'm only voicing my own opinions... or is that not allowed anymore?

JASON: Just be careful Greta. Of course we believe in free speech, but every crime starts with an evil thought. That's the point of The Project. If we can catch these people before they commit the crime, our country will be a lot safer.

GRETA: *(To herself) What an idiot...* Yeah, yeah, whatever you say.

JASON: Good. Now, here are the other dossiers. You'll have to read them thoroughly before school starts and then destroy them. Any questions before you go?

GRETA: Just give me the files. Halle has to go to school. She is a role model you know. She can't arrive late.

JASON: And be sure to keep the daily reports coming. Don't leave anything out. I mean it, Greta. We need to know everything.

GRETA: Halle has to go now. Goodbye.

# AFTER SCHOOL
## INGRID SKJONG

Alexandra stomped into her bedroom, long brown hair flying behind her. It was the end of another day—another *long* day—and, of course, the nine-year-old second-grader was tired. (Though you'd have to wait as long as her day lasted to hear her admit it.) The clock read 10:45 p.m., well past her bedtime, and her mother knew that 6:45 a.m. would come awfully fast.

Alex sat on her bed, her Dora the Explorer bedspread beaming up at her. She yanked one arm out of her flowered turtleneck, then another, and wriggled it up over her head. Her wrinkled brow and scowling face softened as she slid out of her jeans and pulled on her footie pajamas. She paused for a second on the edge of her bed, eyes heavy.

"Alexandra!" her mom called from the bathroom. "Time to brush your teeth now!" "OK, OK!" she answered. Mandolin, the family cat, ambled into the bedroom and jumped up onto the bed with a squawking meow. His dark gray and white body, all 17 pounds of it, flopped against Alexandra. She brightened, laughed, and pushed him back over. "Silly Mandolin."

Alex shuffled out of her bedroom, dragging her feet and humming quietly. She made her way down the short hallway to the bathroom and pulled up in front of the black marble sink. She grabbed her SpongeBob SquarePants toothbrush, reached for the tube of minty toothpaste, and squeezed a ribbon of the blue gel onto the bristles. She passed it under the faucet once, twice, climbed up on the counter, sat on her knees, and got down to work brushing her teeth.

She stared at herself in the mirror. She brushed a little, then smiled big to see how she was doing. She brushed a little more, hummed a little more, smiled big again. Her mom came in, checked on the progress, and signed off on the job. She jumped down off the counter and made her way back to her bedroom. After a short-lived attempt to watch "just two more minutes" of TV, and a visit to the kitchen for a sip of water, she finally made it into bed. And it wasn't long before she was fast asleep, Mandolin tucked in beside her.

# THE ENCHANTED PUDDLE
## JESSICA BORDON

Jessica says: *This fictional piece was inspired by the Mirror of Erised, which, according to Dumbledore from* Harry Potter, *shows "the deepest and most desperate desire of one's heart." Instead of a mirror, however, I've made the reflection be shown through a puddle.*

One afternoon the sun lay on the sky contently, beaming down at earth with a cheery smile. Suddenly, the sun was startled by an extremely loud argument coming from an old cottage at the heart of the woods beneath his body, all ablaze. A man had a young girl by her hair, dragging her ferociously across a front porch. With sudden strength, the girl triumphed her way out of the man's tight grip, leaving behind a clump of tangled brown hair in his fist. She ran into the woods, away from the screaming man. The girl ran for hours, her legs pounding with adrenaline before stopping to rest. She sat down in front of the thick trunk of a tree, catching her breath before spotting a puddle a couple of feet away from her. She pulled herself to the puddle, bending over to slurp the luminous water.

After quenching her thirst, she looked down to see not her reflection, but someone odd standing behind her. Taken aback, she spun around to see nothing but the large tree nesting behind her. The girl glanced into the puddle again, hesitantly. The puddle gleamed once more, shimmering before displaying a woman standing behind her. Leaning in, she identified the beautiful woman as her mother, and with a jolt of joy spun around again only to find the same tree, and nothing more.

Confused, she stared into the puddle for hours before realizing that it was an *enchanted* puddle. From then on, she did nothing but stare into the water's demonstration. The puddle presented her with every scene she had ever dreamed of. In one, she played with her mother and sister along the beach, and the sand so sublimely real and warm that the girl forgot it was a mirage and tried to grab it. She saw herself growing old with her mother, whose complexion did not age at all, as well as her loving sister.

The dreadful stepfather she lived with in the cottage was still working abroad, and had no clue that there was a woman like her mother or a child like her sister. Nothing went wrong in the puddle's reflection. She was never despondent.

The girl and the puddle fancied each other. Day after day the girl wasted away in front of it, staring into the story played within the reflection and the life she craved and desired in replacement of her own. She had forgotten about reality and ignored her stomach's pleas for food or her throat's parched and dusty funnel. She became desperate. Her body was weak and rotting without nurturing, and as she awoke one morning from a light sleep, she felt heavy with an ominous sickness.

She dragged herself to the puddle, but what she saw wasn't the puddle's usual illustration. Scenes of tremendously ill memories flickered across the still water: Her mother screaming in pain through labor, heavy blood pouring across the bed sheets; her newborn sister howling with tears, dying slowly with every breath she took; the funeral the girl went to for her mother and sister filled with unfamiliar relatives, all lamenting and pale.

The puddle washed these away hastily, startling the girl, who always forgot where she was when caught up in a scene. Instead of exhibiting memories or fantasies, the puddle ended its display with scenes the girl did not recognize: Her mother and stepfather laughing with a small, peculiar toddler chasing after a pigeon. The girl realized that the toddler was her sister.

Suddenly she had a thought that made her pause. The scenes were not of reality. They represented the unborn possibility that if she had never been born, her mother and sister would be alive.

Scrambling away from the puddle, she began to rock back and forth, the twigs beneath her pinching her skin violently. She grabbed her neck abruptly and twisted her hands tightly around it. Constricting her breathing, she compressed her throat, her screeching wails echoing through the hollow woods.

The girl tightened her grip, digging her sharp nails into her neck, and the scarlet, warm blood trickled down her chest. At last, she breathed once more, the puddle's illustrations caressing her thoughts one last time before she fell to her side, lifeless.

The sun could not bear the sight of the helpless, cold remains of the girl. His body enflamed and raged with smoldering combustion. Feverish heat swept across the lands as the sun flamed with sympathy and wrath. The puddle, which seemed quite content with his work, began to quiver. Small waves echoed across its body, and the humid warmth slowly dissolved its water.

The sun watched the puddle's body evaporate expeditiously, and finally felt his rage soothe. Just then, the girl's eyes reopened to the gentle touch of a beautiful woman.

# THE GHOST IN THE MIRROR
## KATHERINE NERO

What makes mirrors so creepy, especially in dark rooms? I refuse to look towards any mirror when the lights are off. My imagination didn't always conjure up evil beings in the mirror. My dread of mirrors began when I was five years old, thanks to my sister.

My sister is only five years older than I, but our difference in ages felt like a generation gap back then. After school we weren't allowed to go outside or have company until my mother got home from work. That one hour we had to wait felt like an eternity. However, that did not stop my sister from having her friend Dee over.

I was always making excuses to invade my sister's bedroom whenever she had company. During one of my many interruptions, Dee and my sister were swapping ghost stories. To my delight, my sister allowed me to stay instead of the usual shooing away.

My sister began her scary tale, "The Ghost of Mary Worth." According to the legend, Mary Worth was an old, mean woman with super long fingernails. To see her, you had to stand in front of the mirror with a flashlight in a dark room and repeat "I believe in Mary Worth" 25 times. When you reach 25, the image of Mary Worth was supposed to appear in the mirror. If you were able to face Mary Worth bravely, she would just disappear. However, if you screamed, Mary Worth would scratch out your eyes and haunt you for the rest of your life.

I sat there as my sister and Dee began the Mary Worth chant. When they reached 20, I tore out of there. I doubted that I could see such a scary sight and not scream, and the thought of some old woman haunting me was unbearable. After that, all my sister had to say was "Mary Worth" and I was more than happy to leave immediately.

Even now I think of Mary Worth when I find myself in a darkened room, even though I know she was a creation of my sister's overactive imagination. Her name was borrowed from a newspaper comic strip. Also, I realize that it was a story to keep me from pestering her.

I got my revenge years later when *The Exorcist* came out. My sister initially refused to take me, even with my parents' permission. She claimed that I would get too scared. Well, I saw the movie and slept soundly that night. When I awoke the following morning, I discovered my terrified sister in my bed with me. I remind her of this every chance I get, especially when others are around.

As for how I still feel about mirrors, I believe I'll keep that to myself for now.

#OTHERWORLDS

# A LETTER FROM A DISTANT MOTHER
## KRISTASIAH DANIELS

*Kristasiah says: I took Chapter 1 (from my book "Blood and Fangs") and rewrote it from the perspective of Sadey, Crystal's mother. While Sadey doesn't appear in Chapter 1, it later becomes known that her clairvoyant powers have given her the ability to watch over her daughter throughout her life. Jodi says: I took Kristasiah's Chapter 1 from "Blood and Fangs" and remixed it from Jay's perspective.*

Dear Crystal,

There are great things coming to you. Since you were a child, I took pride in you and knew you were destined for great things. Since your birth, I watched you from afar as your parent, and saw your future as your guardian. You are the brightest, strongest, and kindest warrior of Vampira—or at least you will be. Just like I did for centuries, you will lead many creatures to good things. There are many secrets in you, my sweet. Your power is strong and your heart is pure. Some may say it is only legend that a vampire of two halves of a being can hold the weight of two worlds. A vampire with such pride as this would commit treason to vampire-kind in the eyes of the old or dark, but in return would become a warrior with a power that flows through the blood of three hearts. That is your future, my sweet. You will learn your destiny in due time, but until then, follow your instinct, your judgment, and your heart.

—*SADEY*

# CHAPTER 1 REMIXED
## JODI NARDE

The night was like any other: quiet, except for our breath. I split from the pack and ran miles to our meeting place, but I could've run farther to get to her. She lay still under the brush of gold-green leaves, and as I approached, I swore her whispers were to the trees. "Did you come alone?" I had memorized her hands and reached for them, knowing they would feel heavy and chilled, but smooth like marble. She stood, her eyes meeting mine. Crystal had blue eyes—not like crystals, but more like liquid embers, marine-colored and running into a deep crater-lake in a forgotten Southern country. Despite our bloodlines, deep-rooted ancestry, and recent history, we came together on the first night of every month. Before I knew I could call it love, this girl struck a chord in me that tied our threads together quickly and at once. It was a feeling that felt as familiar as family, as if she belonged to my pack, though she would never run on four legs nor grow fur on her slender arms and neck. "The others went north; I took off westward here." I held her grip firm and tight, still subconsciously expecting she would become warm in my paws. But Crystal would never melt.

She reached into her leather jacket and pulled folds of paper from the inside pocket. "I found this today," she said, opening it up and handing it to me. "It's a letter from my mother." Scanning the pages, I skimmed over the words, reading what I could only barely make out in the moonlight. "She knows about us, Jay. I know it," Crystal whispered. "And it's okay. It's going to be okay." My father's raven eyes flashed in my mind. His garish teeth threatening her neck, sinking into skin, through every vessel, vein, nerve. I couldn't focus, couldn't even begin to feel the kind of calm Crystal was feeling. She had no idea what my pack, what my dad in particular, would do. I began feeling dizzy; my arms reached out in opposite directions, trying to regain balance. My eyes began to close halfway. Crystal grabbed my waist. "Jay! When was the last time you ate?" I wavered, fearing the comfort of the lush, damp ground. "I'm fine." I leaned on the tree, our old oak, our beloved meeting place. "You're the only thing driving me anymore, Crystal, if I'm telling the truth. When it's not you in my thoughts, I'm not sure what's really there." Crystal smiled and held my face in her hands. "I know. I know what you mean...but we have to stay healthy for each other and for ourselves. Listen to your mind—especially when it's trying to tell you what you need. If I can help get it for you, I will." I smiled half-heartedly, and nodded in agreement, my heart pumped like a summer balloon.

# NOVUS
## SAMANTHA YOUNG CHAN

The wind howled through dilapidated buildings, kicking up dust that made the gray atmosphere saturated with the dull color. Thick clouds obscured the sun, lighting the buildings in a hazy glow. The town square was destroyed: the cobblestones cracked, the statue taken over by a blue-tinged fungus. A crowd stood in the square, huddled together, fearful. A huge screen hung from the shell of a building that rocked back and forth with every breath of the wind.

"What do you think this is about?" a man from the crowd asked nervously.

"There's another tornado brewing. I can see it now," the woman next to him said in a quivering voice, pointing towards the horizon. A third companion clutched her arm.

"I don't want to die!" she wailed.

Further away, two girls stood isolated. Their backs faced the people around them, and they kept a distance even from each other.

"Do you think the government has a public announcement?" the taller girl asked. The soft lighting made her jet-black hair look a sickly gray.

Her friend shrugged, boredom overcoming her face. "Probably," she drawled, twirling a strand of her silvery hair. "Why else would we be here? Use your brain, Asako."

Suddenly, the screen before them crackled to life, and a hush overcame the crowd. The screen flashed once, and the image of a man appeared. He was dressed in a slightly rumpled suit, and had receding, gray hair. It seemed as if his mouth was set in a permanent frown framed by wrinkles. His glasses were crooked.

"People of Guanyin!" he boomed. "I have important news for you all. Look at the dying world around you. You have suffered long enough! We will all survive this!" Loud gasps sounded from the people, who looked at each other in shock.

"Our scientific team has discovered a way to save us all," the President continued. "It has been known that every ten thousand years, our planet aligns with another planet in our galaxy. When this happens, a portal opens in the center of our sky and we can travel to the other planet. My people, ten thousand years have now passed, and this time, we will be in alignment with Shen, as our scientists have reported. Citizens of Guanyin, our planet is dying. With this opportunity, we can migrate and survive!" As he spoke, his hands fluttered about him in a frenzied matter.

"Asako, we're actually going to live!" the silver-haired girl exclaimed happily, clutching Asako by the shoulders. Her friend took a step back.

"To be honest, Hanae, how do you know the President is right about this? Guanyin isn't completely dead yet. Maybe it'll have a comeback," she protested. Hanae made an annoyed sound in the back of her throat.

"Are you an idiot or something? Why don't you live here, then, while we all leave? We have no resources left to survive on. Maybe *you* can stay and make your own grave." She glared at Asako.

"Hey, I—" Asako interjected, but was cut off by the static sound of the television once again. The president's image reappeared. He cleared his throat.

"I have been informed that the planets will align in approximately six days!" he announced with a glint in his eyes. "We currently have too many government officials on duty, and I need your assistance right now. I am seeking volunteers to venture to this planet. Any who are interested should come back to this square tomorrow. Remember, our salvation has arrived!" And as quickly as it turned on, the television flickered off. The crowd started up conversation again.

"I'm definitely going to help!" a slight girl with green hair said cheerily.

"I can't believe this is happening," a young man with forest-green eyes whispered in awe.

"Asako, this is a miracle! Will you help?" Hanae cocked her head to the side, with a slightly wicked smile.

"I'm not sure yet...it'll be dangerous, won't it?" she replied, biting her lip.

"You're such a coward," Hanae taunted. "What a baby."

"You don't understand how big a risk this will be, Hanae! Would you actually be a pawn of the government and sacrifice yourself for them?" she snarled. Hanae just sighed and rolled her eyes.

"You over-analyze things all the time. This is something noble to do! You're helping your planet. Do you want everyone to die because you're too selfish to help?"

"We might end up dying anyway! What if this other planet is uninhabitable? You don't understand at all, Hanae!" she screamed, clenching her fists. A few people around them turned to stare.

"I would take the risk, if I were you," Hanae said with a shrug. "I plan on volunteering. If we do discover that we can live on Shen, then that's beneficial to the volunteers." She let out a dreamy sigh. "Think about how famous you could be!" Asako's angry expression faltered.

"I...I'll go with you, but I'm not guaranteeing that I'll take part in anything," she said, shifting her weight around.

"All right, I suppose that's good enough," Hanae replied.

# MARY POTTER AND THE QUIDDVILLE ACADEMY OF MAGIC MARY PORTES

Mary says: *This was a poem based on a free write my mentor Gillian and I did during a pair session. We asked the question: What if Harry Potter never went to a magical school? What if someone else did instead...*

Welcome to the Quiddville Academy of Magic,
Where all your dreams can come true.
Ruled by the infamous Mary Potter,
And her oh so evil crew.
She walks around with her hideous witch crown,
And struts across campus in her ugly purple gown.
Those pointy alligator shoes,
Steely eyes that do not amuse.
But even more pronounced is her pointy nose,
The one thing that is worse than her taste in clothes.
Ask around,
She is the most hated woman to be found
At the Quiddville Academy of Magic.
Isn't that tragic?
Mary Potter, evil principal,
Nowhere near being original.
Supposed founder,
Of the greatest magical school in France,
Brags about it and takes every chance.
A cackling laugh,
A scratchy, deep voice,
Strict and unreasonable rules were set
Rules that make all the students sweat.
Words don't begin to describe her cruelty.
She was trained in evil fluently.

She lived in a small cabin full of junk,
No wonder she was always in a funk.
Broken pipes, and rusty machines,
It was a very dirty house by all means.
The attic was her "room"
Always in a dark, hazy gloom.
Angry, alone, sad, depressed,
All emotions Potter never expressed,
Were held in that dark room of her heart,
Held captive, never meant to depart.
She wanted power and control,
But couldn't get it in that small hole
Of a home, of a place,
In a town that saw her as a disgrace.
She wanted everyone to know how it felt,
To be such a loser, to be so unknown.
When she learned of Harry Portes,
She couldn't wait to steal his magic, his fame
But most of all make someone take the blame.
You bet, she had no shame.
Harry Portes, oh so sweet,
His level of kindness was hard to beat.
Using spells to build houses, and feed the hungry,
He gave back to his whole country!
His parents were the same as he,
They helped a blind wizard begin to see.
As a reward he gave them fame,
Their lives were never to be the same.
Seen as heroes all year round,
It was almost as if they were crowned.
So Mary Potter, she snuck out one night,
Full of evil, full of fright.
To Harry's home she went,
In her clunky car, doors cracked and bent.
Armed with a knife, with a spell memorized,
It was almost like she was hypnotized.
She expected Harry to put up a fight,
Unlike her, he was full of no fright.
With a swift motion of her hand and the chanting of a spell
She was able to steal Harry's power and his parents as well.
By the time he woke up,
It was like in a dream,
He was no longer in his house, and he could not scream.
Help was no longer anywhere near,

He was full of never-ending fear.
Turns out he was inside the Quiddville Academy dorm,
Never to leave or ever see another life form.
His parents were nowhere to be found,
Potter had imprisoned them in a chamber underground.
No one will ever know what happened,
As a result, the whole country was saddened.
Mary Potter's ultimate goal
Includes more magic, and even more control.
To gain access to the whole wizard world
Take all the magic,
And make them do what she wants.
As for Harry,
He will never see his parents again.
But since she erased his memory,
He will never have a chance to complain.
As for the Portes family,
They will be remembered dearly,
For all their good deeds were all done gladly.
Presently, no one knows where they are.
They have searched near and far.
Meanwhile, Harry is forced to stay in the basement,
Forced to stare at pavement,
All day long,
His life is now a never-ending sad song.
All other students don't acknowledge him,
Guess his future is looking pretty grim.
With no memory or knowledge of where he is,
There is no point to this life of his.
Welcome to the Quiddville Academy of Magic,
Where all your dreams can come true.
Ruled by the infamous Mary Potter,
And her oh so evil crew.
Have your memory erased,
And by monsters be chased.
Everything is not what it seems,
Everyone can enter the Quiddville Academy of Magic,
They don't know, it is so tragic.
Everything seems peachy,
Everything seems clean.
But no one gets out.
They will never leave,
They'll forever stay under the reign of an evil Queen.

# A GUIDED TOUR OF MARY POTTER'S QUIDDVILLE ACADEMY OF MAGIC: PART I
## GILLIAN REAGAN

Gillian says: *I took the lead character of my mentee Mary's piece, and turned her into a good principal. I decided to write this piece like a student in the school was giving a new student a guided tour of the academy.*

Welcome to the Quiddville Academy of Magic, where all your dreams come true. Each classroom has a theme THUNKED UP IN DREAM???. See here, that's the biology room and its indoor jungle. There's the crazy-lookin' plants and parrots that snap and the tiger named Tim. But shh, he's snoozing in the corner.

Let's walk real quiet, on our toes and such, and sneak next door. That there's the English room and its crazy-tall library. Lookit all those books! 1.25 million of 'em, I tell ya, on stacks so high, you can't see the top. Which one would ya like to read? Students can spend all day reading if they like. Lookit them climbing the ladders. See, they get their exercise too.

Oh, do ya spy the lady in glasses and a pretty blue sundress reading on that giant green chair in the corner? That's Mary Potter, the founder and principal of the school. She found the abandoned building and got the whole community to pitch in. She's always got a goodie, a brownie or a cookie in that doctor's lab coat of hers to hand out to the smallos like you and me. But let's not bugger her now, we got so much more to see.

Mary Potter, she started the bakery! Lookit, like a grand Candy Land, ain't it? Lookit the barrel-bellied stacks puffing sugar-smelling smoke. Hm, so sweet in your lungs. Them students are bakin' cakes, calzones and brownies. Want to try one? So salty and sticky and sweet, they are. They hand them out to the kiddos who go hungry at night. We can help them later if ya like.

Got a stomach ache from all them sweets? We can go to the health clinic where the care is free. The nurses are nice ladies, no cold fingers on your tum, nope.

Are ya feeling blue? Let's go to the animal hospital next door. There's mangy dogs and one-eyed kittens kept off the streets and fed the finest foods. Lookit them lounging on fluffy couches, wrestling on warm grass. They get extra love at night because we all go down and cuddle them.

Speaking of sleep, maybe it's time for a nap. So much more to see: the math class with dancing numbers (theatrical ones, ya see) and computer school with them giant calculators. But for now let's lie down right here and just rest a laurel or two. I've only just met ya but I want to take care of you.

# MIRROR HORROR
## TEAMARÉ GASTÓN

"This is boring. Let's go outside and do something." With an exaggerated sigh my cousin Liam slid to the left allowing his head to fall on my foot. I paid no attention to him. He sat up and sighed even louder, letting out a huge groan.

"Why would you want to go outside? It's going to rain. Besides, too much sun isn't good for you."

He gave a stern look for a moment and then finally said, "Homebody, you're never up for anything."

I shrugged. Hamlet, my dog, got up from his bed in the corner of the living room and began to bark.

"Rachel, what's up with your dog?"

Hamlet sprung off down the hallway. From the end of the foyer Hamlet barked even louder. I stood and looked at Liam who returned my glance. We both walked down to see what Hamlet was barking at. At the foot of my bedroom door. Hamlet stood on two legs scratching at the base, then looked at us. Liam reached for the doorknob slowly.

"Will you just open it?"

I pushed Liam forward, sending my door flying open. A quick but brisk wind escaped my room. I looked up at the large bay window, yet I noticed that I had not left any of the panes open. I looked down at Hamlet who was growling at my mirror. My reflection in the mirror was me just like always—slender, wide hips, blood shot red hair covering lightly darkened hazel eyes.

Liam finally spoke, breaking my stare from the mirror. "People say that mirrors are doorways to alternate universes. I wonder if it's true."

"That's ridiculous; mirrors are just layers of melted sand."

He smiled at me. "Think what you want." He walked out of my room as I stood looking at my mirror intensely.

*Clink, clink, clink.* I took a step back into the center of my room and looked around. I checked beneath my bed, in my closet and behind my drawer. *Clink! Clink! Clink!* The noise grew louder, and I began turning in circles looking for anything that could be the cause.

"Stop already!" I screamed, panicking a little by this time. I kept flicking my eyes from my drawers to my closet to my floors, but I could not find the source of it. "Stop!"

I stepped back; my ankle bumped into the base of the mirror. Before I could stop, it flew forward and smashed into the ground. I quickly picked it up and stood it upright against the wall. I hurried to pick the pieces of glass off of the floor with my bare hands.

Beyond the few broken shards that stood at the bottom of the mirror I saw myself, except she was not me. Her features were sharp, demonic almost. I turned to run but she grabbed my arms and pulled me into the mirror. I pivoted but her grip on me was too tight. I opened my eyes to find my other self standing before me.

"You have wasted our time long enough!" She smiled revealing her hellish teeth. "You are fired. I will be taking over now."

She lunged at me, her hands reaching for my face. I ducked and grabbed her by the waist and brought her down to the floor.

"You're still trying? Give up!" She grinned. "It's all Renée from here."

Her hand wrapped around my neck as she struggled to get out from beneath me. Her nails dug into my skin. I placed one knee on her chest and with a sudden rush of adrenaline I began to slam my fist into her cheek.

"You are not me!" I screamed.

She grabbed my bangs and in a flash I reached for hers. With all my force I pushed her cranium against the floor making a loud thud. She stopped squirming beneath me, her arms flailed to her sides. Without hesitation I grabbed Renee's arm and pulled her to the mirror.

At that moment her eyes shot open, and she scrambled to her feet. Her eyes red, she swung her arm grabbing the tips of my hair. I ran forward and with my waist pushed her into the mirror. She ripped a chunk of my hair as she stumbled and fell through the mirror. Her eyes met mine one more time before falling into the dark abyss of the mirror.

Wiping the sweat from my forehead, I grabbed the mirror and exited my room. I reached the front door and with one pull opened it. The sunlight washed over me like a warm, victorious embrace. I saw Liam sitting at the foot of the porch with Hamlet.

He looked at me, jumping up in shock. "What happened to you?!"

An emboldened grin crept onto my face. "Let's go to the park. It doesn't look like it's going to rain anytime soon." I threw the mirror into the trash.

Liam now stood gazing at me confused. "You want to go to the park, now?"

I smiled, stretching my arms up. "Sure, why not?"

# IN SOOTH, I KNOW NOT WHY I AM SO SAD SAMANTHA PERSEPHONE MOZES

*This poem was inspired by the relationship between Antonio and Bassanio in Shakespeare's* The Merchant of Venice.

A gondola turned round the wavering street
That shimmered with his laughter, and the floods.
The way he laughs—describe it, analyze it:
A certain backward tossing of the head,
A tremor in the shoulders, how he knows,
Knows with the sureness of a comic hero,
That he will surely get what he deserves.
It is the glad, cruel laughter of a boy,

The sort of laugh to make a man do things
He oughtn't do; for instance, sign away
His heart—quite literally, his very flesh.
It is a laugh to sink at least five ships.
And one, and two, and three, and four, and five.
At last, Antonio's heavy ships are sunk.
And still he bobs, in gay uneven time,
A shimmer in the sinking Venice streets.

# #ANDWE'RE HOME

*Home is where the heart is,* or so the saying goes. But home can be so much more—and so much more complicated—than that.

The stories, memoirs, letters, and poems in this chapter cover topics as varied as returning to a childhood home, trying to feel at home in scary situations, seeking the comfort of home on the page of a book or notebook, and finding a home in one of New York's greatest landmarks as well as in the everyday subway stations and coffee shops of the city.

In fact, many of the pieces in this chapter are about New York City—which is, of course, at least one of the places that all the girls and women of Girls Write Now call home. One member of the GWN family, Lizzie Widdicombe, a reporter at the New Yorker who shared her personal and professional writing experiences at the GWN Journalism workshop, finds inspiration in "the eclectic mix of people you can meet and talk to on a good night out in New York...the East Village in particular...the convenience of the N, Q, R trains...the bedroom in the apartment I just moved out of...hot, humid weather reminding me of Memphis...." For other Girls Write Now writers, inspiration comes from the art and architecture of the city, the crowded subway cars, the excessive noise and bright lights, or even a ukulele player on the street.

And like this great city, the pieces of writing in this chapter are full of both familiarity and surprise. Throughout this anthology, and perhaps especially in this final chapter, the writers of Girls Write Now are speaking to our shared experience as New Yorkers, women, and writers—and yet, there is always something new to discover on each page.

— NORA GROSS
2012 MENTOR AND ANTHOLOGY COMMITTEE MEMBER

# SCHOOL'S CRAZE
## ERIKA ALFARO

Grace says: *During a conversation about fairytales, Erika and I decided to remix the classic story of* Little Red Riding Hood.

Jessie woke up thirty minutes earlier than usual for the first day of Junior High School. It was a special day meant to mark her transition from kid to teenager. But Jessie wasn't excited. Her stomach felt heavy with a mixture of nerves and terror.

She remembered all the stories she had heard during the summer about sixth graders being teased and worried that she had no friends at school that could help in case someone decided she would be the perfect person to be put in a garbage can. Her older brother Michael, who was in high school, told her tales of how he and his friends made two sixth-grade boys make animal noises and dance like fools simply for their own entertainment. "But don't worry Jessie, that kind of stuff only lasts for the first day," he said with a wicked smile.

Before stepping out the door she looked at the mirror hanging on the wall by the kitchen and felt even more nervous and unsure. As if wearing a uniform wasn't bad enough, hers looked as if she had borrowed it from Michael. Her Mom had bought these khaki trousers that looked like something her brother would wear to a formal event. Her legs swam in the oversized pants and her black shoes were less flattering than the orthopedic shoes she wore as a baby. But what terrified her most was the red polo shirt that felt huge on her skinny frame. All sixth graders had to wear one. There was no way she could hide or blend in with the seventh graders because that red shirt was a bull's eye. She was just missing a flashing sign that said, "Tease me!"

Jessie left home with her Mom, who said bye as she rushed to catch the bus for work. She would've liked her to bring her to school on the first day just like in elementary school, but that was impossible. She had to get in early since this was only her second week at that job. Jessie walked as slowly as possible, as if counting her steps. The school was only two blocks away from her house. After seven minutes she was in front of the courtyard, where everyone gathered on the first day. For a moment she thought of going back home but knew she would get in trouble if she did that. There were kids all around. The seventh and eighth graders had already found their friends from last year, and all the kids with red shirts stood quietly to the sides. She stayed close to the gate in case she had to run back home to flee an attacker.

After a few minutes, the teachers came out carrying signs for the different classes. All the kids got into rows according to their class. The eighth graders were surveying the new students to pick out their victims. They whispered and smiled at each other maliciously. After ten minutes they headed inside the school, which looked like a prison to Jessie with its drab gray columns and reddish walls. The windows and the courtyard were all fenced, minimizing any chance of an escape. She walked through the long hallways, memorizing all the exits. She finally arrived at her room and sat in the third seat of the second row. During the first period of class she was given instructions on where to buy gym class uniforms, which were also red. The bell rang, signaling it was time to switch classes. She walked as quickly as possible, but it was hard with all the other kids pushing and running—the typical craze of the first day.

Before she knew it, the end of the day had arrived. Jessie was relieved that she had survived, and that it wasn't as bad as she had imagined it. But when she left school, a group of kids hanging around outside stared at her. She wondered what to do if they chased her. Maybe she would scream, run, or, better yet, call her Dad to pick her up. But home was just two blocks away; how bad could it be? She sped up her pace, fearing that someone was following her. When she turned around, she saw four eighth graders walking behind her. She panicked and ran as fast as she could without looking back. She could hear their steps as they got closer and closer. Her legs felt so heavy that she barely made it.

She stopped at the front door to catch her breath and cautiously look back, but there was no one there, not a soul. She stood there with a blank expression in her eyes, as the September breeze swept through her hair.

The immense building stands its ground before us.

## TO FATHER'S HOUSE [AN EXCERPT]
### GRACE BASTIDAS

Andrea arrived at the airport clutching an old suitcase in one hand and a small piece of paper with her father's address in the other. She wondered if he'd even recognize her. He'd left Honduras seven years ago, when she was still a teenager, and not even the photographs they exchanged could do justice to the woman she'd become. She was able to buy the ticket with the last bit of money he sent in November, before he ended all communication without any explanation. The crimson wool coat was on loan from her boss at the hospital where she worked. She wasn't used to the cold, and the fear that something had happened to her father made the chill even worse as she stepped onto the curb. A gypsy cab driver pulled up, "Señorita, adonde? I will take you," he said. She imagined her dad, busting his tail trying to make a dollar, much like this man who spoke her language. They were both around the same age with a thick head of hair most men would envy. She handed him the note and got in the car, her red hem brushing the new snow resembled an open gash.

# MY ULTIMATE SELF
## LUCY TAN

#ANDWEREHOME

*The Metropolitan Museum of Art.* It is raining. Ceci and I arrive here, disappointed that our previous destination—the Bronx Zoo—wouldn't let us (two young girls both of age 15 out of the life expectancy that is 80) in. Heaving our underage bodies and squeaky sneakers through the crowds, we fill our cameras with pictures of gallery rooms, of foreign coins in fountains, and of ourselves. Two years later, we will pass each other in school hallways with our eyes averted.

*The Metropolitan Museum of Art.* Nick and I go here at the end of December during our Holiday Break. I present to him a holiday gift—his own name artistically drawn and framed. I had meant for him to hang it on his bedroom wall, but unless he is especially egotistical, his name is only something that won't leave my mind. We are in the crowded gallery among European oil paintings—Goya's Manuel de Zuniga stares back at us in his scarlet red jumpsuit. A string dangles playfully from the child's hands, as he stands before caged finches and mischievous cats. "...fleeting nature of innocence and youth," the description plaque reads. Two years later, I will try to make conversation—first eagerly, then halfheartedly—while he gives uninterested one-word answers.

*The Metropolitan Museum of Art.* "I like your metaphors; they're always so unexpected," she says, after reading my poem. Emily and I are sitting above a moat of serene water surrounding Egypt's Temple of Dendur. The colossal window presents to us a great sky, as light pours in, draping over our heads and shoulders, casting shadows upon our necks. We share our stories with each other, surrounded by sublime architecture and history. Two years later, we will be in separate coffee shops, writing different ways.

*The Metropolitan Museum of Art.* "One ticket please," I tell the lady. I get hold of the map, searching for Room 100—the first of many. Three minutes later, I am standing before the mummy of Pharaoh Artemidora, "her support decorated with imagery signifying rebirth." I lean my weight onto my left leg, then my right, moving this way through the gallery rooms—finally examining the art that had always been a backdrop. Then, a voice—"the museum is closing in five minutes." Two years later, I will be able to do the same with my lone self.

The immense building empties from behind me, as visitors trickle down the steps. Snowflakes fall steadfastly like souls from the sky. They vanish against my coat, like dissipating memories, as I walk downwards.

"Heilbrunn Timeline of Art History." *Francisco De Goya Y Lucientes: Manuel Osorio Manrique De Zuniga (1784-1792) (49.7.41).* Web. 5 Mar. 2012. <http://www.metmuseum.org/toah/works-of-art/49.7.41>.

"Mummy of Artemidora." *The Metropolitan Museum of Art.* Web. 5 Mar. 2012. <http://www.metmuseum.org/collections/search-the-collections/100004479>.

# THE ART OF THE MOMENT
## EMILY HAZEL

Before the pyramids, an hour ago,
and before that, Tiffany's glass sunset,
wisteria trailing over the water;
human lives remembered in purest marble;
di Giorgio Martini's ode to detail—
an entire room of two-dimensional illusion,
walls inlaid with precious wood
to mimic cupboards, shuttered doors
swung open, shelves inhabited by objects
fascinating and familiar; before all these,
when we first climbed the steps
to the triptych of doors
between the pillars of history,
the entrance to this sanctuary of art—
neither of us smelled it in the air.

The moment of departure,
like leaving the cool quiet
of an old, stone church, is always an odd leap
back to everyday realities, of which
we have suspended our awareness.
But this time, we return
not to the page where we left off
but to a world transformed.
Stepping outside, we walk into this
surprise party: showers of silent applause
from muffled skies, white confetti
deafening the city. Wonderstruck,
we tilt our faces up to the sky
as if to respond to some unspoken invitation.

Dusk is a tired eyelid growing heavy.
The snow spins slowly
in the glow of street lamps,
as if discovering itself—falling
and rising on gusts, carried on a whim.
Snowflakes whirl like memories
of cherry blossoms, then become
moths and mosquitoes, swarming
under the ballfield lights
on summer nights, then sand
shaken out of a picnic blanket,

then chads emptied carelessly
out of a three-hole punch
in an upstairs classroom,
till they become unsettled dust
from heaven's attic, evidence
there's always someone up there
sorting through the past.

Finally, we descend the steps.
Bound for a downtown express
at 86th, we turn and walk up Fifth,
against the wind now, faces
wet with snow, our footsteps tracing
the eastern seam of Central Park.
The trees lean over us on either side,
over the moss-loved walls
and all along the sidewalk, and we pass
underneath their branches
as if dancing through a tunnel
of outstretched arms—
another moment to be framed.

# COLUMBIA UNIVERSITY CHRISTMAS BASED ON THE POEM, "T'WAS THE NIGHT BEFORE CHRISTMAS" BY CLEMENT CLARKE MOORE [1823]

## GINA DIFRISCO + KATE TREBUSS

Kate says: *Gina and I met at Columbia for a campus tour and pre-Christmas hot chocolate date. I arrived with a copy of Clement Clarke Moore's classic poem* T'was the Night Before Christmas, *which it turned out Gina had never read before! Together Gina and I wrote a parody of the poem based on a quasi-fictional account of our outing.*

T'was the week before Christmas, many presents to wrap,
Kate and Gina met up at Columbia without any map.
They wandered around—Gina thought they'd get lost!—
Looking for a place to sit and write without any cost.

The college students stumbled 'round with eyes open wide,
With exams straight ahead there was no place to hide.
Coffee and soda and sugar to share,
Praying in the library that the exams would be fair.

With the lights getting dim and minutes racing by,
The big day was coming, undergrads starting to cry.
The TAs were ready, marking rubrics in hand,
Gleefully waiting together like a big marching band.

They hoped beyond hope their students wouldn't fail,
But were ready to give 'F's' to anyone, guy or girl.
The cafe was full, noses in books,
Students distracted from studying exchanged desperate looks.

Hot chocolate in hand, Kate sought out two seats.
Gina scanned the horizon for any retreats.
Lost in a labyrinth of chairs, unsure what to do,
The girls wondered if they'd ever find seats for two!

When out from the kitchen there arose such a clatter,
A barista chasing some mice that ran out, pitter patter.
Chairs toppled over, frantic people did shriek,
Half-empty cups flew through the air, landing on computer geeks!

Empty seats all around, after a massive stampede,
The ground puddled with coffee and splattered with tea.
Kate and Gina surveyed the room, what damage was done!
Now, though, there was space for THEM to have THEIR fun!

Happily, they lifted two chairs and set them into place,
Hunkered into their seats with their new found space.
They gave thanks to the mice as they sipped on their drinks,
The event was grand luck for them, whatever anyone else thinks!

Then came the joy of the holiday and much Christmas cheer.
Inspired by thoughts of Girls Write Now, there and here,
Gina and Kate took to writing this poem without any fear,
Only to say Merry Christmas and a Happy New Year!

Ms. Cranky finds that some days everyone seems in utter despair and, then, on others, they're quite cheerful. Take the Saturday before Daylight Savings Time, for instance.

On the subway on the way in from Brooklyn to Manhattan, it seemed that everybody was talking to one another. One conversation (Cranky thinks she might have started the whole thing by asking these guys what they were going to do with the antique shutters they were carrying) began and from there it turned into several conversations and lots of fun.

Then, after Cranky's meeting at GWN, the streets of Manhattan were teeming with people and Ms. Cranky quickly picked up the 'spirit' of the crowd though she was still a bit leery after December on the 'Santa Claus Dress-Up-Day' when she got walloped by a GIANT ELF on 7th Avenue!

But, this night, Saturday eve, was not like that—people were loud and laughing and talking but sweet too or they were quiet like Ms. Cranky and 'in awe' as if they had never seen the lights of Broadway before—but, sometimes, it's like you're all 'new' and it's your first time and you're spellbound all over again. That's how Saturday evening in the city felt—surprising, wondrous.

And, Ms. Cranky treasures many subway stations for their music—and is never disappointed in the "F, N, R" etc. station under Macy's at 34th and 6th Avenue and that Saturday night, the musicians (with lots of horns) were tremendous, and the audience was real happy and moving and grooving. This group really got into it and there was even a tuba player—a tuba player! Ms. Cranky sometimes tips just because the artist has to carry heavy equipment down into a subway station. But, these guys were fabulous and Cranky's real sorry she couldn't get close enough to find out the group's name—next time, promise!!!

Cranky feels honored to live in a city where you never quite know what's going to happen next (which, as we all know, is not always good!), but sometimes it's just one wonderful surprise after another! Ms. Cranky had been previously thinking that everybody looked pretty gloomy and down on their luck, but that Saturday it all changed back and life POPPED UP and talent asserted itself and people carrying antique shutters started several conversations and, then, we all gave helpful tips to tourists.

Life, positive life and music happened and for Ms. CRANKY, at least, the gloom was gone. Musicians performed, people who weren't musicians were friendly and talked and, like the crocuses coming up through the hard wet earth, New York on that Saturday early evening—BLOOMED, zoomed, flowered—came up from under —becoming all that it's capable of being—spirited, thoughtful, kind, funky, mysterious, talented, musical, colorful, ironic, funny, endearing and forever interesting—a bouquet of spring flowers of its very own being.

# I TURNED THE PAGE
## MARIAH TERESA AVILES

Allison says: *I was inspired by the way Mariah used writing as a metaphor throughout her poem, so I decided to write a poem using writing's mirror image — reading — as the structural concept.*

Once I started writing our new chapter, I couldn't help but re-read it over and over again.
Kept writing new pages with new ideas representing new places with new memories,
But as much as I kept writing, I wanted to go back and erase a few words,
A few phrases,
A few periods,
Pauses
Unfortunately, I wrote in pen;
Permanent ink,
So what was said and done simply remained said and done.
It's as if the positive and negative made up two different stories,
Attracting, yet repelling one another.
As I sit back and reminisce, I could remember...
I didn't wanna turn the page;
In fact, I did everything I could not to.
I didn't anyway.
You caressed my hand,
Slowly but surely and towards the end,
Forcefully took it and turned the page
With me,
For me.
You crossed your last *t,*
Dotted your last *i,*
Placed your last period and
Numbered our last page 618, not knowing that was the last,
Dreaming of ending on forever,
Thinking that page,
That story
Was to be edited, added to,
BUT DID YOU FORGET I WAS THE WRITER OF THE STORY,
Yeah, our story?
You made up most of it,
Sometimes adding more characters than it needed
You helped me write it.
And so did they.
But I still give you credit.
Honestly, had this story not been written the way it was,
I wouldn't be here today.
Page 618 is all torn because I keep contemplating whether I should go back and edit,

Keep writing...
Or if I should just turn the page and move on.
When you felt like you should've,
You crossed your last *t*,
Dotted your last *i*,
Placed your last period, and I have done the same.
I have turned the last page of our last chapter,
Our anecdotes,
Our story,
Left written in print, permanent ink,
But our future unwritten,
Never to be published because it will never mean to exist.
Instead, I've started a new page,
A new chapter...numbered 928.
New words,
New phrases,
New sentences,
New songs.
Once again, I am the author of this story.
But maybe this time,
My new character will grab a pen and help me with this one.
Either way, it's being written slowly, already filled with unwanted commas,
Pauses,
But I keep writing,
He keeps humming.
A NEW CHAPTER IS BEING WRITTEN,
My story,
Our story,
Our stories aren't finished...

# READING A GOOD BOOK IN THE CITY
## ALLISON ADAIR ALBERTS

Beginning at page 618,
I sat on a cold metal folding chair in Bryant Park.
The sun filtered through the leaves,
casting intricate patterns on the grass and dirt,
reminding me of snowflakes cut from coffee filters.
Around 723, the afternoon became gray:

the sun wavered, uncertain of itself, finally hiding
behind the big poufs of the cumulonimbus. The rainbow parade,
spread across the lawn in springtime fashions of
reds and blues and pinks and yellows and lilacs,
echoing in their costume the skin of the newborn flowers,
closed their books, packed their picnics, folded their blankets, and left.
The green square became green again in their absence.
I didn't leave. Instead, I walked around the corner and
moved indoors, passed between the lions,
climbed those noble, marble stairs,
and wandered into the reading room, where I read on until 903.
I decided to go home at the end of chapter sixty-three.
Between pages 904 and 928, I rode the train.
Twilight passed in the rainstorm, and the moon had risen behind the clouds.
Bursting out of the tunnel, the train rattled through Harlem,
high above the glossy wet streets. The traffic lights, like glow worms,
benignly changed: green, yellow, red. The river reflected wobbly images
of white light, streetlight fractured into gently floating illuminated discs.
At the second stop, I got off.
It was too dark, and impractical, to read on the walk home.
Instead, I turned the story over and over in my mind, sorting detail with like detail,
rearranging events to illuminate what had previously seemed mysterious.
I climbed my stairs, unlocked my door, and settled into the warmth of the
incandescent light, wrapping myself in a red and green quilt,
plunging deep into the page.

# CAMERA LENS
## SHARLINE DOMINGUEZ

Nancy says: *Our pieces came about from a writing prompt suggested by Sharline where
we had to write about a character in an uncomfortable scenario. We wrote long form pieces
and then used the erasure technique from the poetry workshop to cut various lines, and then
revised from there to create these prose poems.*

Thirty-five minutes ago, she was on the roof of the James Hall building,
counting cigarette butts and cheap, broken lighters.
But now, by the half- frozen pond on campus,
Valerie stands with her hands in her pockets under trees dressed in pink
blossoms and green leaves,

shaded, quiet, clueless, and busy picking her cuticles, sucks blood in
crevices of her fingernails, licks her lips,
unseen by preoccupied college students and teacher assistants.

About two yards across the pond, the school film club's director hears
Valerie feverishly chewing on a dirty fingernail, looks at her from across
the pond, and stops filming his 1940s war movie.
He proceeds to fix cameras on her every move,
spying on Valerie, lonesome Valerie, picking her cuticles under trees
dressed, defying the "conventional" image of beauty.

Capturing this girl is unintended by the camera crew,
but something compels them to draw their digital affections to Valerie.
They aren't the only ones looking at her.
Alex, head of the Jenga club, approaches Valerie, staring in amazement as
she precisely picks her fingertips, her fingers perfect for moving blocks.
Such a strange girl.
Alex holds out his hand to her, and she assures him that it will not be long
before someone else joins them too. Magic.

Simply her own individual, never seeking attention, unlike a camera that
always needs something to focus on. Valerie.

## NEW YORKERS
### NANCY MERCADO

For awhile he had called her "the borscht lady,"
but now she was just Sylvia.

She waited patiently at the lunch counter,
her short legs dangling from her usual circular stool.
Numerous bags were at Sylvia's feet, but she was no bag lady,
just someone who couldn't say no to all of the wonderful books offered to
her by her favorite librarian.

Ruben brought over the soup,
and she closed her eyes and took several loud sips.
She was enjoying the taste, yes,
but he knew that his soup also had the power to transport her
back to her Bubbe's small apartment in Poland. She had told him as much.

In that way, they were both true New Yorkers, thinking of home, while
having made their home elsewhere.

Sylvia reminded him of his own abuelita,
who carried mountains of newspapers in overflowing canvas totes,
and made a consomé Xochitl that Ruben had never been able to replicate with
success.

When the bowl was empty, Sylvia praised the soup as always,
then asked Ruben the usual questions about his children,
and when he would return to Oaxaca to visit that grandmother of his.
The truth

It was funny,
She came in for his soup which reminded her of home,
and he looked forward to her visits because she reminded him of a soup that
he hadn't tasted in years.

Why he was able to make the borscht but not the consommé, he would never know.
Maybe Sylvia just had that kind of effect on people.

Amy says: *Christina's poem was created from fragments of real New York Times headlines in 2012. My piece is a news story created from Christina's fragments, imagining how a poem crafted from glimpses of the news would be reconstituted and reported as news.*

#ANDWEREHOME

No Barrier to Love

In New York  A Poet  Is

Anxiously  Wooing  A

Ukulele Player

Grasping at  and  Hunting for

A Romance With Risk  of a  Brief

Affair

Fantasy

All Over Again

Flashes

in Which Bodies Lurch Backward

in Silence

# MAN, UNTETHERED, BELIEVES THERE IS NO BARRIER TO LOVE AMY DILUNA

NEW YORK - A poet was anxiously wooing a ukulele player Wednesday night on 23rd St.

"He was grasping at and hunting for a romance," said a source close to the situation, who asked that her name not be used.

Conflicting reports have emerged from the incident. Some present say there was risk of a brief affair, while others dismiss the allegations as "fantasy."

This was not the suspect's first foray into these treacherous waters.

Documents obtained by the New York Times indicate the man, described as a "dreamer," has attempted this type of thing before.

"It's happening all over again," said the source. "We're all just wondering: When will he learn?"

According to the police report, the man described to officers what went through his head in that first moment he saw the raven-haired musician in the bar. "There were flashes," he said, as though struck by lightning, or at least, by contact with a loose vacuum cord. As bodies of the other bar patrons "lurched backwards," the woman, it seemed to him, was the only one left standing.

The bar, which had been bustling on the snowy evening, was suddenly blanketed "in silence," the man said.

A psychiatric evaluation has been ordered.

#ANDWEREHOME

# THE LAST LETTER I'LL WRITE YOU
## EMELY PAULINO

Jess says: *Earlier this year, Emely wrote a poem addressed to New York that she felt was a real culmination of the discussions we've had this year about how and why our unique city becomes a character in our writing. I loved the poem so much that I decided to remix it by turning the first line on its head and going from there. Emely then remixed the remix and turned this emotionally charged piece back into a prose letter. We had fun with this one!*

Dear New York,

I love you, with all your arrogance and elegance.

Nothing comes before you, and I'm sure, like so many, I've tried to break through to you. You put yourself on a pedestal, but I didn't care. The way you carried yourself was so misleading. One minute of your time already made me feel like it was forever, but you quickly moved on and my forever was forgotten. Like an idiot, I kept chasing after you even though people warned me to stand clear of your closing doors. Please, don't ever treat me like that again.

I don't know what's worse: The way you treat me, or not hearing from you at all. I hate to say it, but I feel empty without you. Even if I tried to forget you, I'm constantly reminded about you wherever I go. For those few times when we do get to spend time together, you keep me waiting. In the blazing July sun, or brisk December evening; you don't care. The least you could do is walk me home or save me a seat on the train. I don't think I ask for too much. Instead you push me aside, leaving me no choice but to accept that no matter where I go with you, someone has already been there.

And I still wait for you, for that one minute with you when your embrace feels like home.

Love,

*Emely*

## WHY I STAY
### JESS PASTORE

I hate you
with your unexpected beauty,
your unearned grace building out of cacophony.
I hate the expectation of glamour
and the raised eyebrows at the expense.
I hate the trash, the pains you take to tart yourself up,
only to roll in it and sigh a disgusting,
echoing,
satisfied sigh
that leaves everyone I come from
wondering where I'm going,
why I'm so committed to finding that
perfect moment within you.
I hate that the mornings when the shrieks
at the bus stop are already filling my ears,
the days when I revel in giving up and
relegating you to cliché,
are also the days
when the pear trees burst into bloom
along St. Mark's
in a riot of praise for your unexpected moments
and the reason I could never leave you.

Not for a house on a hill surrounded by orchards.

# #BEHINDTHE SCENES

As writers, we spend an awful lot of time alone in front of the blank page, waiting for the muse to strike. But at Girls Write Now workshops, we act as one another's muses, inspiring each other with our mutual presence and the fact that, young or old, we are all here facing the blank page together.

Of course, at GWN workshops, the blank spaces on the page are preceded by thoughtful and innovative writing exercises, specially designed to be open enough to allow us to respond freely, and structured enough so that we can bounce our creativity off the edges. They start with a small piece of writing and then build progressively off one another so that when we leave the workshop, that original building block has turned into the beginning of a longer piece or project. And when we leave, we are tired—the good kind of tired that only comes after a day of good hard work—but energized by the wonderful women around us to keep working in the genre of writing we learned about that day, which is often something, like Crime Fiction, that we have never tried before.

Our overarching theme for the workshops this year was *Remix*. We sought to look at our own writing in a new way, to take our work and transform it into something different and exciting, and, along the way, to learn some of the digital skills that will aid us as writers in this changing world.

We created erasure poetry online at our Found Poetry workshop. We transformed personal stories about eating into blog posts at the Food Memoir workshop. At the Journalism Profiles workshop, we mined our own lives for subjects and then posted online 140-character Twitter versions of the profiles we wrote. At the Transmedia Storytelling workshop, we were moved by a series of multimedia web projects to remix one of our own pieces of writing into a work consisting of social media, video, audio, blog posts, digital images, or animation.

We also began working with Figment, a website where we share our work with the GWN community, receiving or giving comments and critiques on peers' writing, during those lonely times between workshops.

And then, the final remix: all of our experiences over the program year written, rewritten, condensed, and filtered into this book that you hold in your hands. It's been a transformative year at Girls Write Now. We hope you draw inspiration from our endeavors as we draw inspiration from each other. Use these exercises to try a little remixing of your own!

— MAYA FRANK-LEVINE,
PROGRAM ADVISORY COMMITTEE CURRICULUM CO-CHAIR

# FICTION: CRIME WRITING
## OCTOBER

The Crime Fiction Workshop asked mentees and mentors to contemplate what makes a crime novel so compelling? And then they were asked to commit murder.

We fleshed out our characters by writing about their daily routines, favorite outfits, skills, flaws, secret desires—and then murder our beloved new friends. The Crime Fiction Workshop deconstructed key elements that make up a crime novel, and together, mentees and mentors learned how to weave these elements into a complex plot line with twists, turns, suspects, murder weapons and red herrings.

Guest authors Robin Wasserman and Katia Lief shared with us their secret weapons for crafting nail-biting novels.

By the end of the workshop, mentees and mentors had each crafted an original crime novel scene of their own. Luckily, we were feeling warm and fuzzy, having just met our new mentor and mentee partners for the year, because the work we shared aloud was chilling! We headed into our weekly pair sessions bursting with new ideas and appreciation for uncovering the secrets of our characters and ourselves.

## GUEST AUTHORS

KATIA SPIEGELMAN LIEF is the author of nine novels published by both large and small publishers. Best known for her internationally acclaimed crime novels, she has also written women's and young adult fiction. Katia is a graduate of Sarah Lawrence College, with an MFA from The City College of New York, and teaches fiction writing at The New School in Manhattan. She lives with her family in Brooklyn, New York.

ROBIN WASSERMAN'S *Seven Deadly Sins* series, recently adapted into a Lifetime original movie, features seven teens "determined to get what they want when they want it." Other books include *Hacking Harvard, Chasing Yesterday,* and the dystopian *Cold Awakening Trilogy.* She's putting the finishing touches on her new novel, *The Book of Blood and Shadow,* a murder mystery that crosses continents and centuries.

#BEHINDTHESCENES

## FROM THE WORKSHOP

The dresser had an arranged line of pictures in silver frames. Various faces of her family trapped in each one. In the middle, it was her in a long white strapless wedding dress. The top wrapped tightly against her breasts. A strip of diamond separated the upper portion from the rest of the dress. Its elegance displayed against the white marble steps. Little flower patterns ran down the dress in the back. Her hair was out, flowing and framing her shoulders. Next to her stood her husband. He looked insignificant. His smile seemed empty, his body nothing more than average. Their bodies did not fit together, his hand awkward around her waist. He had a crooked smile with eyes that squinted too much. There was a clear imbalance of passion. She was such a passionate person, flawed but that never had any effect on her. I wondered why she had chosen him. We had spent so many years in each other's company yet she had faded away to

JOANNE LIN

marry him. Of course, she had come back to sleep with me. She had this innate desire for danger and adventure. I ground my teeth together as I stared at the picture. Her husband wasn't the foe here, he was a victim. The fact that she hadn't devoted herself to me, as I had to her, made my eyes sting with tears. Her face seemed cold and empty now, her body closed off from me. I sat up and a noise escaped from her.

"Joe?" she whispered, her voice weak.

I swung my legs to my portion of the bed and picked up my jeans. My hands trembled as I pulled out an object wrapped in a black leather case.

"Joe? What's wrong?" She sat up and began to move her body towards me. The bed creaked with every motion.

I quickly pulled out the knife from the case and ran it against my palm. Blood oozed out. There was no pain, just a sting as the oxygen seeped into the rip of my skin. I turned to her and placed my hand on her arm. She looked confused, her eyebrows slightly raised. She bit her bottom lip and her eyes darted to where I had left my mark. A line of blood trickled down diagonally across her pale skin.

# BLOG REVIEW:
# SUSPENSE, PERSPECTIVE, AND WRITING ADVICE
# GEORGIA SOARES

The lights fade out and dim sunlight enters through the windows. From far behind, a woman comes silently, dressed in a discreet beige coat. She looks around suspiciously, keeping her hands in her pockets. As soon as she reaches the front, she turns back and takes out a magnifying glass, as if to search for clues, announcing: "Don't move! FBI!" She looks serious and alert, as if she really were from the FBI.

This is how our first Girls Write Now workshop about crime fiction opened, as a way to personify the investigation and suspense we would talk about. The workshop was a great opportunity to learn about how to write a story full of suspense, crime and details that draws the reader's attention. We learned how to insert essential plot elements, and we had the delight of hearing Katia Lief's advice on how to write books. It was invaluable to learn how details serve as the catcher of attention and how the first page can determine whether a reader will be engaged to continue—or not.

Using the elements of crime fiction in an unusual way can make a story stand out. For instance, try to create a different setting. Write about a crime scene somewhere unpredictable, like on an airplane or during a football game. Mislead the reader into believing the wrong suspect is the killer and surprise them with the truth. The killer could be the investigator himself who is trying to point the case in the wrong direction. Pay attention to whether it makes sense, though—the killer cannot be the elderly neighbor who only knitted throughout the story! Using creativity to write an unexpected story will make you stand out.

"From a poem comes a poem," began the Found Poetry Workshop. Mentees and mentors spent the day finding inspiration where they least expected it—in a phrase read backwards, in scientific text, in the unknown words of a Swedish poem, in lines we borrowed from one another—and used them like pieces of a collage to paste together a surprisingly new and original poem.

We learned what an erasure poem is: you start with a source text and delete words or phrases not wanted until what remains is a poem. Using a website designed to create erasure poems, 60 poets painstakingly deleted one word at a time until we were left with beautiful relics like this:

> *this bellowing comes every hundred years*
> *And the mountain is sick*

Poet Matthea Harvey shared with us her unique perspective on words, and poet Idra Novey spoke of the power of poetry to take us out of our own lives and into another's, if only for a stanza or two.

We translated from Swedish, using only the look and sound of the words, and formed groups, taking turns writing line after line until a collaborative poem was born. Then we each selected another author's line, on which to base a brand new found poem. We lost our old preconceptions about poetry, and we found a new way to be inspired.

*This year's Found Poetry workshop was held in honor of poet, mentor, and teacher Audry McGinn.*

## GUEST AUTHORS

MATTHEA HARVEY is the author of *Sad Little Breathing Machine* (Graywolf, 2004) and *Pity the Bathtub Its Forced Embrace of the Human Form* (Alice James Books, 2000). Her third book of poems, *Modern Life* (Graywolf, 2007) was a finalist for the National Book Critics Circle Award and a New York Times Notable Book. Her first children's book, *The Little General and the Giant Snowflake*, illustrated by Elizabeth Zechel, was published by Tin House Books in 2009.

IDRA NOVEY is an American poet, professor, and translator. She is author of *The Next Country* (Alice James Books, 2008), which was a Kinereth Gensler Award winner and received a starred review in Publishers Weekly, and the translation *The Clean Shirt of It*, which won a PEN Translation Fund Award. Her honors include the 2008 Amy Award from Poets & Writers, and fellowships from the Poetry Society of America Chapbook Series and the National Endowment of the Arts.

#BEHINDTHESCENES

SOPHIA CHAN

Scraps will beg
someday I will see
farewell my son
some joke
battling in rags
constant cry of bitter passion
*tie me down*
*some bliss*
*unknown heaven*
heartfelt kindness
no longer will I sit silent
decked out in drag

#BEHINDTHESCENES

## BLOG REVIEW:
## TRUTH. LOVE. LAUGHTER. LIFE.
## MARCELA GRILLO

At our Girls Write Now Found Poetry Workshop, I was reminded of why I love poetry so much: it's honest, unadorned, and so rich with feeling. Being a writer you kind of figure that poetry is just spilling out what you feel onto a page, but often the most inspiring words are the most unexpected. A poem about your favorite place becomes a sacred memory: in this workshop my grandfather became a beacon to lost traveling souls, and his porch in Puerto Rico became a safe haven.

What if a poet comes up with a line you fall in love with, a line you cannot forget? What if it is a line that sparks you to create your own poem? Amazingly, such a type of poetry exists. Found Poetry is poetry that takes words from somewhere else and reorganizes them to form a new creation. Whether with a single line or a whole paragraph, we writers have this innate ability to let our unique voices be heard, separately or together.

My fellow talents and I (mentees and mentors) sat together in a circle and faced a large paragraph of words we hadn't seen before. We then crafted what is called an erasure poem, which is created by removing words from another author's piece. In those moments, when we yelled out to get rid of this word, or leave that word, I felt that I was a part of something fabulous. It was the first time that I was getting to know my peers through their writing.

You hold out your hand, and close your eyes. Something light and delicate is placed in your palm. It smells faintly, deliciously. You put the item in your mouth. Your tongue picks up the taste of cocoa powder, then, quickly, the heavy flavor of dark chocolate fills your mouth. You succumb to your temptations and bite through the chocolate truffle to find a rich creamy filling. You open your eyes to a room full of mentees and mentors, eyes closed, chewing thoughtfully.

The Food Memoir Workshop used our memories of favorite meals or sought after treats and our sense of taste to access deep memories connected to childhood, family, relationships. We used these memories to tell a story of growth, writing from the moment of the memory and then reflecting on how the meaning of the moment has changed over time, has taught us something about ourselves. Inspired by the writings of guest author Julie Powell, and the courage of guest authors Gabrielle Hamilton and Cheryl Lu-Lien Tan, we closed the workshop by turning our short memoirs into blog posts, considering the implications, and power, of sharing our memories with the rest of the world.

## FROM THE WORKSHOP

SHANNON DANIELS

"Remember Kenneth's wedding?" Mommy would ask the table, wearing a smile waiting to be born into a laugh.

"Oh God, who could forget that?" my Yee Ma would mutter with a chuckle.

She wasn't really my Yee Ma, my mother's sister; she was my cousin's. But everyone on my mother's side of the family was so close that it didn't even matter. Distant relatives smiled upon me like uncles and aunts, and I was tied to cousins like they were sisters.

One cousin, Nina, would interject right on cue. "Can we please not talk about this? Just thinking about what grandma did to that chicken makes me queasy."

"What happened?" I'd urge my mother, even though

## GUEST AUTHORS

GABRIELLE HAMILTON is the chef/owner of PRUNE, which she opened in New York City's East Village in October 1999. PRUNE has been recognized in all major press, both nationally and internationally, and is regularly cited in the top 100 lists of all major food magazines. She is most recently the author of the *New York Times* bestseller *Blood, Bones & Butter: The Inadvertent Education of a Reluctant Chef.*

After a misspent youth involving loads of dead-end jobs and several questionable decisions, JULIE POWELL, author of *Julie & Julia*—made into a major motion picture by Nora Ephron starring Meryl Streep and Amy Adams—has found her calling as a writer-cum-butcher. She lives in Long Island City, Queens, when she isn't in Kingston, NY, cutting up animals.

CHERYL LU-LIEN TAN is the New York-based author of *A Tiger in the Kitchen*, a memoir about discovering her Singaporean family by learning to cook with them. She was a staff writer at the *Wall Street Journal*, *In Style* magazine and the *Baltimore Sun*. In March/April 2010 and also in December 2010, she was an artist in residence at the Yaddo artists' colony, where she completed her memoir.

I'd already heard the story thousands of times. I loved to hear it, but I loved even more to hear her tell it.

"Years ago–you were too young to remember–your uncle and aunt got married and received all sorts of gifts: bouquets of gladiolas, baskets of oranges..." she waved her hand at each detail, tossing them into the air.

"And a chicken," Nina would say, "a whole, live chicken!"

"A Chinese tradition," Mommy would explain. "But anyway, Po Po prepared the cutting board," her voice grew longer and deeper, "and raised her thick, black kitchen knife..."

She'd pause and watched my horrified, but mesmerized face. Then she'd drag me in further.

"–and off with his head!"

I winced.

"But, that chicken wouldn't give up without a fight."

"I was there!" Nina would moan. "It ran around the living room, headless, dripping blood all over the linoleum." She'd turn to Mommy. "Can you believe it? Po Po wanted us to catch the thing!"

Then, forgetting the tension of the story for just a second, the table erupted into laughter over the pure hilarity of the situation. A chicken, I thought, shaking my head. A whole, live chicken.

"And did you?" I beseeched.

"No," her cheeks were scarlet, "but Po Po did."

I could definitely imagine that. Not once had I ever seen her face shape into anything remotely close to disgust or fear. Po Po took the job–whatever it was–and the job got done.

Thinking about her always reminds me that she isn't with us now. I try not to imagine her in that place where lost things, lost people, go–the place I can never really seem to find no matter how hard I look. But there's something about the way my mother's eyes shine when she tells a story, how she shares that same fearlessness of embracing the truth. And when I see that, it's like the lost hide-and-seek games, the misplaced cell phone, the disappeared hats don't matter anymore.

When I see my mother tell a story, I know that I've found that place. It's not a place where lost things go; it's a place where things that wait for you go. When you're finally ready to see them, they appear to you, in that fresh, crisp way only the unpredictable can master. Sometimes it happens in a flash. Sometimes it just brews.

## BLOG REVIEW:
## AN AWE-INSPIRING CRAFT TALK WITH JULIE POWELL
## LARISSA HERON

The December Craft Talk with Julie Powell was one-of-a-kind with humor and wit. She told the Girls Write Now community about the trials and tribulations of becoming a successful writer, and entranced us all. She spoke of her experiences while writing *Julie & Julia*, including her obsession with cooking (and blogging) every recipe in Julia Child's *Mastering the Art of French Cooking* in one year. From loosely-written blog posts came a national bestseller, which inspired the popular movie of the same name.

Listening to such a well-known writer talk about the writing and editing process was a fascinating experience. She stated that there is a fine line between being sensitive to people in her memoir and telling the honest truth. She learned early on in her memoir career that even if changing a story works for the book, it could damage friendships and turn the story into something dangerously untrue.

Julie was one of the first writers to turn her blog posts into a book. She started something new—something worth recognizing. However, many publishing companies wanted to simply print the blog posts as a book, which she rejected. When she finally had the opportunity to rewrite the blog posts and turn them into a full-length book, she gladly took the challenge. Nevertheless, she soon realized that creating a book rather than writing blog posts was much more difficult. Julia succeeded because of her unique style. She inspired us all to do something extraordinarily new and original, like no one before us.

## GUEST AUTHORS

VANESSA GRIGORIADIS is an award-winning, long-form magazine writer whose body of work includes numerous feature articles and cover stories (many of them profiles). She is a contributing editor at *Vanity Fair, Rolling Stone* and *New York Magazine*, where she began her career. Vanessa's profile of fashion designer Karl Lagerfeld for *New York Magazine* won a National Magazine Award in Profile Writing in 2007.

LIZZIE WIDDICOMBE has been working in the Talk of the Town department at *The New Yorker* since 2006. At Harvard, Lizzie studied 19th-century American Literature and wrote her thesis on the American writer, Henry James. She has said, "It turns out that History and Literature were good preparation for journalism. If you substituted, say, Carla Bruni for Henry James, you could argue that things are more or less the same."

## JOURNALISM: PROFILES MARCH

The Journalism Profiles Workshop explored the art of using the fine details of a person's life to tell a meaningful story about her or his character.

We began the workshop writing about the morning routine of a person we knew well, describing their choice of breakfast, their outfit, and their mood. We then explored examples of print, online, and audio profiles, studying the use of "telling details," the specific details that evoke a strong sense of mood or personality. We expanded the profiles we started with our own telling details, then dove in deeper, thinking about *why* we chose the subject we did; what about her or him makes their story compelling to others.

Guest authors Vanessa Grigoriadis and Lizzie Widdicombe shared with us stories from the field, Vanessa of her interview with Justin Bieber, and Lizzie of her day with Taylor Swift. Our own team of journalism mentors joined into the conversation to share their tried and true methods for conducting successful interviews. The take away: Always have two audio recorders running!

Although the room was fluorescently lit, the lights seemed to dim once he cleared his throat. A hush came over the audience, and Ryan Dieringer introduced what he was about to sing to his SAT class. "How about some Lauryn Hill?" The girls automatically nodded their heads in unison —-- they didn't care what came out of his mouth; they just wanted to hear it. With another throat-clearing, the show began. "You're just too good to be true..." His voice was light as air, and as he continued, the crowd's eyes widened in awe while his eyes closed in concentration. "Can't take my eyes off of you. You'd be like heaven to touch, I wanna hold you so much..." Whether Ryan knew it or not, his soft-spoken, melodic voice had officially put everyone under a trance—a trance that would soon be broken once he hit the chorus. "I need you baby! And if it's quite alright, I need you baby, to warm a lonely night!" he bellowed out. His raspy acoustics bounced off every wall of the room and into the girls' spines, who sat alert at the sudden change. In that moment, with his eyes shut tight, hands clenched and vocal chords pulsing through the veins of his neck, Ryan Dieringer's two lives—SAT teacher by day, indie rocker by night—collided.

Having grown up in New Jersey and New York, Ryan's musical journey began in the church choir he attended weekly as a child. Even though he had been singing his whole life, it never became a serious, personal thing until his sophomore year in high school. "By the time I was a senior, I had a band with my friends," he says. "That's when things started to get really fun, and I started to think that maybe music was for me." The very band that was formed in his senior year has transformed into Ryan's biggest passion. After a name change and several style transitions, the group, which includes drummer Sam McDougle and guitarist Daniel Maroti, is now known as The Powder Kegs. "We started off playing folk and that was the first time I started to play fiddle music," he recalls. However, The Powder Kegs weren't playing traditional folk— they brought a punk rock feel to it, which was vital to their first performances, on the sidewalks of New York and beyond. "We started off being street performers, busking in the streets, and we did that for years. We'd play super fast because it attracted large crowds."

That frenetic energy—along with the civil war imagery an actual powder keg conjures—inspired the name. On the street, more energy meant more money. "We would sing at the top of our lungs. This is the kind of stuff that you do to get money on the street but we also did it on stage. The Powder Kegs was the kind of energetic image that we wanted."

Besides providing The Powder Kegs with his vocals and bass playing skills, Ryan is also the songwriter for the band. Surprisingly enough, he doesn't typically write pen to paper, but rather thinks of things and manages to remember them later. "I write very much from the subconscious, so I'll discover as I go, things that are on my mind," he says. "You don't have to solve big problems in your songs. You just have to express a feeling, a moment, so that's a non-premeditated kind of experience." Ryan believes it's important that a song is a place of discovery for the artist, "not a place where they tell you something that they've already discovered, but that they join you in the process."

CHRISTINA BUTAN

#BEHINDTHESCENES

# BLOG REVIEW:
## A MENTEE REFLECTION ON GWN'S JOURNALISM: PROFILES WORKSHOP
### YODALIN PERALTA

The March 10th Girls Write Now Journalism Profiles Workshop was an amazing experience. Award-winning writer Vanessa Grigoriadis (of *Rolling Stone* and other publications) not only gave us tips on how to write a strong profile, but she also talked to us about how to be a good reporter, and how to get all the right info without going too deep into the personal issues of your subject. One of her most profound bits of advice was that, as a journalist, your story's focus should be on all the things you'd be dying to tell your friends right after an interview.

These exercises influenced me to write more profiles, and they helped me organize my thoughts; they even helped me write this to help you write a better profile of someone! During the workshop, we were assigned to write a daily routine of someone we are familiar with, someone we know really well. I decided to write about my sister, whose schedule I know perfectly and who's always keeping track of what she wears and what she does. After that, we had the option to choose from one of four prompts to elaborate more on our subject.

Before the workshop, to me, journalism was just writers taking people's privacy and making it public, which seemed unfair. But the way Vanessa explained her experience writing a profile on Justin Bieber made my thoughts expand. For example, Vanessa mentioned that in the middle of their interview, Justin Bieber had to fly to Los Angeles, and she went along with him last-minute. I see that as a journalist it could be really hard if you're not making your subject feel comfortable—she had to ask him questions in front of people on an airplane, probably they were all staring or there was too much talking, which could make it really hard to concentrate. I admire Vanessa and many other journalists because they risk their own personal comfort zones to ask hard questions, all in the hopes of entertaining people. Also, she mentioned that sometimes you might get nervous asking questions, so just be honest, make eye contact, establish trust, and hopefully the subject should feel you trying to create a character, to show their humanity. This made me realize that journalism is not as bad as it sometimes seems; it's actually very entertaining and it takes effort and courage.

#BEHINDTHESCENES

Girl meets boy—"meet cute." Boy is hopelessly shy and can't talk to girl—obstacle. Boy finally opens up and professes his love for girl through song and dance in front of a national audience—grand gesture. That's all there is to it, right?

Our Screenwriting Team, and guest authors Jennifer Westfeldt and Sabrina Dhawan, taught us that there is a lot more to a good romantic comedy than meets the eye. It takes realistic characters, struggles, desires, and a good sprinkling of comedic twists. We wrote our own "meet cutes," the moment when your two characters first meet and a spark is born, followed by an obstacle, when it seems like your characters are doomed to live a life of solitude and despair, and last, the grand gesture, when one character does something dramatic to prove her or his love.

We didn't just talk the Rom Com talk, we walked the walk. The workshop closed with mentees and mentors getting up in front of the room and acting out their hilarious "meet cutes" and tear-jerking grand gestures. By the end of the day, our fate was sealed, we'd fallen in love with Romantic Comedy.

**#BEHINDTHESCENES**

## GUEST AUTHORS

SABRINA DHAWAN is the producer of *Monsoon Wedding,* directed by Oscar-nominated Mira Nair, was awarded the Golden Lion at the Venice Film Festival in 2002 and was nominated for a Golden Globe for "Best Film in a Foreign Language." Sabrina is currently working on a Broadway musical adaptation of the movie *Monsoon Wedding* and on a feature film for ABC.

JENNIFER WESTFELDT is best known for co-writing, co-producing, and playing the title role in the award-winning 2002 indie hit, *Kissing Jessica Stein,* released by Fox Searchlight Pictures. Jennifer and her longtime partner, Jon Hamm, formed their production company, *Points West Pictures,* in 2009. Their first feature is *Friends with Kids,* written, produced and for the first time, directed by Jennifer.

## FROM THE WORKSHOP

*GINA DIFRISCO*

*MILLY and LEO are walking down the staircase leading from an art room after school.*

LEO: Hey Milly, I know I've always been a jerk to you—

MILLY: More than a jerk. You're a total ass! I don't know even know why I talk to you when you're always bullying me.

*LEO stops in the middle of the staircase. LEO reaches for MILLY'S arm to stop her and turn her to face him.*

LEO: I know, and I'm sorry. It's just... You know how people say guys bully the girls they like? I act that way 'cause...

MILLY: Are you saying you call me names and agree with every mean thing Jayson says about me because you like me?!

*LEO lets go of MILLY'S arm and shakes his head to say 'yes.'*

LEO: I really like you Milly. I know we were "dating" in elementary school, but we didn't know what dating was back then.

MILLY: Leo, we never dated. I told someone I had a crush on you and someone else asked if you knew. You said yes and called that dating.

*MILLY starts walking down the stairs, leaving LEO.*

# BLOG REVIEW:
# IMAGINATION TRUMPS EXPERIENCE
# BRE'ANN NEWSOME

Last week at GWN headquarters, a workshop was hosted, and like previous months, we were presented with a brand new kind of writing style: screenwriting. We had a lineup of experienced mentors in this area—mine included!—and one very special guest author. This author was none other than Sabrina Dhawan, best known for her romantic comedy *Monsoon Wedding*. When she walked into the room, she took a poll. She asked who was interested in screenwriting and she wanted us to answer honestly. Out of 60 or so mentees and mentors, about 10 to 12 hands shot up. Mine was not one included at all. Don't get me wrong, I find nothing wrong with screenwriting. I just felt I wasn't really good at it. This writing style takes imagination and common social skills because you have to figure out what each character would say to each other. But every time I'd try to start writing dialogue, the dark rain cloud of writer's block poured over me. I think I have a healthy imagination, but each time I looked down at my ever-so-taunting blank sheet of paper, not one unicorn rode through my mind.

My opinion changed drastically by the end of the workshop. *Characters!* Yeah, that's right. Made up people, animals or any inanimate objects we create come to life through description. Sabrina gave us some tips on how to make our characters more believable and three-dimensional. She asked us to start our characters from scratch, and to make them as realistic as possible, to the point that we as readers believe they exist in a distant place we haven't heard of or don't know about yet. We gave them traits, created their likes, dislikes, personalities, and characteristics.

Once we got down to the basics of our characters, we had to take into consideration things like what the character *wants* as opposed to what they *need*. This is a common dilemma in real life and we learned that's what makes fictional characters more relatable. The genre of romantic comedy gave us a lot of room to be creative, but it also meant that we had to meet some requirements. Original questions like *what* do they want and *what* do they need, evolved into *who* do they want and *who* do they need.

Sabrina also reminded us that the old saying, "opposites attract," may very well be true. That's when it got fun! We, as the authors, got to play matchmaker with our characters.

For example, my character came from a wealthy background, and by some weird fate, she meets someone from a less privileged family and falls in love. The conflict in this scenario was that my character's family didn't find her love interest worthy enough, instead selecting for her the "ideal man" they believed she should have. In this case, I had to find a way to get the two who were truly in love together.

Before departing, Sabrina left us with a quote: "The more specific you are, the more universal you become." To me, this means that, the more effort I put into my character's personality, the more they can relate to my audience. This is the best advice I've heard regarding screenwriting so far. I strongly suggest everyone try this writing style and see where it takes them. Any writing that you create is part of you, describing you. Why not put on a mask for a while and watch what's in your mind come to life through writing and performance?

# WILDCARD: TRANSMEDIA STORYTELLING
## MAY

Transmedia storytelling, the technique of telling a story across multiple platforms and formats, was the perfect way to conclude this year's theme of *Remix*.

At this workshop , we experimented with six different forms of digital media, viewing examples of video as journalism, poetry created in conversation on Twitter and Tumblr, and memoir in hypertext. We then used these as inspiration to plan, plot, outline, and write a first draft of a remixed piece based on original writing from a year's worth of portfolio work spanning fiction, poetry, journalism, memoir and screenwriting.

Some of the tools we provided:

- Video or animation: a storyboarding template to plot out key frames
- Audio: a cue sheet, to plan out possible dialogue or sound effects
- Social media: a Facebook timeline template and a Twitter template
- Blogging: a simple, generic blog template
- Digital Images: blank paper and various arts supplies

As we generated a striking mix of fictional character profiles, digital identities, animation storyboards, twitter poems, movie scripts and more, we constantly asked ourselves, how do these different mediums inform or give new meaning to a piece of writing?

Our Craft Talk guest authors were a panel of our very own GWN mentors and mentees, fresh from a GWN digital media spring semester pilot, to share their new expertise and screen their remixed writing in the form of video, photo, animation and sound.

# THE GIRLS WRITE NOW DIGITAL REMIX PORTFOLIO PILOT SPRING 2012

This spring, eight mentee/mentor pairs embarked on a digital remix adventure. Parting ways with the rest of the GWN crew for the months of February, March, and April, these *Remixers* attended *dorkshops* (digitally focused workshops) created with our partners, Parsons, The New School for Design, and Figment, in collaboration with the GWN Youth Board and GWN teaching artists. The pilot was supported by the MacArthur Foundation and the Hive Digital Media Learning Fund in The New York Community Trust. Remixers learned digital photography, video editing, animation, audio production, and online sharing. Running with the theme of Remix, participants reimagined written work—from their own portfolio, from over 200 pieces submitted by the Figment community, and from their GWN peers—in the form of multi-media pieces, like a series of audio diary entries from a story's two main characters, a stop-motion animation based on a freewrite, and a video of photos with animated text of a poem!

## SAMANTHA + ALEX FROM THE DORKSHOPS

*SAMANTHA YOUNG CHAN*

Since my original story, Novus, was constantly being remixed on its own throughout the year, I decided to use it once again, this time in the form of audio diary entries. Originally a radio play, Novus follows the journey of two different girls from two very contrasting worlds as they discover more about themselves, each other, and the vast problems that exist around them. I used Audacity to mix all of the sound effects and music found online together with the original audio files to create the final product. What inspired me was the idea of exploring people's personalities through their inner thoughts and personal possessions. I was interested in really developing both Hana and Asako, the two protagonists in my story, through a personal medium, and that's when I thought of having it in journal format. I instantly knew I wanted to do this through audio, since that was the intended medium from the beginning.

## DIGITAL BIOS

MENTEE SAMANTHA YOUNG CHAN: An amateur voice actress and fandub producer who also loves to roleplay, create digital art, and explore different worlds through writing.

MENTOR ALEX BERG: Video junkie meets chameleon journalist pounding the pavement, camera in tow, to create stories in the uncharted web territory.

## CHANTAREYA + ALISSA
## FROM THE DORKSHOPS

*ALISSA RICCARDELLI*

My remix post was made using iMovie, which isn't something I've ever used before! My mentee TT and I had gone out to take photographs based on a poem I had written about my hometown in the fall poetry workshop. But, being from the Hudson Valley, NYC's landscape didn't lend to the images I was trying to capture that cold afternoon. I ended up going home one weekend and taking pictures around town to better match the mood. All of the shots were taken on River Road and along the seawall in Grassy Point, NY.

## DIGITAL BIOS

MENTEE CHANTAREYA PAREDES: I don't do a lot of computer stuff other than typing on the computer 24/7. I love to take pictures and I enjoy playing virtual reality games.

MENTOR ALISSA RICCARDELLI: Sharing prose excerpts, observations, and flash in a sleepy Tumblr community.

## CHANDRA + CLAUDIA
## FROM THE DORKSHOPS

*CHANDRA HUGHES*

The piece I used is called "If These Wings Could Fly" by Allysen Graf and published on Figment. As soon as my mentor, Claudia, found it, I knew it was perfect to remix using video, audio and animation. Allysen's poem conveys the feelings of wanting to be free from the emotions that constrict her. Anyone who wishes they could just fly away and feel stress-free might relate.

For my remix, I decided to alter the meaning of the poem to be depressing instead of hopeful. The last lines of the poem are, "I'd think then just maybe, I'd be okay", leaving the reader on a positive note. Since I wanted my viewers to understand the feeling of being "caged in", my video shows enclosure, ending with a closed gate and a lock on it. I also included text in the form of remixed lines from the poem.

## DIGITAL BIOS

MENTEE CHANDRA HUGHES: Using Sony Vegas Pro, I mix radio plays and fandubs, create amvs and openings, add visual elements to writing and that's my world!

MENTOR CLAUDIA PARSONS: Email rules my life, hundreds every day. I'm a journalist who tweets and blogs occasionally and dreams of writing something creative.

## ELAINE + MONICA FROM THE DORKSHOPS

MONICA CHIN

My remix project was made using After Affects. The original piece, "A Postcard", was a poem I had submitted to the Scholastic Art and Writing Awards. I was inspired to remix this because I could imagine it visually. The original poem had a double meaning: the literal meaning was about a love letter that the speaker could not send, and the figurative meaning was about a person contemplating suicide. I could picture a postcard swaying in the air on a perilous journey.

## DIGITAL BIOS

**MENTEE MONICA CHIN:** I am not a stalker, a hacker, or even a computer wizard; I am just a Facebook, AIM, Hulu type of girl.

**MENTOR ELAINE STUART-SHAH:** Print journalist turned multimedia pioneer! I don't blog or tweet and have yet to succeed in making a professional web site, but I'm eager to become a more active (and adept) participant in the digital world.

## SADE + LINDA FROM THE DORKSHOPS

SADE SWIFT

My remix piece was inspired by real life events. Through digital media I was able to capture those moments from real life in such a way that they'll live with me forever. I've quickly come to see that in the world we live in today, we are losing a sense of creativity because everything we can possibly need is at the click of a button. With these dorkshops I was able to use my own imagination to create a piece that really reflects a moment in time, that hopefully others can relate to. I learned that digital media can be used in such a way that it doesn't degrade our imagination, rather it enriches it.

## DIGITAL BIOS

**MENTEE SADE SWIFT:** I am a dynamic well-rounded illustration of words and pictures trying to tell a story. I don't look to impress anyone, I don't look to change anything, I simply look to influence the views, inspire the thoughts and help discover. I like when people read my things or see my pictures and assume I'm one way then get completely surprised when I turn out different, exceed expectations.

**MENTOR LINDA CORMAN:** My digital self is episodic, sporadic, reluctant, skeptical, and a little intrigued. If being digital is a screenful of blips, I am one blip that flashes infrequently.

## GEORGIA + KAREN FROM THE DORKSHOPS

*GEORGIA SOARES*

Some say that adolescence is the transitional stage when doubts arise the most; questions open doors to new discoveries and adventures, maturity and wisdom. My writing "Entangled in Darkness" is about facing the unknown and questioning life's purpose. I decided to translate this reflective piece into a video because of its meaningful message delivered through powerful language and imagery. The story narrated seemed to be relatable, and video is one of the best ways to inspire and provoke thought in others. This piece was done in After Affects and iMovie, and I additionally used Audacity to incorporate audio. I hope that the video can touch people's hearts and give them a meaningful message about questioning life.

## DIGITAL BIOS

MENTEE GEORGIA SOARES:
I'm an active blogger and curious Figment writer who shares stories with Brazilian and American teens, and also I'm addicted to Tumblr reblogging.

MENTOR KAREN KAWAGUCHI:
I am a writer, curious about new media. A bit hesitant but I want to explore and learn. How does remixing affect the meaning of the written word? How does it affect the way we communicate?

## KATHRYN + THERESE FROM THE DORKSHOPS

*THERESE COX*

Book trailers right now are a little bit like slap bracelets or skinny jeans: a trend that will either pass and leave us all wondering, "What were we thinking?" or else a staple that's here to stay. I decided to risk it and create my own for my (currently unpublished) novel, DEAR DIRTY DUBLIN. It's all about creating "buzz," right? I used iMovie to create the trailer, using photos, video footage, hand-drawn maps, and text I had created and captured over six years of research trips to Dublin. I took my inspiration from the city itself, hoping to capture both the urgency of my story's narrative and the grittiness of modern-day Dublin: its maze of streets, crumbling grey stone, and splashes of street art bearing messages both comforting and sinister. At the Remix orientation, menteeChandra Hughes first suggested I make a book trailer. Once this whim was recorded as my "audio contract," I knew I had thrown myself into the deep end. But then again, I write novels. I don't do shallow.

## DIGITAL BIOS

MENTEE KATHRYN JAGAI:
When I was nine, I decided that I was going to be a famous writer just like the J.K. Harry Potter lady! Somehow, my parents failed to dispute me of this notion because you can still find me writing poetry, short stories, novels and anything else whenever I can find the time.

MENTOR THERESE COX:
Eavesdropper, snarkitect, book freak, hockey dork, accordionista. I love Dublin, blog at &7, tweet @ ThereseCox, and write novels.

## IDAMARIS + DEMETRIA FROM THE DORKSHOPS

*DEMETRIA IRWIN*

My remix project is based on a handwritten piece I wrote during a pair session. A lot of times, my mentee Ida and I will use word prompts from an app on my phone (It's called Word Prompts!!) and time ourselves writing based on those prompts. One of the scenario prompts required using magic, a post office, a small town, bird cages and a new car smell. In our 10-minute time limit, I wrote a little more than a page in my Moleskine about a guy in a small town who wanted to be a magician but nobody believed in his dream and he was just ready to leave. When I did the remix, using iMovie and Audacity, I realized that the character I made up wanted to use magic to make his life better and easier. It made me think about how magic would improve my life. As a freelance writer, my computer is a critical part of my existence. So, I made a stop motion animation that shows my laptop literally eating my bills. That's really what it does so I decided to make it more literal.

## DIGITAL BIOS

**MENTEE IDAMARIS PEREZ:** I'm not tech savvy, but I sure am an enthusiastic tech girl. I'm a text addict, Wikispaces social justice writer, and an iPod Touch lover. I'm hooked on my Nook. Enjoy watching YouTube. In other ways, I'm like a baby robin bird still learning how to navigate through this vast world of technology.

**MENTOR DEMETRIA IRWIN:** Writer, prolific link putter-upper on FB, queen of shameless plugs on Twitter.

#BEHINDTHESCENES

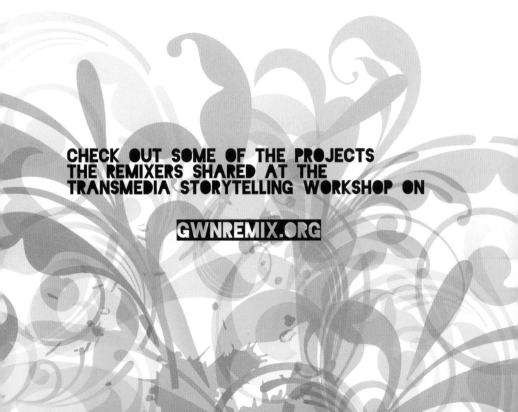

## CHECK OUT SOME OF THE PROJECTS THE REMIXERS SHARED AT THE TRANSMEDIA STORYTELLING WORKSHOP ON

## GWNREMIX.ORG

We are grateful to the countless institutions and individuals for their generous donations. While space restricts the number of donors we can recognize here, each and every gift has allowed our organization to grow and thrive.

Girls Write Now would like to thank Amazon.com, which provided the charitable contribution that made possible this year's anthology.

2011-12 INSTITUTIONAL SUPPORTERS

ADCO Foundation, American Express Charitable Fund, Assurant Foundation, Baird Foundation, Inc., Bartle Bogle Hegarty, The Bay & Paul Foundations, Brooklyn Community Foundation, The Catalog for Giving of New York City, Colgate-Palmolive Inner City Education Fund, The Concordia Foundation, Crosswicks Foundation, The DEBS NYC, Ferris Greeney Family Foundation, Find Your Light Foundation, Fondation Femme Debut, Fractured Atlas, Friedman Family Foundation, Hammer Family Charitable Foundation, Hive Digital Media Learning Fund in The New York Community Trust, The Hyde & Watson Foundation, Impact Investing Foundation, The Rona Jaffe Foundation, Manhattan Borough President's Office, Amy Morrill Charitable Trust, New York Women's Foundation, Palisade Capital Management, The Patrina Foundation, The Pinkerton Foundation, Random House, Inc., The Edmond de Rothschild Foundations, Ruth Asset Management Co LLC, Siegel + Gale, SJL Attorney Search LLC, The South Wind Foundation, The Taproot Foundation, The Treats Truck, Union Square Awards, a project of the Tides Center, Youth, I.N.C.

Thank you to Open Road Integrated Media, lead sponsor of our 2012 CHAPTERS Reading Series: Remix.

OPEN ROAD
INTEGRATED MEDIA

2011-12 LITERARY PARTNERS

Alliance for Young Artists & Writers, Marci Alboher and Friends, Center for Literary Translation, Figment, Hachette Book Group, HarperCollins, Hive Learning Network NYC, John Street Church, Largehearted Boy, Macmillan, The Mentoring Partnership of New York, *The New Yorker*, Parsons the New School for Design, Poets Out Loud at Fordham University, Poetry Society of America, Poets & Writers Magazine, SheWrites, Volume 1 Brooklyn, Cristi Young, Young to Publishing Group, Youth Development Institute, a program of the Tides Center

The anthology is supported, in part, by public funds from the National Endowment for the Arts; the New York State Council on the Arts, a State Agency; and the New York City Department of Cultural Affairs, in partnership with the City Council.

State of the Arts

NYSCA

NYCULTURE
CITY OF NEW YORK

NATIONAL
ENDOWMENT
FOR THE ARTS
A great nation
deserves great art.

SPREADTHEWORD

## BUILDING A COMMUNITY OF WRITERS, ONE GIRL AT A TIME

From young women first exploring writing to seasoned professionals practicing their craft every day, Girls Write Now is building a vibrant and growing community of women writers grounded in unique mentoring relationships where every writer learns to develop her creative, independent voice.

## MENTOR. WRITE. GIVE.
GIRLSWRITENOW.ORG